FOOTPRINTS OF
GAUTAMA THE BUDDHA

The Western world is becoming more and more interested in the wisdom of the East and many people are learning to appreciate the teachings of the Buddha, whose message is as applicable in today's world as it was when he lived two and a half thousand years ago. The author of this book says "I want the stories of the Buddha's ministerial life to tell of his teaching in the circumstances in which it was actually given — not as abstract philosophy to scholars but to suffering men and women."

Here Marie Byles draws for us a vivid picture of a man with a very lively sense of humor, with a sun-like compassion which few could resist. This is the Buddha his disciples knew. Everything about the narrative, told through the lips of the disciple Yasa, has a relevance to life.

Although written as the experience of one of the Buddha's disciples, with a beautiful simplicity, the book is nonetheless a work of scholarship, and at the end of each chapter a list of sources is given. Sir Lalita Rajapakse, former Minister of Justice in Ceylon, has written the foreword.

By making her own pilgrimage to the principal places of his ministry, Marie Byles has proved herself to be as true a disciple as the men and women who followed directly in the steps of Gautama the Buddha across the hot plains of India and up into the pure air of the lofty Himalayas.

Footprints of
Gautama the Buddha

BEING THE STORY OF THE BUDDHA HIS DISCIPLES KNEW
DESCRIBING PORTIONS OF HIS MINISTERIAL LIFE

by

MARIE BEUZEVILLE BYLES

A QUEST BOOK
Published under a grant from The Kern Foundation

THE THEOSOPHICAL PUBLISHING HOUSE
Wheaton, Ill., U.S.A.
Madras, India / London, England

First published 1957

Quest Book edition 1967, published by The Theosophical
Publishing House, Wheaton, Ill., a department of The
Theosophical Society in America

Second Quest Book Printing 1972

ISBN: 0-8356-0399-7.

Library of Congress Catalog Card Number 68-5855

Manufactured in the United States of America

To

ERIKA WOHLWILL

ACKNOWLEDGEMENTS

It is a pleasure to record my thanks to those who have helped me. Mrs. Erika Wohlwill is almost part author. She read the manuscript many times as it proceeded to completion, and was infallible in putting her finger on spiritual, moral and literary inaptitudes. There can be few so fortunate as to have a collaborator like her. Miss I. B. Horner, who is one of the leading Pali scholars of today, gave invaluable criticism and help, and spared the time to read and critically examine about half the manuscript: that there are not more *faux pas* from the scholar's angle is entirely due to her, and I cannot sufficiently express my indebtedness. At the same time, it is only fair to state that with many of my interpretations and translations, and to some extent with my conception of the Buddha's teaching, Miss Horner does not find herself in agreement. The late Mr. F. L. Woodward, also one of the leading Pali scholars, helped in the same manner as Miss Horner, and was indefatigable in answering questions up to a few weeks of his death. Miss Hilda Mackaness and Mrs. Marjorie Fitzpatrick gave useful help from the literary angle. Mr. David Maurice, of Burma, very kindly arranged for a bhikkhu in that country to read and criticize the chapters on the Vinaya rules. The Librarian of the Victorian Public Library, who had the foresight to place in that Library the Pali text translations of the sacred books of the Buddhists when they were in print, is particularly deserving of recognition. No other library in Australia had them and, as many were then temporarily out of print, I am more indebted to this librarian than to any other. At the same time I could hardly have succeeded without the help of Miss Florence James who handled the manuscript for me in England, and Sir Lalita Rajapakse who introduces it to Ceylon. That an orthodox Buddhist should introduce the book is not only a tribute to the kindness of Sir Lalita, but far more to the traditional tolerance and understanding of Buddhism itself. Acknowledgement is also made to *Vedanta and the West, The Aryan Path* and the *Fellowship of the Friends of Truth*, in which portions of the manuscript have previously appeared.

The making of statues of the Buddha is a late development. In early Buddhist times, the presence of the Buddha was indicated by footprints only. Hence the title.

As few Pali and Sanskrit words as possible have been used; when used, the word most likely to be familiar has been chosen, irrespective of whether Pali or Sanskrit, and it has not been put in a different type, because inquiry shows that a word in a different type is "skipped" by a person to whom it is not familiar while the one, to whom it is, finds it hinders the easy flow of the narrative.

CONTENTS

FOREWORD

by Sir Lalita Rajapakse, q.c., b.a., ll.d.
(Minister of Justice, Ceylon, 1947–53)

Miss Marie Beuzeville Byles was born in England and went to Australia while she was still a child, and made it her home. She had a distinguished career in the University of Sydney where she obtained a degree in Arts and Law. Having an incisive mind she directed her talents quite early to the study of Law. She passed out as a Solicitor of the Supreme Court of New South Wales, and in course of time acquired success in the legal profession. Her spare time was spent in the wide open spaces of the countryside as well as on the mountains she dearly loved. Her early expeditions were on the mountains of New Zealand and China.

A Christian by birth Miss Byles was brought up in a Christian atmosphere. She became really interested in religion in 1940, and read widely of other religions. She found the greatest appeal in the teaching of the Buddha. A surgical operation on her feet took away the possibility of further mountaineering; and ill-health which followed, involved her in several years of physical suffering. She spent this period in reading more and more of the Buddha Dhamma from which she derived immense solace and comfort of mind.

In 1950 she conceived the idea of writing this book and, while getting the manuscripts ready, she spent the year 1954 in North India to help her to obtain first-hand knowledge of the land trod by the Master himself twenty-five centuries ago. She returned to Australia *via* Ceylon, and has now produced *The Footprints of Gautama the Buddha*.

Every Buddhist has heard of the first five disciples of the Tatha-gatha. They had been his erstwhile followers. Yasa was the sixth disciple, and in one sense the first of those who had not met the Buddha before he attained Enlightenment. Yasa was the son of a millionaire, and his parents became the first lay disciples of the Buddha. The "Footprints" is an attempt to portray through the lips of Yasa the life of the Buddha and of his more illustrious disciples as they lived it. It is somewhat different from the "Evaṁ mē sutaṁ" text that one is familiar with. It is a kind of "Evaṁ mē ditthaṁ".

In describing the travels of the Buddha from Benares to Kapilavattu the capital of his father's principality, to Kosambi across the Jumna tributary of the River Ganges, to Vesali, Uruwela, Nalanda, Rajagaha, to Savatti where Anatha Pindika, another millionaire, donated the beautiful Jeta-Park to the Maha Sangha, and finally to Kusinara where the Buddha drew his last mortal breath, the authoress has given the reader a realistic picture of the topography of North India right up to the Himalayan mountain ranges.

The vivid details of the day-to-day life of the Buddha among his disciples enable the reader to get not only a general comprehension of the rules contained in the Vinaya Pitakas, but also an insight into the character and temperament of his chief disciples. In a style which is both elegant and interesting, one is introduced to the two great disciples, Sariputta of outstanding wisdom, and Moggalla of extra-ordinary super-normal powers; to the amiable attendant of the Master, Ananda of remarkable retentive memory; to the forest dweller Maha Kassapa, whose austerity and meticulous regard for form earned him "fearful" respect; to jealous Devadatta, and the remarkable Angulimala.

Naturally, Miss Byles focuses attention on an aspect which a male is apt not to emphasize very much—namely the attitude of the Buddha towards women, and the part played by them in the development of the Dhamma. One gets to know and remember the conversion of the beautiful Khema, the queen of Bimbisara, of the noble Pajapathi, the first of the Bhikkuni Sasana, of Patacara, proficient in the rules of discipline, of Bhadda, skilled in debate, and of gentle Visakha, famed for her munificence.

Throughout the book the doctrine of the Buddha is woven into the narrative with fascinating anecdotes which leave an indelible impression upon the mind of the reader. If at times one does not agree with some of the views of the authoress or her interpretation of the Dhamma, it does help one to focus attention on certain matters of the Doctrine as it is understood by a disciple who has been nurtured in a theistic environment. If the idea that Miss Byles had in the back of her mind was to stimulate the interest of the reader to a critical study of the Word of the Buddha, undoubtedly the *Footprints of Gautama the Buddha* has achieved that object. She says "The best memorials to the Master are not the cairns erected over His ashes, but lives well lived in the Dhamma". That certainly is the true spirit of the Buddha Dhamma.

AUTHOR'S FOREWORD

In the sixth century B.C., when Solon promulgated his famous laws in Greece, when Nebuchadnezzar's reign marked the height of Chaldean civilization and when Confucius taught wisdom to China, Siddhartha Gautama, afterwards known as the Buddha, was born on the plains to the north of India in what today is South Nepal, the son and heir of the raja of the local clan. He was born into a land where there was general well-being and prosperity, an India very different from that of today, which for the average Westerner conjures up a picture of the extremes of wealth and poverty, of squalor, starvation and lethargy. In the Buddha's day it was a land of well-balanced activity, containing a society with no extremes of wealth and poverty, and firm-based upon a well-to-do farming class. There were slaves, but they were members of the household and did not remotely resemble the negro slaves or slaves of the Roman Empire. There was no hard and fast line between the classes, which could then hardly be called castes. The Brahmins claimed to be the repository of sacred wisdom and to have a monopoly of sacrificial rites; they were certainly respected but they lived as others, and the people most respected were not the Brahmins, but the "holy ones", the hermits who lived in the forest and the "wanderers" who went about the countryside expounding their particular doctrines. It was an age which took religion very much for granted and so was prepared to support "holy ones". Gautama represented the high-water mark of a very high tide of religious endeavour. It was also an age of religious tolerance, which may partly account for the fact that the Buddhist religion has never persecuted, nor waged war in the name of its Founder.

The family was the basis of the social organization, wives going to their husbands' homes on marriage. The courtesan was a professional companion and occupied a respectable status. There appears to have been no obsession with sex (such as we have today); the allusions to sex in the Buddhist scriptures are often crude, but it obviously did not dominate men's minds.

Beautiful legends have gathered around the birth, boyhood and young manhood of Siddhartha Gautama, telling how, despite his happy, protected life within the palace, he discovered that sorrow,

disease and death are universal; how at the age of twenty-nine he left
his home, his wife and new-born son, and went away alone into the
forest to find the way to end man's suffering. During the six years
that followed (when he was a "hermit"), he experimented with self-
tortures and starvation without finding the answer to his quest. Then
he took food and, sitting in meditation on what is believed to have
been the full moon of May (Wesak), he found the answer and became
a Buddha, an Awakened or Enlightened One. There followed forty-
five years of active preaching life (when he was a "wanderer"), during
which he went about the country, showing men and women how
they might find the ending of ill, discord and suffering, and the same
imperturbable joy that he himself had found.

The early life of Gautama before he became a Buddha is probably
partly legendary and symbolic. It is his later life, his ministerial life,
that his early disciple, Yasa, unfolds in these pages. And the purpose
of this book is to let Yasa tell the teaching of the Buddha in the
setting in which it was actually given. It was not given to learned
philosophers in abstract discourses, but to suffering human beings
whose problems were not so very different from our own. The stories
Yasa tells are drawn principally from translations of the Pali texts,
the oldest written records of the Buddha's words, but translations
from the Sanskrit, which are later, have not been ignored. Because it
is earnestly hoped the reader will peruse the translations for himself,
the principal sources are given at the end of each chapter, and given
so that they can be found by ordinary readers and not, as is usually
the case, by scholars only.

The earliest records of the Buddha's words were collected by
monks, that is, by men, and by celibates. A tremendous debt is owing
to these monks for their work, but with the best will to be truthful
they naturally gave the records their own "slant", and tended to
belittle both the householder and the other sex. A Westerner,
especially one trained in the sifting of legal evidence, suspicious of
miracles and without the background of Buddhist sacred tradition,
must inevitably put a different "slant" on the stories, for when there
is contradiction within the records—as there often is—he must take
the report which is against the monk's interest. It is hoped that there
will not, on this account, be anything in the following pages not
acceptable to the orthodox Buddhist; if there is, all that can be said in
extenuation is that the author is a sincere disciple of the Buddha.

The Buddha, like most great spiritual Teachers, took for granted the cosmology accepted by the people around him, or, more correctly, he expounded the Dhamma, the moral and spiritual Law, within their own terminology relating to the super-sensual world, a world with devas (angels), petas (ghosts), Brahma, the Creator, its heavens and its hells, and, above all, its certainty of reincarnation. All these things may be said to form part of Buddhism. But none of them are the essential teaching of the Buddha, whose Four Noble Truths and the Eightfold Way (see Appendix) can just as well be grafted on to our modern cosmology with its scientific and psychological terminology relating to a super-sensual world of atoms and subconscious forces.

The Four Noble Truths and the Noble Eightfold Way can also be grafted on to the Christian cosmology, but in this case there is the difficulty of terminology, for, to the Buddhist, the terms "God" and "spiritual" pertain to the world of spirits, the devas, Brahma, the Creator, Sakka, King of the Gods, and the like; beings who exist, but who, like human beings, are held within the Dhamma, the Good Law, and also, like human beings, are transient and subject to suffering. But the teaching of the Buddha is eternally true and must not be confused with Buddhist terminology.

Whether the Westerner, who first approaches the Buddha's teaching, be accustomed to modern scientific or to Christian terminology, he should always bear in mind that the Buddha was not interested in the existence or non-existence of a Supreme Being or any other abstract philosophical proposition. He was interested only in the Way, the practical way, by which suffering may be ended both here and hereafter.

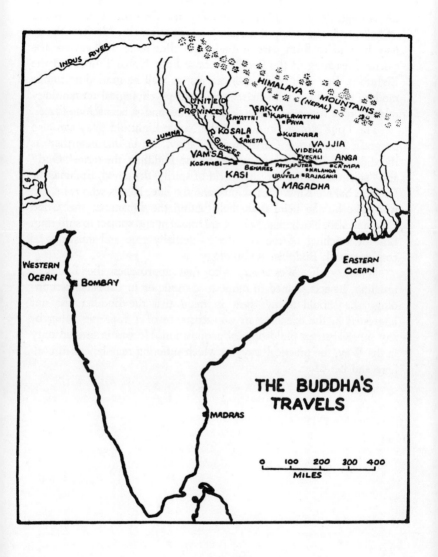

CHAPTER I

THE FIRST DISCIPLES

I, YASA, was the sixth disciple whom the Master, Gautama, the Buddha, called to follow him, and who understood his teaching and answered that call. I was the son of a nobleman of Banaras and like the Master I had known all pleasures a life of luxury can bring. For some weeks before the time of which I now tell, a vague feeling of unrest had possessed me, as when we hear the faint strains of distant music and strive to catch it but cannot. In the same way did I seem to hear a music not of this earth, but when I tried to grasp it, the music fled and was gone. All that I now knew was that the life of pleasure with which I was surrounded no longer satisfied me. It was empty and hollow, useless as a rice field into which the water has not been run. Then it happened that one night I woke and, continuing wakeful, I went forth into the outer rooms where I beheld the maidservants of the household lying in sleep. They who were as flowers of beauty in the daytime now lay in disorder upon the couches snoring and with dress dishevelled and soiled. A sense of great misery overwhelmed me that what had seemed so lovely should be so repellent. I could rest no longer. I put on my gilt slippers and went forth into the night. Something, I know not what, drew me towards the deer park of Isipatana. As I walked in the night, I felt I could never rest again. What was life to me when underneath all its glitter was the sordidness of those recumbent bodies? No rest! No peace! What endless chain of wretchedness! I kicked off my gilded slippers in disgust. Then I seemed to feel a cool breath of peace stealing over me, as if in my fever I had plunged into a cool, pellucid lake. I heard a gentle voice answering my thoughts, "Nirvana is refreshing, cool, and free from sorrow."

Almost as in a dream I found myself seated beside a man I had never met before and yet seemed to have known all my life as my Master. He was older than I, but how much older I could not have said, for he seemed to have lived a long time and yet was still young. I cannot remember what he said. Perhaps he did not even speak. But my misery slipped from off me as the old skin is slipped from off a snake. I saw stretch out before me the Way to the Great Peace. Then I noticed my jewelled garments glittering in the starlight. I felt ashamed. I was glad that I had at least kicked off my gilded slippers. The Master read my thoughts and said:

'Those ornamented with jewels need not be the slaves of their senses. It is not the outward garb that matters; it is the inward heart. A man may have the garments of a beggar and dwell in lonely places, and yet his heart may be filled with desires and worldly thoughts. If you look with an equal eye on all, having no preference either for jewels or for rags, then, though you live in the world, you are yet liberated from it.'

Many more things the Master said, and when he rose, I followed him as a young calf follows its mother. The tall palms were silhouetted against the orange dawn; three white birds of the waterlands stood silently in the mud on the edge of a pool waiting for their prey; and beyond stretched out the rice-fields like the patchwork rags of the gown of him I followed.

He led me to a mango grove not far from the deer park, and there I met the first five disciples, Kondanna, Vappa, Bhaddiya, Mahanama and Assaji. They were all much older than I who was only twenty years of age, but I was at once one of them, as if I had always been of their Brotherhood. Kondanna was the eldest. He had been one of the eight Brahmins summoned by the Raja Suddhodana at the birth of his son to foretell the future of the babe. With inner sight he had perceived that the child was destined to become a Buddha. Twenty-nine years later, when he heard that this young Prince Siddhartha Gautama had taken to the homeless life, he himself also left home, and, joined by Vappa and the three others, followed the princely hermit into the forest to seek with him for the Way, the Light and the Truth. They had thought that these things would be found if they fasted and tortured their bodies, so that, the flesh being subdued, the spirit might mount towards celestial things. For a long time the Master had set them the example, excelling them in severity of starvation and self-torture, and they had revered him accordingly. When he had broken his fast and fed as other men, they were angry at his seeming failure and deserted him. Now they told the story of how they became his disciples.

When they had seen him coming towards them, they had talked together and decided that this Gautama, having taken food like men living in the world, had no claim to the hospitality it is customary for one monk to extend to another. So far as was possible they would ignore him, and if that were not wholly possible, they would treat him in an off-hand manner. They would not offer him a seat, nor look after his comfort.

But as the Master drew closer, a subtle sense of power and peace seemed to sweep towards them. Before they knew what they were doing, one had taken his robe, another had offered him a seat, a third had got water to wash his feet. Then they all sat down respectfully to listen to him as they would to an honoured teacher. But having sat down, the spell was broken; they remembered their vow not to pay him any respect, and in a feeble, half-hearted manner they began to speak to him familiarly, telling him how deeply disappointed in him they had been, when he fell away from the high ideal of austerity. But one by one their protests died away under his calm, serene countenance. In a little while they stopped talking and the Master spoke:

'There are two extremes. On the one hand, there are those who gratify their sensual desires and live a life of luxury and self-indulgence. Such ones cannot even understand their Sacred Sayings; how much less can they understand the Way to liberation from sorrow and the door to immortal life. On the other hand, there are those who torture their bodies by starving or injuring them in other ways. Such ones cannot think about worldly matters; how much less can they understand heavenly wisdom! The emaciated monk is like a woman striving to light a lamp with water instead of oil, or a man trying to make a good fire of rotten wood.

'The Way to Truth is not either of these. But there is a middle way, a way that lies between these two extremes. On the one hand, luxury and indulgence are avoided. A simple life is lived so that the body has what is necessary for its health and strength, but no more. Along the middle way is the Way to Truth.'

They told me that the Master spoke to them with an authority they had never heard from other teachers. It was not what he had learned from others, nor what might be heard in the Sacred Sayings. He spoke of what he himself knew from his own experience. He had tried both these extremes and found that they failed. He had tried the middle way and found it did not fail. But there was something besides experience in what he said, or perhaps it was the way he said it. There was indescribable gentleness and understanding, but also a sense of beyond-time-ness. They tried to explain the effect that he had had upon them, but they could not. All that they knew was that the ill-will which had chilled their hearts melted away and that they became his disciples. They were the first five of the many thousands who listened to the Four Great Truths and the Noble Eightfold Way that transform the lives of men and women who listen and follow, and for whom opens up the path of loving kindness to the Great Peace of Nirvana.

.   .   .   .   .   .

When I did not return home, my mother missed me and sent my father to see what had become of me. My father saw the gilded slippers I had cast away and, recognizing them, he then followed my bare footprints and came upon me seated with those five first disciples listening to the teaching that was to liberate the world. When I told him that it was my intention to leave home and become a wanderer as the disciple of the Master, he did not seem surprised, for he saw at once that the Teacher I followed had found the Truth. He told me that my mother was full of lamentation because of my failure to return home, but he did not press me to go back to her. Instead, he invited the Master and the first five disciples as well as me to take food at his house.

The next day, as soon as my mother saw the Master, the clouds lifted from her brow and she grieved for me no more. My wife, too, rejoiced that I had chosen the homeless life, for in our household we regarded this calling of complete renunciation as the highest of all callings. It is true I was leaving home earlier than was usual, for I had not yet reared a family, but there were others able to perform my duties as a householder, and in later years my wife followed my example and joined the Sisterhood. After the meal was over, the Master talked to the whole household of the great Truths; thus my mother and father and their household became the first lay disciples of the Master.

Partly because of my skill in the playing of music, I had been a leader among the gay youths of Banaras. When my former companions saw me dressed in yellow rags and with shaven head, they were greatly astonished. On hearing the reason, they came to see the Master who had wrought such a change in my life, and hearing him teach they lost their astonishment, and many of them likewise shaved their hair and went forth from home. The Master told us that when he attained enlightenment he was tempted by Mara, that is, of his individual self which desires happiness, to depart alone into the wilderness as a hermit to enjoy the bliss he had won, for none would understand the Truth he had found. But already was Mara proved wrong, for thus early he had gathered to him disciples, both lay and ordained, who understood his message.

Chapter I—Sources

Vinaya—S. B. East, XIII, p. 89

Vinaya—*Book of Discipline*, IV—S. B. Buddhists, vol. 14, pp. 13 and 21

Fo-Sho-Hing-Tsan-King—S. B. East, XIX, p. 168

Jennings, p. 60

Theragatha—*Psalms of the Brethren*—Pali Text, vol. 4, pp. 62 and 284

Woodward—pp. 27 and 30

NOTE: The meeting of Yasa and the first five disciples are an elaboration on the Texts, likewise Yasa's wife. Yasa's name never appears again in the Texts after the Buddha visited his home.

CHAPTER II

ESTABLISHING THE KINGDOM OF TRUTH

WHEN a number of men had become ordained as Brothers of the Order, the Master gathered us together in the Deer Park near Banaras and said to us:

'Go now and wander through the land as teachers filled with compassion for this pain-riven world. Let not two of you go the same way. Preach the Dhamma wherever you go, the Dhamma, which is glorious in the beginning, glorious at the end both in the letter and spirit. Show the possibility of a life of goodness, holiness and happiness. There are some whose eyes are clouded with only a little dust, and when they hear they will understand.'

The Master always perceived with his inward eye those whose eyes were clouded with only a little dust, and to them he would go great distances to impart the Dhamma. When he now told us he would go first to Uruvela, near Gaya, where he had found enlightenment, and thence to Rajagaha, where we might rejoin him when the cold season commenced, we knew that he had already perceived with his inward eye that there were those at Uruvela and at Rajagaha, who were very ready to receive the Dhamma. What happened to him after he left Banaras I later heard from others, and this is as I heard it:

When the Master came to Uruvela, he left the road and entered a certain grove where he sat at the foot of a tree to meditate. Into that same grove had also come a party of young men of wealth together with their wives for the purpose of picnic and pleasure. One of them was not married, and so that their numbers might be equal they had invited a courtesan, a professional companion of great beauty and charm. Now, while they were sporting in this grove, looking into lotus lily ponds and watching a peacock spreading his tail, the courtesan took up their belongings, which they had left strewn upon the ground, and ran off with them. When those young men and women saw what had happened, they were angry, and set forth in various directions seeking to find the courtesan and recover their belongings. Thus roaming to and fro they came upon the Master seated in meditation, and one of them went up to him, saying:

'Venerable Sir, is it possible you have seen a woman pass this way?'

'A woman?' asked the Master, looking up from his meditation. 'What have you young men to do with a woman that you seek her?'

Then that young man explained to the Master the reason for desiring to find the courtesan.

The Master said: 'Now what think you? Which would be better for you and of more profit, to go in search of a woman and your belongings, the sport of a passing hour, which you yourselves have found brings distress, or to go in search of the True Self of you, which is imperishable, and to find which, brings joy?'

The young man who had first spoken, and who later joined the Order, told me that had any ordinary holy man spoken this, they might have been moved only to secret laughter, but that there was something about the Master which restrained ridicule, and called up before the mind a vision of what seemed more to be desired than anything they had yet sought.

It was this young man who answered the Master, saying: 'It were better, Venerable Sir, that we should go in search of the True Self of us.'

'But what is the True Self?' asked another young man.

Then the Master bade the young men and their wives be seated, and he explained to them how seeking to fulfil the desires of this perishable individual self brings sorrow, and that in denying those desires and utterly destroying them, is found the True Self and perfect joy.

When he had spoken, the young men and their wives rejoiced and departed, determined to follow the Way he had shown them. They were young, but even the eyes of youth may be clouded with only a little dust.

From that grove the Master went to the grotto of the Fire-god, whose sacred flames were guarded by certain Matted-Haired Ascetics, men well versed in the Vedic lore, and given to great austerity and self-mortification. Their leader was named Kassapa, and on account of his great penances he was esteemed the holiest of all men.

It was evening when the Master approached Kassapa, and said: 'If it be not disagreeable to you, Brother, I would spend the night in the grotto where burns the sacred fire.'

'You know not what you say, Brother: the Fire-god is a great and venomous serpent. I would not have him harm you. Even I who am the holiest of all men, do not venture into the sacred grotto after night has fallen.'

'None the less, I beseech you,' pleaded the Master.

'I dislike controversy,' replied Kassapa. 'On your own head rest your death. Be it as you ask.'

The Master thanked Kassapa and went into the grotto, sitting cross-legged in meditation until the second watch of the night. When the Fire-god sent forth a cloud of smoke and flame, the Master would send forth a greater flame of love and goodwill, and the smoke and flame of the Fire-god would be quenched. Kassapa, turning in his uneasy slumber and seeing only the great blaze of light within the grotto, muttered to himself: "Truly the countenance of this distinguished visitor is very beautiful, but the Fire-god will do him great harm."

When morning came Kassapa arose, and, seeing the Master still unharmed, he marvelled, and the Master, reading his thought, said to him; 'The fire of the Fire-god has been quenched by the greater radiations of love and goodwill.' And he held forth his bowl in which the serpent lay peacefully sleeping.

Kassapa marvelled more than ever, saying to himself, "Truly this distinguished visitor has great magical powers, and he knows not fear—none the less he is not as holy as I am."

A second night did the Master fearlessly enter the shrine of the Fire-god and a second time were the flames of the Fire-god overcome by the greater flame of his love and goodwill. And Kassapa conceived an affection for his visitor and said: 'Stay with me and I will provide you with food, for the villagers are bountiful in the food they give to the one they regard as the holiest of all men.' The Master agreed, and on the following night devas came and the whole grove was filled with the beauty of their light. Kassapa marvelled more and more, although still saying to himself that the Master was not as holy as he.

There then approached the day on which Kassapa was accustomed to celebrate a great sacrifice when large numbers of people from Anga and Magadha came, bringing with them abundant food. Now Kassapa feared that if the Master were present at the sacrifice, he would distract the attention of the people with his magic, and that gain and honour would accrue to the Master and that his own gain and honour would diminish. The Master, perceiving his thoughts, said:

'Tomorrow, Brother, it were fitting that I should take my meal and spend the day in meditation by the waters of the lake.'

'That were fitting indeed,' said Kassapa, mightily relieved, and as the Master left him, he muttered to himself: "This Brother is a good man with keen perception—but of course he is not as holy as I am."

During the days that followed the Master performed many tasks of humble service for Kassapa. He made a convenient bathing and washing pool by the banks of the stream and placed a stone on which the washing could be done. He picked large quantities of fruit, fragrant and full of flavour, and he split firewood for the sacred fire, five hundred pieces in all. And Kassapa was pleased, saying: 'This Brother is truly most kind and thoughtful—but of course he is not as holy as I am.'

At that time a heavy rain fell out of season, and the spit of sand with the mango grove where the Master used to meditate, became surrounded by water. Kassapa was afraid that the water, still rising, would carry his guest away. He, who until now, had never known tenderness or concern for another, found his heart heavy within him at the thought that the Blessed One might be drowned. He therefore hastened to the village to procure a boat and take the Master in safety to dry land. He rejoiced greatly at the kindness he was able to do, though he still muttered to himself that his guest was not as holy as he.

The Master, knowing that Kassapa's heart was now softened and pliant, and ready for conversion said to him: 'These many weeks, Kassapa, you have been saying to yourself that I am not as holy as you. But can you in solemn truth tell me that you are fully enlightened and know not the meaning of fear?'

Kassapa hesitated a while; then his heart was entirely softened by the emanations of the Master's loving friendship, and he bowed before him saying: 'No, Master, I am not fully enlightened; I am still filled with fear; I am not more holy than you.' He went into the sacred grotto and, taking the vessels of sacrifice he threw them into the river, and coming back he sat at the Master's feet and asked him to tell him of the way whereby he could free himself from fear and find inner sight.

Now other of the Ascetics of the Matted Hair, seeing the vessels of sacrifice carried down the river, became afraid lest some misfortune should have befallen their leader. They came hastening to the sacred grotto, where they saw Kassapa sitting at the feet of the Master and listening to his teaching. And they, too, sat down and listened.

'That Fire-demon whom you feared,' the Master was saying, 'is within your own hearts, the Fire-demon of desire, of pride, of self-importance. It is the fire of lust which is burning. When the senses touch sense objects and the thoughts touch thought objects, the fires of lust and desire are kindled. Your ears hear praises of yourselves, and then your thoughts think of self-importance and you are fearful lest you lose that self-importance. You forget that this self is not the True Self of you which is Universal and Deathless.'

At this point Kassapa heaved a great sigh of relief, for, as the Master spoke, a vision of the Great Peace opened before him. The Master continued: 'Pondering on these things you become weary of the fires that are kindled by your senses and your thoughts, and then the fires of desire die down. The true sacrifice is the sacrifice of desire, the flame of it is man's will well-tamed, and the true altar is the altar of humility.'

After those Ascetics of the Matted Hair had listened to the Master, they asked that they might become members of the Order, and the Master consenting, they cut off their hair. He then ordained them and they travelled with him from Uruvela to Rajagaha.

The reason for the Master's decision to go next to Rajagaha was this:

In the days when he, who was then the Prince Siddhartha, had left home and was yet seeking for the Truth, he chanced to enter Rajagaha as King Bimbisara was about to offer a great sacrifice with the slaughter of many animals. Prince Siddhartha preached to the King and his ministers concerning the oneness of all that lives, and the King was moved by Prince Siddhartha's compassion and bade the animals be freed. Thereafter the King perceived great qualities of kingship in the young prince and desired him to stay and share his kingdom with him. But Prince Siddhartha replied:

'Your majesty, I seek a greater kingdom than yours, greater than any earthly kingdom. I seek a kingdom not of this world, the Kingdom of Truth. When I have found that kingdom I will return and share it with you.'

The king was sad at these words, but he knew that the young prince was right and let him depart unhindered.

It was in fulfilment of this promise that the Master, now having found the Kingdom of Truth, set forth for Rajagaha, taking with him Kassapa of Uruvela and other of the Matted-Haired ascetics.

The Master lodged near the shrine of Supatittha, about six miles outside the city of Rajagaha, a pleasant city set about with hills, the mightiest of which is Vultures Peak. There are always shelters for wandering monks outside cities and villages and none takes much account of their coming except to do honour to them. But when King Bimbisara heard that Gautama, an ascetic of the Sakyan tribe, had arrived at Supatittha, he at once made ready to visit him, for he was certain that this was the same Prince Siddhartha, who had found the Kingdom of Truth he was seeking and had come to share it.

Now, as the King and a large retinue of courtiers and householders approached Supatittha, they saw that Kassapa of Uruvela was seated beside the Master, and some said that this ascetic, Gautama, must surely have become the disciple of Kassapa, who was renowned for being the holiest of all men. But others who had heard of the great holiness of the Exalted One, considered that Kassapa must have become the disciple of the Master. They were still disputing this matter when they came into his presence and introduced themselves.

When they were seated, the Master turned to Kassapa saying: 'Will you explain to this assembly what knowledge you have gained that has induced you, who were renowned for your penances and known as the emaciated ascetic, to forsake such penances and to desert the sacrificial fire.'

'The sacrifices I performed and the penances I underwent,' replied Kassapa, 'were concerned with things visible, and sought for rewards within this world or within the deva-world, worlds of sights and sounds and thinking. The rewards that are offered for such sacrifices and penances do not extend beyond the world of the individual's pride and egoism, which is bound for ever upon the wheel of suffering. That is why I have forsaken all penances and deserted the sacrificial fire.'

'And if your mind no more delights in these things, Kassapa, what is it in the world of men and gods in which your mind does find delight?' asked the Master.

And Kassapa again replied: 'I have seen the state of peace, Nirvana, when the individual self is laid aside and all thoughts of "I" and "me", and which is in nowise attached to sensual or material existence either in this world or in any other. This state of peace knows nothing of becoming or changing. It knows not death. Why, then, should I any more perform sacrifices and penances for rewards either of earth or heaven, for these are for ever coming-to-be, changing and decaying?' On saying this Kassapa arose and bowed low at the Master's feet, adding: 'My Teacher is the Blessed One. I am his pupil.'

King Bimbisara told me how deeply impressed were those that listened, for when a man who has held himself foremost, bows low, folk know that he has found the Truth. It was not until Kassapa sat down again that they turned to one another saying: 'The great Kassapa of Uruvela, he that was the holiest of all men, has placed himself under the direction of the great ascetic Gautama. Surely Gautama must have shown him the greatest of all blessings.'

Then the Master preached to those that were assembled more concerning the great truths that Kassapa had told of, and the Way to the finding of the Kingdom of Truth. When he had finished, King Bimbisara bowed and thanked him saying, that when he was a young man he had five wishes all of which had now been fulfilled. The first was that he might become king, the second that a holy Buddha might come into his kingdom, the third that he might bow before him, the fourth that the Buddha might preach the Dhamma to him and the fifth that he might understand.

The King then invited the Master and those that were formerly Matted-Haired Ascetics, to take of food with him. After the meal was over the King took a gold vessel with water in it, and pouring it over the Master's hand he said: 'I give up the Bamboo Grove, Veluvana pleasure garden, near the north gate of the city, to the Blessed Buddha and the Fraternity. May it be accepted.' And the Master accepted it, and that was the first park given to the Order. Many times the Master stayed in that Bamboo Grove, and folk came there with their problems and their sorrows.

Chapter II—Sources

Vinaya—S. B. East, XIII, pp. 116, 118 and 136
Vinaya—*Book of Discipline*, IV—S. B. Buddhists, vol. 14, p. 31
Fo-Sho-Hing-Tsan-King—S. B. East, vol. XIX, p. 183
Coomaraswamy and Horner, p. 133 (true fire sacrifice)
Samyutta Nikaya—*Kindred Sayings*, I—Pali Text, vol. 7, p. 212 (true fire sacrifice)
Note: The miraculous elements in the Texts have been omitted in view of the Buddha's strong denunciation of display of miracles.

CHAPTER III

THE TWO GREAT DISCIPLES

SHORTLY after King Bimbisara presented Veluvana Pleasance to the Order, most of the Brothers whom the Master had sent forth from Banaras made their way towards Rajagaha to rejoin him there.

Flat is the land around my ancestral home near Banaras, flat the sandy banks of the sacred River Ganges, and flat the patch-work of the rice-fields which stretch away to Isipatana deer forest. But when we approached the town of Gaya on the way to Rajagaha, we saw hills rising before us. Assaji pointed out certain of these and said that it was among the caves of these hills that the Master and those who had been the first five disciples, had practised austerities. Never before had I seen such high land, and I persuaded Assaji to scramble with me through the prickly undergrowth to the top. On the other side, we looked down upon the wide sandy bed of the river which meandered lazily among the sands and round an occasional grove of mango trees. On the other side, Assaji told me, was one of the twenty-four places near Gaya where oblations are offered to the ancestors. 'It was under a Bodhi tree over there,' he said, pointing across the river, 'that the Master sat when he found enlightenment.' I would have crossed that sandy waste to see that tree, but Assaji reminded me that travelling with this object was not part of the serious purpose we had before us. We therefore descended and proceeded on our way a further twenty miles or thereabouts, until we saw the pleasant hills which surround the city of Rajagaha on all sides like natural fortifications. We went through a gap to the south of them. Rajagaha was a city of greater opulence and gaiety than Banaras. On all sides there were merchants selling wares many of which I had not seen before, such as jewelled girdles, gorgeously embroidered silks, and leather saddles worked with very beautiful designs. We were directed right through the city to the north where there are hot springs. A short way beyond these was Veluvana Pleasance, its giant bamboos overhanging a lovely little lake. Through the arches of the bamboos we looked out on to the fields and a place excavated for the making of bricks, which were lying out in the sun to dry.

Now it happened that at this time there was residing in Rajagaha a wandering ascetic named Sanjaya with a large company of disciples including two friends, Sariputta and Moggallana. These two friends were serious in their search to find that which lies beyond this shadow world of time and space, and often they talked about the matter. One day they climbed to the top of a hill which overlooked both the city and the plains to the north. They saw the people moving to and fro at their work in the paddy fields and the streets, and the thought came to them that, in a hundred years, all those beings would have fallen a prey to death. They were deeply smitten by this thought and proceeded for a long time in silence. Then one of them said to the other: 'If there be a universal principle of death and ceaseless tendency towards destruction, there must also be an opposite principle of not-dying, a tendency towards escaping from destruction.' 'Yes,' replied the other, 'let it be our resolve to search for the secret of the way to Deathlessness.' 'And, furthermore,' said the first, 'let him who first finds that Way, tell the secret of it to the other.' And thus was a pact made between them.

They first went to their teacher, Sanjaya, but he had already taught them all he knew, and he could not reveal to them the secret of the way to that which does not die.

Then it chanced one day, as Sariputta was going for alms, that he saw Assaji also going for alms. Assaji walked with modesty and downcast eyes, and bore upon his face the marks of serenity and inward peace, and Sariputta was certain that this monk had found the secret he and Moggallana sought. Sariputta followed him when he returned from alms-gathering, and waited respectfully while he ate and then washed his hands. After this, Sariputta went up to him, saying:

'Your countenance is serene, friend, who is your teacher? And what does he teach you?'

Assaji's face glowed with love and veneration as he replied: 'Gautama, the Buddha, is my Teacher. Have you not heard of the illustrious Buddha?'

'He who recently came to Rajagaha? What doctrine does he hold? What doctrine is it that he teaches you?'

Assaji was never able to express himself in words, and now words failed him more than ever. He understood what the Master taught, but it was an inward experience and he could not put it into speech. At length he replied: 'I am but a new disciple. I have but recently received ordination. I know that the Master's teaching is true, but I cannot explain it fully.'

Sariputta was more certain than ever that the teacher of Assaji could tell him the secret of Deathlessness, and he continued to question him.

'Could you not tell me even a little? I want but the spirit of it. The letter matters not.'

Assaji thought a long time and then he said: 'The Master teaches that everything that has a beginning has also an ending.'

It was not an answer that would have convinced those sages who wandered about the countryside, seeking to cross intellectual swords with anyone who would challenge them, but Sariputta was not one of these. For a long time he had been seeking that inward experience, and as Assaji spoke, the light suddenly flashed upon him and he said:

'That which is born must die?'

'Yes,' said Assaji.

'And behind existence and non-existence, behind birth and death, is the Deathless?'

'Yes,' again replied Assaji.

'The ending of the cycle of birth and death,' continued Sariputta, more to himself than to Assaji, 'and the finding of the Immortal— birth and death and all that exists and ceases to exist—ripples on the pools of time—coming to be only to cease to be—and in the depths beneath, Deathlessness! Friend, you have shown me the secret of the Deathless, the secret of the Griefless.'

'Not I!' protested Assaji, 'but the Master. Come with me and I will take you to him.'

'Very gladly will I come,' answered Sariputta, 'but first I must go to my friend, Moggallana, and bring him also. We two have made a compact that he who first sees the light of Deathlessness will tell the other.'

Assaji told Sariputta where the Master was lodging, and Sariputta sought out Moggallana and told him of his meeting with Assaji. Moggallana rejoiced, saying: 'Let us go, friend, and join Gautama, the Blessed One, that he may become our Teacher.'

But Sariputta replied: 'It is largely on our account, friend, that so many wandering ascetics in this town follow Sanjaya. Let us first inform them of our intention that they may do what they think fit.'

Moggallana agreed, and the two friends went to those wandering ascetics and told them of the Teacher who taught the secret of Deathlessness, and having great regard for Sariputta and Moggallana, those ascetics decided that they would also take the Master for their Teacher. After that, the two friends went to Sanjaya and told him also of their intention. He begged them not to leave him but to stay and share with him the leadership of those wandering ascetics, but they would not, and they left him, and all those wandering ascetics followed after them. When Sanjaya saw them departing, he grew red with rage and vomited hot blood.

When the Master saw Sariputta and Moggallana coming, he turned to us, saying, 'You see those two companions arriving? Mark them. They will become the greatest of my disciples.' And it happened even as he said, for they became foremost within the Order, and second only to the Master himself.

Since the Master had come to Rajagaha, he had won to him the Matted-Haired ascetics, who had followed Kassapa of Uruvela, and the wandering ascetics, who had followed Sanjaya, and also many distinguished young noblemen. And now people began to murmur and get angry, saying he was taking away everyone else's disciples and leaving families fatherless. When we told the Master this, he said: 'This noise will not last long. Make no account of it. The Giver of Deathlessness leads men by the power of truth. Who will murmur long at the power of truth?'

Again it happened as the Master said. At the end of seven days, people ceased murmuring, and the noise died down.

Now before I tell more concerning the Establishment of the Kingdom of Truth, let me say something of these two great disciples Sariputta and Moggallana.

Sariputta had the deeper wisdom and understanding, and he had inner sight, surpassing any except the Master. He could defeat anyone in argument if he so willed, but he would not engage in debate unless some purpose would be served, for he knew, even as Assaji knew, that the deepest things cannot be expressed in words, and that, if one's mind is so disposed. one can find the secret of Deathlessness through that one thought of the transiency of all things of earth. Yet for all his learning and knowledge, there was something humble and almost childlike about Sariputta. He admired the Master as a child might admire a great hero. Once, when we were staying at Nalanda, he burst forth:

'Master, such faith have I in you that I think there never has been, and never will be, nor is there now, any other who is greater and wiser than you.'

The Master smiled one of his merry smiles and replied: 'Grand and bold are your words, Sariputta. You have roared a veritable lion's roar in this that you have said. Of course, then you have known all the enlightened ones, all the saints and sages of past times, and have known, too, their innermost minds, their conduct, their doctrine, and the freedom to which they had attained?'

'Not so, Master,' replied Sariputta humbly.

The Master went on with gentle irony: 'Of course then you have known all the enlightened ones who in long ages of the future will be saints and sages, knowing, too, what will be their innermost minds, their conduct, doctrine, and mode of life, and the freedom to which they will attain?'

'Not so, Master,' again replied Sariputta smiling.

'But at least, Sariputta, you know my innermost mind, my conduct, my doctrine, and the freedom to which I have attained?'

We were all laughing when Sariputta again answered, no!

'Then, Sariputta, no knowledge have you concerning enlightened ones, saints and sages, either past, future, or present. Why then are your words so grand and bold? Why have you roared this all-comprehensive lion's roar?'

'Master,' said Sariputta, 'I admit I have no knowledge concerning the minds of enlightened ones, past, future, or present. I only know what is in conformity with Dhamma.'

'And that is enough to know,' replied the Master approvingly.

'But I also know,' said Sariputta boldly, 'that the gate into the city of Dhamma is hard to find, that enlightened ones, saints and sages of the past have found it, that those of the future will also find it, and I know too,' and he spoke with mock sternness, 'that Gautama, the Buddha, he, likewise, has found it!'

We laughed and the Master smiled with apparent pleasure that the joke had been turned against him. After his death, those that had not known him sometimes contended that he was always dignified, remote and distant. Those who said these things had never witnessed the merriment between him and his disciples. It is true, he spoke against laughter which is uncontrolled and shows the teeth, saying: 'it is enough to show one's pleasure by smiling.' But there was nothing of gravity about his manner, and he appeared to be glad when there were such as Sariputta, who could turn his own words against him in pleasant banter.

Sariputta's humbleness, which was shown on this occasion, was also shown when he first met Punna, who had been a slave before he joined the Order. On hearing the Master say that Punna had attained the higher life, he who had been a Brahmin followed him who had been a slave into the forest, waited patiently while Punna sat in meditation, and then questioned him. When Punna had explained, Sariputta expressed his delight at the teaching.

'And what is your name, Venerable Sir?' asked Punna.

When Sariputta told Punna who he was, Punna said: 'And here have I been talking to Sariputta without knowing it was Sariputta, the disciple whom men liken to the Master himself. Had I known it was Sariputta, I should certainly not have presumed to have explained things. None the less, it has been a great thing for me to have had speech with Sariputta, and from whom to have learned humility.'

Indeed, it was Sariputta's humility which made him approachable in a way that people of great knowledge seldom are. I did not hesitate to tell him my problems and ask his advice, and always he was followed by the novices, even before he was appointed their teacher.

Sariputta's friend, Moggallana, was utterly different. He had the inward eye, the second sight that could see into men's hearts, scan distances, and visit the realms of gods and devas, and I was a little fearful of his supernormal powers. When he smiled a strange and distant smile, we knew he was seeing things which other men saw not; I would shudder as he told us of visions he had had, as that of a skeleton going through the air with crows and falcons pecking at it while it uttered cries of pain. And I was not happier when the vision was explained as that of a cattle-butcher who was suffering for the many dumb creatures he had slain. For Moggallana there was sometimes the temptation of Mara to be caught up in his interest in non-human beings, and once the Master admonished him, he told us, to be steadfast in the practice of meditation, of the Aryian silence. Too often do those with this second sight forget that not in communion with gods and devas, whose lives are as transient as our own, is the Goal Beyond which is Nirvana and Deathlessness. Nirvana is found only through the silencing of all thoughts as well as of all desires. The greatness of Moggallana lay in that having these powers of supernormal vision, he did not let them dim his vision of the Goal Beyond. And often those powers were of great use, as when he found

one in the assembly who was not pure, even though wearing the
yellow robes, and he took him by the arm and led him forth from
the gathering. Sometimes, I fear, it was admiration of Moggallana's
supernormal powers that moved young men to join the Order, but
maybe I misjudge and that it was rather the bright joyousness of his
countenance. Moggallana was not a leader like Sariputta and if there
is less to tell of him than of his friend, it is for this reason. More I shall
report concerning them as I proceed.

Chapter III—SOURCES

Vinaya—S. B. East, vol. XIII, pp. 144 and 168

Digha-Nikaya—*Dialogues of the Buddha*, vol. 3—S. B. Buddhists,
   vol. 4, p. 95 (Sariputta's admiration)

Majjhima-Nikaya—*Further Dialogues*, Pt. I—S. B. Buddhists, vol.
   5, p. 103 (Punna and Sariputta)

Vinaya—*Book of Discipline*, vol. I—S. B. Buddhists, vol. 10, p. 181
   (skeleton)

Vinaya—*Book of Discipline*, vol. IV—S. B. Buddhists, vol. 14, p. 52
   (meeting with Assaji)

Samyutta-Nikaya—*Kindred Sayings*, II—Pali Text, vol. 10, p. 169
   (skeleton)

Udana—*Verses of Uplift*—S. B. Buddhists, vol. 33, p. 62 (Moggallana
   and the impure one)

Woodward—p. 237 (Moggallana and the impure one)

Bigandet, Ch. VII, p. 158 (meeting with Assaji)

NOTE: The twenty-four places around Gaya where oblations are
   offered, are not mentioned in the Texts but are factual, and explain
   why Buddha Gaya is sacred to both Buddhists and Hindus. The
   part Yasa plays in this chapter and in all subsequent chapters is
   an elaboration on the Texts.

CHAPTER IV

RETURN TO HIS OWN KINSFOLK

SUDDHODANA, the father of the Master, was the Raja of the Sakyan tribe whose capital was at Kapilavatthu and sad had he been when the young prince, Siddhartha, had left his home, his wife and young child and had set forth into the forest to live as a hermit, there seeking the Raja knew not what. News came of the great bodily mortifications and austerities his son had undertaken, and Suddhodana's heart ached. Once he sent a messenger to bid his son return and forsake his foolish quest, but his son hearkened not and the messenger returned alone. Some years later news had come that his son had started preaching and was drawing large crowds to him. Then he heard that he had gone to Rajagaha, the capital of the kingdom of Magadha. Though this was a long way from Kapilavatthu and separated by the River Ganges, a great longing came upon him to see his son again before he died, and he called one of his trusted noblemen saying: 'Take with you servants and go to the city of Rajagaha. Tell my son that I am now much advanced in years, and that I desire to see him again before I die. Beseech him to return with you to Kapilavatthu.'

The nobleman did as he was commanded, and in due course he came to the Bamboo Grove outside Rajagaha where a great multitude was listening to the teaching of the Master. Being unwilling to disturb those listening, the nobleman remained on the outskirts of the crowd with his retinue, and listened also. Soon he forgot all save the words of truth that flowed from the Master's lips. He spoke, not as other holy men and Brahmins, with clever argument, but with an authority that came from a realm beyond reason. Peace and gladness filled their hearts as they listened, and the world and its treasures became as things that mattered not. He forgot Suddhodana's message, and when the Master had done speaking, he pressed his way through the throng and asked to join the Order.

When the nobleman did not return, Suddhodana sent another, but it happened to him even as to the first. Suddhodana then sent for Kaludayin, who had been born on the same day as his son and had been his companion. The Raja told him of the two noblemen who had gone and not returned, and begged him to return and bring news even though the news might be that his son would never come back. This Kaludayin promised provided he might afterwards join the Order.

Kaludayin also fell under the spell of the Teaching. But he also remembered Suddhodana's message and had compassion for the aged father. Some days after his arrival, he therefore approached the Master in order to deliver this message. Two months had the Blessed One been in Rajagaha, and it was five months since he had left the deer park near Banaras, where he had preached the good news of the Way to those first five disciples. When Kaludayin came into his presence Kaludayin spoke thus:

'The cold season is nearly over. The warm season is about to begin. This is a fitting time to travel through the countryside. Nature is clothed in fresh green; the trees of the forest are adorned with flowers; the roads are lined with fragrant blooms; the peacock proudly spreads his tail; the birds fill the air with song.'

'And for what reason have you given this delightful picture of the countryside in springtime?' asked the Master, amused.

'Your father, Master, has a great longing to see you again before he dies, and your family would rejoice were you to preach the Dhamma in their midst.'

'So be it,' he replied.

Kaludayin hastened ahead to give the good tidings to Suddhodana. For us, who travelled slowly, it took sixty days from Rajagaha in the south to Kapilavatthu which lies at the foot of the Himalaya mountains.

I shall always remember that journey with the Master from Rajagaha to his home town. Those were the happiest days I had known and the happiest I was to know for many a long and weary year. At nearly every village the Master would stay awhile in the cool shade of the mango grove and the villagers would gather round him. The ground is open in these groves and the trees evenly spaced, and they are more convenient for gatherings of people than the sacred groves of wild forest which adjoin them. The countryside was as beautiful as Kaludayin had painted it and wherever the Master passed he kindled, as it were, the incense of happiness among the villagers to whom he talked, and the aroma of it spread like the perfume of flowers by the hedgeways. Sometimes the peasants were bowed with toil and poverty, but, as the Blessed One spoke to them, worry would be smoothed from their faces, and when he left they would find that things they had been anxious about were not as they had thought, and that from out of their difficulties there were ways they had not known. It was joy to see the care lifted from the faces of the people among whom he sojourned. But the greatest joy of all was to be near the Master.

At length we reached the River Ganges. The boat by which men usually crossed had been swept away in a sudden storm, but certain people were making a raft to serve instead. They had cut down trees and when we arrived they were binding them together with creepers and covering them with leaves and grass. The raft was soon ready and we crossed the river upon it. The men paddled with their hands and feet so that it took a long time to cross the wide waters. When we arrived upon the farther shore the raftsmen pulled the raft out of the water, left it on the shore and proceeded on their way.

After we had crossed the river it chanced that we fell in with a wandering ascetic. One of the newly ordained Brothers started conversing with him, and from conversing they fell to arguing, and the newly ordained one was hot in defending the teachings of the Dhamma as the Master had shown it to him, and neither one convinced the other, but the newly ordained one lost his equanimity, and we were glad when that wandering ascetic turned into another path. The peace of the afternoon had been broken by the arguments of those two.

That evening when we gathered around the Master for Dhamma talk he told us the parable of the raft.

'Suppose the man who made that raft, on reaching the farther shore were to say: "This raft has been of great use to me. Resting on this raft and paddling with hands and feet, I have crossed the river. Suppose now I were to keep this raft with me, lift it on my shoulders and carry it with me." What would you think of such a man?'

We laughed by way of answer and the Master continued:

'Even so, Brothers, is this Dhamma which I teach. It is the means by which you cross to the farther shore, to Nirvana, the means whereby you find inward peace. Do not become attached to it. When you have used the means to find that farther shore, leave it behind. If you regard it as an end in itself, it will become a crushing burden in the same way as the raft would become a burden to the raftsman were he to put it upon his head and carry it with him.'

'Are we not then to convince others, Master, concerning the Dhamma?' asked the newly ordained one.

'The Dhamma is not a creed or doctrine about which to wrangle and debate,' replied the Master. 'It is a way of life that leads to the abandonment of delusions and passions, and the attainment of inner peace and serenity. He who has found liberation and inward calm has no theories to pit against other theories, no ideas to pit against other ideas. For he has risen above all compounded things of earth. He has left the raft behind.'

We now lost sight of the Ganges and journeyed north through Vesali, the capital of the Vajjian confederacy and the land of the Licchavi lords. We did not linger there but turned north-west passing through Devadha, the head town of the Koliyan clan, the clan of the Master's mother. It was here that we first caught sight of the mighty Himalayan mountains. I had not been so far north before, and not before had I seen mountains of eternal snow. Great exultation filled my heart at the sight. They were utterly pure and perfect—utterly beyond my reach. They seemed as pure and perfect as Nirvana— was Nirvana equally beyond my reach? This was the first time such a doubt had crossed my mind. It was a doubt that very soon was to deepen.

We now passed through the lovely parkland of Lumbini, where the Master told us he was born, the birth-pangs having come upon his mother before she reached her home-town of Devadha. There was a pool of pure water overhung by sacred bodhi trees. White cattle grazed nearby and in the distance were the purer snows of the Himalayas, clear in the April sunlight before the dust of summer shrouded them. Then at last we reached Kapilavatthu, a walled town strongly fortified, beside which runs the River Rohini through the pleasure gardens in which the Master wandered during his youth.

On the day we arrived at Kapilavatthu, a town far smaller than Rajagaha, it was reported to the Raja that a yellow-robed beggar, who was surely none other than the Prince Siddhartha, had entered the city with a number of disciples and was holding out his bowl for alms among the bamboo cottages in the poorest quarter. Suddhodana knew that the life the Master had chosen would mean that he depended upon beggar's scraps for food, but the fact that his son was begging in his own city, made resentment surge up. Kaludayin told me later that the Raja had wanted to disown his son, but that affection was too strong. He went forth to meet him. When they met his anger flared up again.

'Is it thus necessary to beg your food from door to door? Could not a more decent way be resorted to for supplying your wants?'

The Master replied gently: 'My noble father, it is proper that Truth-finders should take what scraps of food may be given to them.'

The Raja was a little mollified by the Master's gentleness, but it was still with indignation that he continued: 'Are we not of the princely Sakyan line? Has any one of our race before acted in so indecorous a manner?'

'Nay, my noble father,' replied the Master even more gently, 'but I am also of the noble line of Truth-finders, and the way of Truth-finders is to receive scraps of food that are left over, even as beggars do.'

The Raja's anger melted and he said: 'Then, my son, if you so insist, let me be among those that give you food.'

'So be it, my noble father. Tomorrow the Brothers and I will come to your house.' Suddhodana had to be satisfied with this small boon, and he departed.

The next day his household arrayed themselves in brilliant attire to receive their former Prince and give food to him. After the meal was over the Raja sat beside his son, but he did not ask him to preach to those present as did others who invited the Master to partake of food. Instead he sat looking at him. The day before I had not noticed how worn and furrowed was his brow. For a moment I wondered if the Master had any regret, but my doubt faded as soon as it arose, for I felt the Master's compassion smoothing that furrowed brow. Gradually a quietness fell upon the assembled people. A happiness that did not seem to belong to earth began to flow over them. I could almost feel their petty cares and troubles fading away. These no longer seemed to matter. Another day perhaps they might solve their problems, but now let them bask awhile in this subtle and unearthly joy. It was the Raja who at length broke the silence. It was probably not the speech he had prepared, for his pride and resentment had died. There was only anguish and self-pity in his voice.

'Oh son, how could you have dealt thus with me? How could you have left me to bear the burden of rulership alone? When I heard you were coming I looked forward to meeting you as a weary traveller in a desert looks forward to a fountain of pure water. He hastens towards it, but when he reaches it the fountain dries up and disappears. I see my son with the well-known features of old. But his heart—' his voice dropped to a whisper—'where has your heart gone? I am a thirsty man before a dried-up fountain.' The old man did not weep. His disappointment and self-pity were too deep for tears.

The Master said nothing. The people were utterly quiet. I knew that they were not thinking of the Raja; they were only wishing that this joy of the Master's presence might last for ever.

Then at length the Master spoke. 'My father, I bring you the living water of immortal life. But before you can drink of those waters of immortality, the springs of personal affection and possessive love must be dry. All desires must die.'

The agony on the King's face only deepened. I could see he knew the Master spoke the truth, but he knew, too, that he was asking him to give up his son, to give up his ancient ideals of family possessive love, and princely duty. He could not meet the Master's eyes. He must have time to think about it. He rose and left the hall amid pin-drop silence. Soon the Master rose likewise and also left. The spell was broken. As we passed out of the door I heard people discussing what they had witnessed. Whence had the young Prince Siddhartha got that strange power? What had he meant about the living water of immortal life? Why had not the Raja asked him to preach to them, as was customary? The only thing they were all agreed upon was what they had experienced, they would give up all to experience again.

Kaludayin, who stayed near the old Raja, told me how that night the Raja could not sleep. All the arguments he ought to have used repeated themselves over and over again. How his son had been trained to rule the world, how a man's duty demanded he should do the work to which his birth had assigned him, how he had deserted that duty. But in the background of all his arguments to justify himself, there arose an ever-increasing sense of something he needed more than his son, and in the morning he told Kaludayin to ask the Master to preach his Dhamma to the household and such of his people as would listen.

The crowd that came to hear the Master's message had been gathering since before noon. They knew very little of their Prince Siddhartha, who had been brought up in seclusion. They heard he had become a Buddha, an all-enlightened-one. And now they heard of his strange and wonderful influence on the Raja's household.

When he entered, with one accord they rose and saluted him with joined palms. Yet his eyes were downcast and he was humble in mien. When he opened his lips a stir of expectancy swept across them like a wind across the rice-fields. His voice was clear as a distant bell and even those on the outskirts of the crowd could hear every word he said, and it seemed to each as if he were speaking to that one alone.

'This is my home where I lived in enjoyment of all things that earth can provide. But happiness does not spring from having things.' A buzz of questioning passed through the crowd. Surely they always had been taught that if one did good deeds and performed sacrifices, one would be reborn in the next life having more of the good things of earth and therefore happier! Now they were told that happiness does not come from having things! I watched them turning to each other with their questioning. 'No,' he continued, reading their thoughts. 'Because of your good deeds you may be reborn in a higher state of life than that in which you now live. But that does not mean the ending of suffering, for all suffer. The prince and nobleman suffer even as do the menial and the slave. If a prince loses his son by death, does he not suffer even as the servant who loses his? All are kin in blood and tears.'

I turned my eyes to the Raja. Like everyone else he felt that the Master was speaking to him and to him alone. After a little pause the Master went on: 'Suffering is bound up with birth and with life on earth. Old age, disease and death for ever follow birth. Decay is the everlasting inheritance of all. As a young man I saw suffering all around me, and I wept with the tears of my brothers and sisters. Surely, I thought, there must be some way out of this vale of tears. For if there is not, then life is a state too terrible to contemplate and the scheme of things a discord no harmony can heal. But I have found there is no discord but such as we make for ourselves; the soul of things is lovely and the heart of all is bliss and peace.'

As the Master uttered the word "peace", the last questioning died away. All were still. They were drinking in this new teaching. They were experiencing in their own beings that peace of which the Master told. It was a long time before he spoke again.

'There is Dhamma, the living law which holds all. To pit your desires against it means endless suffering. To yield your will to it brings peace and joy. And the way to the heart of Dhamma is impersonal all-embracing Love which asks nothing for oneself and gives all. When there is no longer any thought of "I" and "mine" there is bliss unspeakable, and suffering is left behind forever. . . . That is the living water of life which I bring you.' Then the Master taught them more fully of the Four Great Truths and Noble Eightfold Way. He spoke for a long time, but none stirred nor knew how the time went. The sun was sinking when he ceased speaking and a great gladness lit the faces of the people as if a lamp had been brought into a dark room. Suddhodana was weeping silently. All his pride, disappointment and self-pity had fallen from him. He was now as a little child who sought to be led by his own son into that Way which had been opened up before him.

'Can a Raja tread that way?' he asked.

'All can follow the Way,' replied the Master.

The Raja's face lighted with great joy; his eyes were opened, and he took the first step, which we call by the name of entering the stream which flows onward to Nirvana.

.   .   .   .   .   .

Yasodara, the wife of the Master before he left the world, was not among those of Suddhodana's household who had gathered to hear him. Proud and hurt she had remained apart saying: 'He is my husband; let him come to me.' When first she heard how he had cut his hair and donned the robes of a mendicant, sleeping on the ground and eating only one meal daily, she had sought to do the same. But it was not because of self-renunciation that she had done these things; it was only that she might show she was his equal in austerity and therefore worthy of him, and so that he would forsake the life of a wanderer and return to her as her husband. Now he had come, but she would not humble herself and go to him.

The Master, knowing what was passing in her mind, said to us: 'When my former wife meets me and clings to me as a fond wife to her husband, let her do as she will.' Had not the Master spoken thus, we should indeed have sought to prevent her from troubling him, for no woman may touch one who wears the yellow robes.

It happened as the Master had foreseen. After he had departed from his father's presence he went into Yasodara's apartments, and she with passionate heart-burning flung herself upon him, clinging to him and weeping and laughing as if she could not contain herself. The Master stood silently until her passion abated. She now repented that she had not come to listen with the others to his teaching, and she said humbly:

'My husband that was, teach me, even me, as you have taught the others of the household.' And the Master taught her as he had the others. When he had done speaking she said: 'My Lord and Master, I follow you.'

Thereafter, Yasodara continued her austerities, not from pride as before, but from the gladness of knowing that in wanting little she would find the ending of sorrow.

After the Master left Yasodara's apartments, he happened to pass his half-brother, Nanda, the son of his own foster-mother, Pajapati. Nanda was about to be married and publicly proclaimed as the Raja-to-be. The Master asked him to take his bowl. He did so. As they went out they were seen by the noble lady who was to marry him. She was combing her long, glossy hair. She paused in her task and I saw a look of anxious foreboding spread over her face. Nanda told me that when he took the Master's bowl, he had no intention of joining the Order, but that when he reached his lodging a strange peace filled his heart. The life of a Raja no longer appealed to him. He stayed with the Master and on the third day he asked that he might be ordained.

Yasodara, hearing of the ordination of Nanda, dressed her young son Rahula in his richest clothing, and pointing to the Master, said to him:

'Yonder shaven monk, my son, is your father. Go to him and ask him to give you your inheritance.'

Rahula was only eight years old, and he knew not the deep meaning of his mother's words, not the ache that lay in her heart knowing she was parting from him whom she loved the best. But even as she had followed her husband's example of austerity, now she sent her son that he might receive the greatest of all gifts.

The boy Rahula came to the Master with innocent charm of childhood and spoke as his mother had bidden him. The Master looked at him for a long time without speaking. He was a very young child to leave the world. Then Rahula looked up at his father with trust and love saying: 'It is bliss to be even within your shadow, Holy One.'

The Master's doubts faded and he said: 'Yes, my child, I will give you your inheritance. You shall share with me in those goods which I gathered at the foot of the Bodhi tree when I attained enlightenment.' He turned to Sariputta and added: 'Let him be ordained.' In this manner Rahula became a pupil of Sariputta who taught him the Dhamma according to his age and as he was able to receive it.

When Suddhodana heard that both Nanda and Rahula had donned the yellow robe and gone forth from the householder's life, he was exceedingly sad. He went to the Master saying: 'When I heard that Nanda had left I consoled myself for the loss of my two sons by the thought that I had still my grandson. But he has gone forth also and the princely line of descent is rent asunder. The love for a son cuts into the skin, into the flesh, into the very bones. I know that what you say is right concerning possessive love, but it is a bond hard to break, and I ask that you, my son, who are now my Master, should declare that ordination should not henceforth be conferred upon a son without his father's and mother's consent.' The Master consented and made the rule even as his father asked.

The Raja thanked the Master and departed. As he was much advanced in years the Clan was summoned to the mote hall, to appoint a successor. After due deliberation it was decided that Bhaddiya, the cousin of the Master, should succeed Suddhodana as chief of the Sakyan Clan. Thereafter, Suddhodana applied himself with zeal to following the Dhamma as the Master had shown it to him.

Chapter IV—SOURCES

Vinaya—S. B. East, XIII, p. 208 (Rahula)

Vinaya—*Book of Discipline*, IV—S. B. Buddhists, vol. 14, p. 103 (Rahula)

Theragatha—*Psalms of the Brethren*—Pali Text, vol. 4, p. 248 (Kaludayin)

Bigandet, Ch. VIII (return to kinsfolk)

Woodward—p. 316 (raft)

Sutta-Nipatta—Harvard O. S., vol. 37, p. 193 *et seq.*

Fo-Sho-Hing-Tsan-King—S. B. East, XIX, p. 218 (meeting of father and son)

Majjhima-Nikaya—*Further Dialogues*, I—S. B. Buddhists, vol. 5, p. 94 (raft)

Majjhima-Nikaya—*Middle Length Sayings*, I—Pali Text No. 29, p. 173

NOTE: The Texts are elaborated but not substantially added to. Most commentators assume Rahula's mother sent her son to induce the Buddha to return home; but the present interpretation is equally consistent with the Texts.

CHAPTER V

SECOND VISIT TO RAJAGAHA

MAHA-KASSAPA—ANATHAPINDIKA—KHEMA

WHEN the Master had stayed at Kapilivatthu as long as seemed fit to him, he left to go again to Rajagaha. I did not accompany him, and I was sad; I knew that each must labour with diligence and depend upon none save himself. But now that I was away from the Master, this did not seem easy. After the Master's death, it was reported that all of his first disciples attained to enlightenment and sainthood within the space of a few months. But this report was greatly in error. As the Master said: 'Progress on the way is gradual. The Dhamma is like a mighty ocean. It deepens only gradually, sloping down in hollow after hollow, not plunging down by sudden precipice. Even so this Dhamma-discipline—there is no sudden penetration into insight.' When trials and difficulties now began to beset me, I realized only too well the truth of this. However, it is not my purpose to tell of my own doings, except in so far as they show forth the Dhamma, and I shall now tell not of them, but of what befell the Master after he left Kapilivatthu, and of the three most renowned who became his disciples on his second visit to Rajagaha.

Before reaching Rajagaha, he passed through the town of Nalanda, from which the hills around Rajagaha can be seen, and a short way beyond this, he withdrew from the road to a wayside shrine to meditate. It was here that Kassapa, afterwards known as Maha-Kassapa, or Kassapa the Elder, came upon him. Maha-Kassapa, he who called together the Council after the Master's death, must not be confused with Kassapa, he of the matted-hair, of Uruvela, who had claimed to be the holiest of all men.

Maha-Kassapa's early life had been unusual. He had been the son of a Brahmin householder. In later years he was accused of having belonged to another sect, which may well have been. But he always asserted that, after he cut off his hair and beard, he recognized none except the Buddha Gautama as his Teacher. He told us that, even before he became a householder, the thought came to him that the household life is thronged full of many things that prevent purity of living, and that it is not easy for one living as a householder to live an altogether pure, radiant, and Brahma-faring life, and that dwelling in the open air is the best way to attain to renunciation. He therefore decided not to marry but to go forth from the world. His mother, however, had decided otherwise, and by means of a ruse, she had him married to a maiden called Bhadda of the Kapilas. Now it happened that she too, had determined not to marry but to go forth from the world. Finding each other to be of the same mind, they spent the night of their marriage separated by a chain of flowers, and their marriage was never consummated. As soon as Kassapa's mother died, they cut off each other's hair and went forth from the world together, separating at the cross-roads. Five years Baddha sought wisdom before she joined the Order, but Kassapa became a disciple almost immediately.

The manner of Kassapa's meeting with the Master between Nalanda and Rajagaha he told us many times. He came upon him seated by that wayside shrine. He at once recognized him as his Teacher and fell at his feet, saying he was his disciple. The Master accepted him and conversed with him. Afterwards, Kassapa lived for seven days as before, begging his alms. Then on the eighth day, he said, insight arose within him. When he next saw the Master stepping off the highway to meditate at the root of a tree, he folded his robe of rags, which happened to be soft and comfortable, and placing it on the ground invited him to be seated on it. The Master accepted the invitation, remarking:

'Soft indeed, Kassapa, is this your under-robe of rags.'

Kassapa did not realize that this comment was a gentle rebuke, and he was overjoyed, saying: 'Master, will you accept as a present this soft under-robe of rags?'

Kassapa's joy knew no bounds when the Master replied that he would, adding: 'Then Kassapa, will you wear my coarse patchwork cast-off robes?'

Kassapa replied: 'I will indeed, Lord, wear the Exalted One's coarse patchwork cast-off robes.'

So he gave the Master his soft under-robe of rags and joyfully accepted in return the cast-off robes. Thereafter, Kassapa wore none except the coarsest and roughest of rags. Knowing the Master, we knew how he must have smiled indulgently at Kassapa's enthusiasm, but Kassapa had no sense of humour and he talked about the matter ever after, boasting how the Giver-of-Deathlessness had changed clothes with him, and how he was therefore his true son, born of his lips and begotten of the Dhamma. Kassapa also used to boast how he could attain to the four ecstasies of meditation, that he possessed supernormal powers, that he was free from the asavas of earthly life, that he could no more hide these attainments than an elephant nine cubits high could be hidden by a bit of palm leaf. Kassapa was not well loved within the Order, but none could deny that he excelled in asceticism and indifference to bodily comfort. He once took food from the hand of a leper and ate it, even while he watched the finger that had put food into his bowl, mortifying, break away and fall off from the leper's hand. But asceticism is no virtue in itself, and though Kassapa did not actually ill-treat his body, he would boast of his indifference to it, and there was a streak of hardness in his nature in consequence of this. He had overcome with ease the temptations of the flesh which usually assail men and he had no sympathy with those that were weaker than himself in such matters. There was nothing of compassion in him so far as human beings were concerned. And yet, as regards Nature, he had depths of understanding that few possessed except the Master himself. His great delight was to dwell alone in the forest or climb the crags like a deer to meditate upon some high and solitary place. His muscles were tough as leather and he was tireless in his walking and climbing, and the ways of all the wild things he knew, the cries of the crested creatures, and the homes of the herds, and the habits of the white-faced apes and the timid deer. He knew when the roseapple trees would bloom and the irises open by the water-brooks. The cries of the jackals at night had no sinister meaning for him. He was at home with all Nature. But he was not at home with men. When he came among men, his long silence in the wilds seemed to give him the urge to talk, and he would talk mainly about himself and how he excelled. But he was listened to and respected on account of his hard work and sincerity as well as his lengthy talking.

After meeting the Master on this memorable occasion, Maha-Kassapa accompanied him back to Rajagaha where he was lodging in the Veluvana Pleasance or Bamboo Grove that King Bimbisara had given to the Order on the previous visit. Many came to wait upon the Master there, both rich and poor. Among the rich who came was the great merchant of Rajagaha who was married to the sister of Anathapindika, the great merchant of Savatthi, which lies to the west of the Master's birthplace. Anathapindika of Savatthi was known as the friend of the orphan and destitute, for everyone in need of help came to him. His heart was as great as his wealth and there was no limit to his charity. All praised him and told him he would be reborn in a heaven of bliss. But he himself was not entirely satisfied. He told me later that he felt there was something he lacked.

Now it came about that he went to see his sister or his brother-in-law on some business or other, and arrived in Rajagaha soon after the Master had taken up his abode in the Bamboo Grove. Wherever Anathapindika went, men were accustomed to lay aside what they were doing, and welcome him as an honoured guest. But on this occasion his brother-in-law scarcely noticed that he had come, and continued directing his servants in the preparation of what appeared to be a great feast. In the main-hall the servants were spreading fresh liquid cow-dung to make the floor bright and shiny. In the kitchen his brother-in-law was saying: 'Now, men, make sure that every speck of black is taken out of the rice, that the boiled rice is neither too wet nor too dry and that the curries are not over-strong, and the sweetmeats fit to be served to the King.'

Anathapindika thought to himself: " 'Tis strange, my brother-in-law's conduct! In former times he would put aside everything to greet me in friendly talk, but now he seems quite beside himself, ordering his servants about. What can be the cause of this? Is he giving a wife in marriage, or preparing for a great sacrifice, or perhaps he has invited King Bimbisara himself and all the court to tomorrow's meal."

Anathapindika waited until his brother-in-law had finished giving his orders and then came up to him and told him of the thoughts that had passed through his mind.

'No,' replied his brother-in-law, 'it is for none of these purposes that I am preparing a great feast. But it is indeed as if it were for a great sacrifice, for I have invited the Buddha and his Order of Brothers for tomorrow's meal.'

'What! A Buddha! Said you, an All-Enlightened, All-Awakened-One?' Anathapindika could hardly believe what he had heard.

'Yes! I said "the Buddha",' replied his host.

Anathapindika could still not believe it. He repeated his question twice and got the same reply. Then he said:

'A Buddha! It is seldom indeed that one even hears that word, but that a Buddha should actually be in this town! Do you mean, brother-in-law, that it is possible for me at this very moment to go and see one who is wholly enlightened?'

'Yes, it is possible, but now is not the fitting time. Wait until tomorrow. Then you may see him.'

Anathapindika lay down to rest that night with his mind full of the thought that in the morning he would actually, with his own eyes, behold an all-enlightened-one. He could not sleep for the wonder of it. Twice he got up, thinking it was dawn, and found it was not. On the third time, he was certain he could see the first faint light, and he set forth at once towards the Bamboo Pleasance where, his brother-in-law had told him, the Master was staying. As he left the city and entered the forest, the light faded. Perhaps the moon had set, but he thought not of any natural explanation. The fading light seemed to portend a great disaster; he thought of his vast possessions and that they might be destroyed. He grew afraid and a great trembling came upon him. Almost he turned back; then he thought he heard a voice saying:

'Go on, householder, go on. Better for you to go on than to go back. Hundreds of elephants, hundreds of horses, hundreds of chariots, hundreds of thousands of maidens decked in jewels—none of these, nor any wealth, is worth one stride towards the Goal.'

Then indeed did the dawn begin to show, and his fear faded. He went on unafraid towards the grove where the Master was walking up and down in the fresh air of the early morning. He saw Anathapindika when he was still far off, and sat down, calling to him to come and, addressing him by his own name of "Sudatta", which few knew of.

Anathapindika's joy was even greater than he could have thought. He bowed at the feet of the Master and took the dust from them. When he rose, the Master said to him:

'But for what come you thus early, when most of those of active life like yours would still be sleeping?'

'Deliverance!' Anathapindika replied. 'All my life I have given charity to others. Now I ask charity for myself. I seek the gift of Nirvana, the great peace.'

'Are you not satisfied that your good works will gain you the highest heaven of bliss?'

'It may be, Master, I do not know. It is to learn this that I come to you.'

'Your doubts are right, Sudatta,' said the Master. "All ways of life can be the means of deliverance, and the Great Peace. But on one condition only.' The Teacher paused.

'And that condition, Master?' asked Anathapindika impatiently.

'That they are untainted by any thought of self. It is not enough to give up your wealth. As long as the least thought of self remains, it will spoil all your beneficence. Thoughts of self shade even the loftiest aim, as ashes conceal the fire, treading on which the foot is burned.'

'But, Master, surely I have given without thought of my own needs, my own comfort and security.'

'Had you no thought, Sudatta, of men's approbation, nor of reward in a heaven of bliss?'

Anathapindika did not reply at once. He thought awhile and then said: 'I had such thoughts, Master.'

'Good works will win you heaven,' said the Master softly, 'but heaven and life among the devas is not Nirvana. Those that dwell in heaven abide there but a while. They, too, are subject to change, decay and death, yes, and suffering, also. Nirvana, the peace that is beyond understanding, alone is outside change, decay and death, and it can be found here and now as well as hereafter.'

'And how, Master, how?' Impatient had Anathapindika been as he waited for the dawning of the day. But far more impatient was he to learn of the dawning of the light of Nirvana.

'Selflessness and selflessness alone will take you to it,' replied the Master. 'If you take your refuge in Dhamma, you will find that it demands the giving-up of all desire for happiness both here and after death and the giving-up also of even the desire to do good.'

'But how may I free myself from that desire, especially the desire to do good?' asked Anathapindika eagerly.

'Cease listening to the praises that people give you, Sudatta. Cease thinking that your good works will do anyone any good, and do them simply because to do them is your work, even as scavenging is the work of another. To begin with, it would be wise to cease doing good works on a large scale; do them on a small scale proportionate to your surrender of self to Dhamma.'

'That will be difficult,' replied Anathapindika. 'It will be hard to hear the words of others when I give less than I have been accustomed to give.'

'That does not matter,' replied the Master. 'It is only good works done without thought of self that can bring lasting good to man, because selfless works alone can spread the gift of the Dhamma, and the gift of the Dhamma is the greatest of all gifts.'

'I cannot see, Master, how I can give the gift of the Dhamma to a destitute man who is starving.'

'You cannot,' replied the Master. 'Hunger is a sore sickness, and the mind of a hungry man can understand nothing except food. But of what use is food if it merely perpetuates his life in a world of ceaseless suffering? Food alone will not release him from the suffering which is bound up with the cycle of life and death. Food will help him lastingly only if it is given by the hand of a man who is utterly selfless. For then, whether he teaches in words or in silence, he will shine with the light of the Dhamma, and through him will the one helped gain a glimpse of Not-Self, which is the True Self, in knowledge of which alone is found the Immortal, and the ending of sorrow and suffering.'

Anathapindika remained a long while in silence, pondering on what the Master had said. Then he rose and took the dust from his feet, saying:

'It shall be as you have said. But will you and the Brothers take food with me tomorrow and teach me about the Way?' The Master silently agreed, and Anathapindika departed.

When the great merchant of Rajagaha heard that his brother-in-law had invited the Buddha to the morrow's meal, he offered him the means of providing it, since he was a visitor in that city. And King Bimbisara and also the chief citizen made the same offer. But Anathapindika would give to none the joy of serving the Buddha. He himself helped to prepare the food, and when the Master and the Brothers arrived, he served them with his own hands. The meal over, he asked him if he would spend the rainy season at Savatthi.

'Savatthi is a large town,' he replied, 'and those faring on the way to Truth like solitude.'

'I understand, Master; it shall be arranged accordingly.'

Now Anathapindika had many friends and acquaintances in Rajagaha and all were desirous of meeting him. It was, therefore, some time before he had finished his business there, and returned to Savatthi where he was able to learn in solitude the meaning of the sacrifice, not of wealth, but of himself and his desire for men's approbation. When he resumed his charitable deeds, he gave with reverence, making himself humbler than the people to whom he gave, so that, as well as the gift of food, he might give to them the gift of the Dhamma, the greatest of all gifts, and knowing, too, that only because of his loving friendship would the hungry forgive him for the rice he gave.

. . . . . .

Another notable person to be converted on this, the Master's second visit to Rajagaha, was King Bimbisara's queen, Khema. She was very vain of her beauty, and fearing that the great Teacher would condemn her for her vanity, she would not even visit him. I never heard rightly how the King arranged that she should unwittingly do so. But meet him she did. As she sat near him, there came to her a vision of an ancient woman, wrinkled, old, and ugly, and she knew that this was her own body as it would become. Looking upon that vision, there arose within her the knowledge that all things pass away and die. Then she listened to the Master's teaching, saw with the Pure and Spotless Eye of Truth, and entered the stream that leads to Nirvana.

In those days, the Sisterhood had not been organized but Khema obtained her husband's permission to go forth from home, and become a wandering teacher and preacher like those of other sects, especially those of the Niganthas, turning her great gifts of eloquence and wit to spreading the Dhamma. In due time, alone and in solitude and earnestly striving, she found full enlightenment and became widely known as a saint of great wisdom.

The Master did not go straight to Savatthi when he left Rajagaha after the conversion of Queen Khema. Before accepting Anathapindika's invitation, he decided to go once again to Kapilavatthu, partly because his father was about to die, and partly to consolidate the Kingdom of Truth among his own people, the Sakyan clan. Maha-Kassapa stayed behind in Rajagaha and travelled through Magadha. It was thus some considerable time before I met the one who was to become the leader of the Order after the Master's death.

Chapter V—Sources

Fo-Sho-Hing-Tsan-King — S. B. East, XIX, pp. 201 and · 262 (Anathapindika)

Samyutta-Nikaya—*Kindred Sayings*, I—Pali Text, vol. 7, p. 271 (Anathapindika)

Woodward—*Some Sayings*, p. 141 (Anathapindika), p. 115 (Kassapa)

Anguttara-Nikaya—*Gradual Sayings*, V—Pali Text No. 27, pp. 119 and 127

Therigatha—*Psalms of the Sisters*—Pali Text, vol. I, p. 47 (Bhadda), p. 81 (Khema)

Theragatha—*Psalms of the Brethren*—Pali Text, vol. 4, p. 359 (Kassapa)

Vinaya—*Book of Discipline*, V—S. B. Buddhists, vol. 20, p. 216

Vinaya—S. B. East, XX, p. 187 (Anathapindika)

NOTE: The Texts are silent on whether Khema joined before or after the organization of the Order of Nuns, but it was probably before for she is not mentioned in connexion with the nuns, except the one she herself ordained.

CHAPTER VI

SAKYAN NOBLES JOIN THE ORDER

WHEN the Master returned to Kapilavatthu the second time, the countryside was suffering greatly from drought. The waters of the River Rohini, with which the rice-fields were irrigated, were not enough to cover them all, and the young rice was likely to die. Now the Rohini separates the district of the Sakyan clan from the district of the Koliyans, the clan of the Master's mother. Each clan claimed the right to have the whole of the waters led into its fields and into its fields alone. The feeling between the two clans spread like a forest fire and their Rajas called upon them to arm themselves and make ready for war. As the Master approached, he could see the flashing of their weapons, and with his inward eye he had already perceived the cause of their quarrel. Having compassion upon them because of their blindness and their folly, he hastened that he might arrive before they commenced to slaughter one another.

The opposing armies likewise saw the Master approaching, or perhaps they felt the aura of peace he cast before him. They delayed their hostilities until he came up, and standing on the banks of the River Rohini, he spoke thus to their leaders:

'Princes and warriors! Which is of more value, a small quantity of water, or the lives of many people—the lives of princes and great ones?'

'The lives of people,' they replied, 'more especially the lives of princes and great ones!'

'Therefore,' replied the Master, 'lay aside your passions; throw away your weapons of destruction; conquer your anger instead of your foe, bear loving kindness one to the other. Then you will find the means to divide the waters equally between you, and so live at peace.'

Always hatred and anger died down in the Master's presence, and his words seemed to them good. Indeed they marvelled that they had not before thought of the matter thus. They laid aside their weapons, and their leaders met one another and agreed how the waters of the

Rohini might be used so that the paddy-fields on either side received one-half.

After averting this warfare, the Master went to his father, Suddhodana, who was an old man and dying. The Master spoke to him concerning the transiency of things of earth and the way to the Immortal. And the Raja died having found his being with the Deathless.

Pajapati, the wife of the Raja, and the foster-mother of the Master after the death of his own mother, now asked that she might shave her hair and go forth from home. But the Master, probably mindful that three of his family had already left home, refused her request. Concerning her, I shall have more to tell later.

Prince Bhaddiya now became Raja of the Sakyan clan, and he encouraged all people to listen to the teaching of the Master, so that the good news of the way to the ending of suffering spread far and wide on this, the Master's second visit to his own people. Indeed, it spread to such an extent that a great family felt ashamed if not one of its members wore the yellow robes. Hence it came about that we were often invited to the homes of the nobles of the land to partake of food.

Now I know not whether it was because the wheel of time had turned, or whether it was because I now came into contact with the life I had formerly lived, but I found that the way to liberation no longer pursued the happy path I had known before the Master set forth for Rajagaha on the second occasion, while I stayed behind in Kapilvatthu. Those early years had been ones of sunshine and gladness. The Master had opened up for me a vision of the path of selfless love, and surely loving friendship is a magic which transforms things to gold. Everything seemed to take on a new life and wonder. If sometimes I wandered from the way, very quickly would a look or gesture from the Master recall me. I was happy beyond all measure in the homeless life and the abandonment of earthly ties.

But now I perceived that, though earthly ties had been abandoned outwardly, yet within my heart their abandonment was yet a long way off, and that the fullness of love and understanding is found only when there is complete renunciation of self and detachment from all things of the world. At the same time, there crept back upon me an intense longing for that which in the world I had cherished most. This was not the passion of sex, which so often beset the young Brothers. I had been married young, as was the custom, but of this passion I knew nearly nothing. My lust, my craving, had been for music. I remember how one of my companions had lost his hearing and how I thought to myself that I could never have endured so cruel a fate. After I joined the Order, I of course ceased to attend dances, dramas and other shows at which music is played. But though I ceased seeking for music, it was around me everywhere, and I still delighted to listen to it and to make music for myself. It seemed to me that the wonder of music flowed from the Dhamma itself. What I did not realize then was that my passionate attachment to it was leading me into discord with the Dhamma.

One day it happened that I was invited to take food with Anuruddha, the younger brother of one of the great families. I was taken into the open courtyard surrounded by a veranda. Anuruddha was sitting on a string bed, reclining against cushions and listening to the strains of lovely music to which fair girls were dancing. He rose to salute me, motioned the servants to bring out another string bed and cushions for me, and when they had done so, again reclined back and listened to the music. I soon found myself enthralled by the delicate loveliness which the dancers and musicians unfolded before me, and I forgot that Brothers of the Order should not visit pageants or plays lest they be led into the temptation of sensual joys.

Eventually the dancers paused and Mahanama, the elder brother, came in. He saluted me reverently, sat down, and started talking to Anuruddha before the players could recommence.

'My dear Anuruddha,' he said: "it is fitting that this Venerable Brother should be present while I open to you a matter that has been troubling me for many moons.'

'Say on, my dear brother,' Anuruddha was in a happy mood from the music to which he had been listening, and he had no suspicion as to what lay in Mahanama's mind.

Mahanama continued: 'For many moons I have been feeling it to be a disgrace to our family that not one of us has donned the yellow robes and gone forth from home as a disciple of the Lord Buddha. It is true that we give lavishly of alms, but that is not enough. We must give of our very selves to spread the Dhamma throughout the world.'

'Do you then propose to don the yellow robes?' asked Anuruddha with no great interest in the matter.

'I would willingly do so,' replied the brother, 'but my time is occupied with the management of the farm and the household, and I could not be spared. My duty is clear.'

'You do not suggest that I should go forth?' broke in Anuruddha, now for the first time both interested and disturbed.

'That is exactly what I had in mind,' said Mahanama firmly. 'For the honour of our family one of us must go forth, and you can be spared more readily than I.'

Anuruddha sat up, genuinely alarmed. 'But I have been delicately nurtured, as you know full well. I have had different residences for summer and winter, and in winter I have never gone forth at all. I have been waited upon by many servants, and my wearing apparel has been provided. How could I possibly stand the rigours of the homeless life? My stomach would turn if I had to live on vile scraps and leavings, and as for making my own clothes of rags or sleeping out of doors—oh no! Mahanama, it would be impossible.' He sank back again on the cushions.

'Very well, Anuruddha, will you take over the work of the householder and set me free to go forth?'

'What does the work of a householder involve?' asked Anuruddha. 'I doubt if that either would be suited to my temperament and upbringing.'

'The work of a householder,' said Mahanama, 'means this: First you have to get your fields ploughed. When this is done, you have to get them sown. Then you have to get the water led down over them. After this, you have to have the water led off again. When this is done, you have to get the weeds pulled up. Then you have to arrange for someone to mount the high look-out and guard the crops all night against marauding animals. Then the crop has to be reaped. But that is not the end: the crop has to be arranged in bundles, threshed, carried away.' Mahanama's voice was getting purposely weary. 'The chaff has to be removed. Then you have to get it winnowed and garnered into barns.' He waved his arms wearily towards the huge round bins at the end of the courtyard. 'Having finished that, you have to do the same thing all over again next year, and the next year, and the next. The work is never done. There is no end to one's labours. Vainly does the householder ask when he may enjoy the pleasures of the five senses—listening to music or seeing dancing. He never has the time. His work, beloved Anuruddha, is *never* over. The householder dies and still the work is not finished. But if you would prefer it——'

Anuruddha got up and walked to and fro, 'You have made me see that the householder's life is not for me. And you have also made me see that my mother has indulged me foolishly and that I have not been taking my share of the family responsibilities in the life I have been leading. But to go forth to the homeless life, surely that would be an even greater responsibility and far beyond my abilities. Can you think of no other manner in which I might fulfil my duty to our family?'

'No, Anuruddha,' said Mahanama decidedly. 'There are two ways and no more: either to live in the home as the householder, or to go forth from home as the disciple of the All-Enlightened-One and Blessed Buddha in whose presence there is perfect bliss and joy.'

'It seems that the second is the only one that is possible for me. Be it as you say. I will go forth to the homeless life of Gautama's Order of Brothers.'

'Thank you, my dear Anuruddha, I am most glad. I shall have the honour of presenting you with the robes, and this Venerable one will take you to the Master for ordination, will you not?' Mahanama turned to me and I nodded assent.

I agreed because I could not do otherwise. But my heart was heavy within me. When I had become enraptured with that music, it had suddenly been borne in upon my consciousness that one half of myself was still with the music to which I had been so passionately attached and that its delights were preventing me from comprehending the Dhamma. There also arose within me a longing to return to the life of the world, and doubts as to whether I had even been right to leave it.

And now, here was Anuruddha doing exactly the same as I had done, and I was helping him. Yet, how could I act differently? As one who wore the yellow robes, all assumed that I was free from sensual longings and would wish others to be free also. Thus was, therefore, now added to the conflict already in my heart a new conflict, because my actions were not those of strict truthfulness. In the darkest depression I accepted the food that was put into my bowl and ate with downcast eyes which onlookers interpreted as modesty, but which was really shame lest any should see the uncleanness which now seemed to lie within my heart.

When I rose to go, Anuruddha said to me: 'Before I leave home, I must of course obtain my mother's consent. Please come hither, Venerable Sir, at the same hour tomorrow, and if all goes as I expect, I shall be ready to accompany you to the Master.'

I bowed my assent and left. It was then that I entered a valley of dark shadows. During the next days, indeed during the next years, I carried on a ceaseless argument with myself. At one time I would persuade myself it was necessary for me to give up my passionate attachment to music; at another I would argue that I could use it to lift myself and others towards the understanding of the Dhamma. But the light of the Way had faded and I was alone in a dark and night-enveloped forest which seemed to have no ending.

The next day, I went back to Anuruddha as arranged, and he told me his mother had not been willing to give her consent, for he was her favourite son, but that he had eventually persuaded her to agree that, if Prince Bhaddiya, the head of the clan, joined the Order, then he, too, might join.

'And do you think he will?' I asked.

'I am determined that he shall,' said Anuruddha with such forcefulness that it was hard to believe he was the same young man I had seen only the day before lying lazily upon cushions and listening to music.

'Are you certain you have made the right decision?' I spoke hesitatingly, but he did not suspect the storm of uncertainty that was raging in my heart, making me wonder whether it would not have been better had I stayed at home, whether indeed it would not be better if I now took off the yellow robes.

'Of course I am certain, Venerable Sir, why do you ask?'

'No particular reason,' I said, once again practising that deception which was so hateful. 'But you were hardly of that mind when I entered your presence yesterday.'

'Ah, but my eyes have been opened since then, Venerable Sir. Come with me to the Raja Bhaddiya, and you will see just how determined I am.'

I accompanied him to the Raja, and in spite of my own misery and depression, I could not help smiling at his method of approach.

He bowed shortly to the Raja and said: 'You are obstructing me from donning the yellow robes and joining Gautama's Order.'

'I?' asked the Raja, very surprised.

'You and no other!'

'Heaven forbid!' exclaimed the Raja. 'So far from obstructing another from joining, I would join the Order myself.'

'If that is so, all is well,' said Anuruddha jubilantly. 'Now that you will join, my mother will give her consent to my joining, also.'

'Oh!' said the Raja, abashed at being taken at his word. 'I did not mean that seriously. I have many tasks which I must first fulfil. I will join the Order in seven years, when the first period in office as chief of the clan has expired.'

'No, that would be too long,' said Anuruddha. 'You would be obstructing me from joining the Order until seven years had elapsed, and you would not have that, would you?'

'I would not obstruct you from doing what is right and proper for you to do, my friend, but I could not possibly join the Order at once. It would be a gross breach of my obligations as chief of the clan. Perhaps in seven months I could join.'

'That would be a great help,' said Anuruddha. 'But even seven months is too long. It would mean that you were obstructing me from joining the Order until that period had elapsed, and who knows what may happen before then. *You* were elected in place of Suddhodana, and another chief can be elected in place of you, and this you well know. Will you agree to delay no longer than seven days?'

It was with reluctance that Prince Bhaddiya agreed, and he agreed only because no member of the Sakyan clan would go back on his word. Throughout the land, the Sakyans were known as those who always spoke the truth and kept their troth. It was for this reason, and not because she approved, that Anuruddha's mother now gave her consent.

Because of Prince Bhaddiya joining, it was seven days before Anuruddha was ready to leave, and when we met at the appointed place at the end of this time, I found he had persuaded four other young lords to come, too, among them being Ananda and Devadatta, younger cousins of the Master. They had also arranged for the poor barber, Upali, to come with them so that he might return with their fine clothes and jewels after they had been ordained. The young lords were in high spirits, as is often so, when men have set their minds to some great sacrifice. But I was still plunged into the darkness to which there seemed no ending, a night made darker in contrast with their exultant spirits.

Upali seemed to be greatly drawn to me and as we travelled towards Anukiya, a town belonging to the Mallas, where the Master was staying, he asked me about the Order and what it meant and whether it was open to all, even poor and ignorant people of such a humble calling as a barber's. I answered him that truly within the Order there was no distinction of class or caste, and how the Master had often said that, as the great rivers on reaching the mighty ocean renounce their former names and all are reckoned as the mighty ocean, even so do those of all classes, who go forth from home under the Dhamma discipline, lose their class and become one. I also told him how any could join, provided only such a one obtained the consent of those to whom he was responsible. Upali became more and more attracted to the life within the Order as I painted it, although why, I could not understand, for surely I could not have made it seem a life to be sought after when it had plunged me into such misery. But perhaps the Dhamma shines through us when we know it not. So impressed was Upali with the idea of homelessness that before we reached the Master, he announced to the young lords that he himself would also join the Order. They were delighted at his decision, and arranged that I should present him for ordination before I presented them, to signify that the pride of the Sakyans was humbled, and that there was equality within the Order. It happened as the young lords had planned, and that day there were seven new members of the Order, including the poor barber, Upali, who afterwards became an elder and renowned for his power of debate.

When the new members departed to their lodgings, I stayed behind with the Master. I knew he could read my heart, and that there was no need to tell him of the agony of that inner conflict through which I was passing. He looked upon me with under-standing, and as my eyes met his, the conflict ceased awhile, for I saw into the depths of that eternity he carried with him. Then he said:

'Buddhas only show the way. I cannot still the conflict in your heart, Yasa. You alone can find the means to do that. But find the way you will, and in the end the conflict will cease. You will find there is a bliss in renunciation of self you never found in music.'

After I left the Master, my heart was at peace again, and the loveliness of the Way once more opened before me, and the mountains of renunciation seemed clear and the approach to them easy. But it was not for long. Soon the darkness closed in again, and through the months that followed, there was seldom any gleam of light. It was then that I came to know Ananda, the cousin of the Master, whose coming into the Order brought a kindliness which made him beloved by all, both the members of the Order and the lay men and lay women. Not until after the death of the Master did he make an ending of all attachments, and very bitterly would he sorrow when he lost those that were dear to him. But he was open in his affection for all, and when I passed from the beauty of the light into inner darkness, it was to Ananda that I would turn to remind me of the light I had once seen.

Chapter VI—Sources

Dhammapada Commentary—Harvard O. S., vol. 30, p. 70 (prevention of war)

Bigandet, vol. I, Ch. IX, p. 204 (prevention of war)

Samyutta—Nikaya—*Kindred Sayings*, I—Pali Text, vol. 7, p. 109 (folly of war)

Vinaya—S. B. East, XX, p. 224 (Sakyans join)

Vinaya—*Book of Discipline*, V. S. B. Buddhists, vol. 22, p. 253 (Sakyans join)

Woodward—p. 250 (ocean?)

NOTE: The averting of the war is found only in the Legendary Sources, but is referred to in the Theragatha which is canonical. Yasa's part is of course imaginary.

CHAPTER VII

SAVATTHI AND JETA GROVE

ANATHAPINDIKA, the friend of the orphan and destitute, returned
to his home-town of Savatthi in the north-west, the capital of Kosala,
ruled over by King Pasenadi. He pondered on what the Master had
said concerning solitude and quietness. The Queen, Mallika, had set
aside a garden for the use of Wanderers, but the hall within it was
always the centre of endless talk and argument. It was not hard to
find quiet places near Savatthi in the forest which stretches away to
the Himalayas, but other things were also required. The place for the
Master must be not too far from a village, nor too near, easy of
approach for folk who sought to visit him, yet not too much frequented
by day and free from noise by night. It must also be sheltered from the
cold winds from the Himalayas. Surveying the surroundings, Anathapindika observed that Prince Jeta's park, less than a mile from the
city, had all these requirements. He therefore went to the Prince and
said:

'Young master, let me, I beg, have your park to make a residence
for Gautama, the Buddha, and his Order.'

'Nay, householder, my park is not for sale,' replied the Prince
adding with a laugh, 'to purchase my park I should require to have
the purchase money spread all over it.'

'Then that is an offer, young master, and I accept it. The purchase
money shall be so spread.'

'No, no!' exclaimed the Prince. 'That is not a contract. I spoke
only by way of a joke.'

But Anathapindika would not have it that way, and after some
further discussion they agreed to place the matter before the city
councillors and let them decide whether there was a contract or not.
This was done, and the councillors held that the Prince had named
the price and that Anathapindika had accepted it, so that there did
exist a contract between them. Whereupon Anathapindika had the
copper coins brought in carts and spread all over the ground until
they covered the whole of it, except a small space near the entrance.

Anathapindika told his men to go back and fetch more money that this space also might be covered. But Prince Jeta, who had watched the laying on of the coins, was by that time convinced that this could be no ordinary holy man for whom Anathapindika was expending so much wealth, and he said:

'Stay, householder, cover not this space. Let this space be my gift.'

Anathapindika agreed, for he said to himself that the Prince was a man of great influence, and widely known, and that if he became a disciple of the Master he would have great opportunity for spreading the Dhamma.

Having secured the ground Anathapindika proceeded to erect the necessary lodgings for the Brothers with cells, storerooms, service halls, rooms for fires, wells, lavatories, bathrooms and all conveniences. Thus it was that when the Master first arrived at Savatthi he found a spacious monastery ready built for him, and folk, knowing the manner of the purchase of Jeta Grove, flocked from near and far to listen to his teaching. Prince Jeta was among these and brought with him Queen Mallika, the chief consort of the King. Queen Mallika had respect for all wandering ascetics and gave alms to all alike, but she at once became a disciple of the Master.

Now it happened that soon after this, King Pasenadi, going in procession around the city, cast adulterous eyes at a certain beautiful woman. That night he was haunted by a nightmare and woke in fear and trembling hearing loud and fearful sounds. He could not sleep after that for thinking of these ghostly shrieks. In the morning he called to him the Brahmin priest of the palace and asked him the meaning of his dream and whether it portended the end of his kingdom, of his queen or of himself. The Brahmin priest did not understand the meaning of the dream, but he said it meant that the King must die unless he offered a sacrifice of every kind of living creature including human beings. The King, in mortal fear, had his servants gather together great numbers of every living creature—elephants, horses, bulls, cows, asses, rams, fowls, pigs, and boys and girls. And great was the lamentation of the people when they heard of the sacrifice that was to be performed, for not in anyone's memory had human sacrifice been heard of.

Queen Mallika, hearing that noise and ascertaining the reason, went to the King, and told him that, though he was a great King he had very little sense. She said:

'Did you ever hear of a man saving his life by causing another to be killed? Because a foolish Brahmin told you to do so, is that any reason for overwhelming your people with suffering? Now in Jeta Grove there is a Teacher who abounds in wisdom. Ask him concerning your dream and he will advise you.'

Thus it was that King Pasenadi also came to the Master, who, when he heard of his dream, told him of sufferings that arise because of lustful thoughts, and the King perceived that his dream had arisen because of the conflict in his mind between his adulterous thoughts and his desire to rule wisely. He departed to bid his servants release all those living creatures from their bonds, and great was the rejoicing of the people, who went about exclaiming: 'Long live our wise and gracious Queen Mallika.'

But Anathapindika rejoiced more than any that the word of the Master should be spread abroad and that the King and Queen had become foremost among his disciples. He who had given lavishly of his substance to succour those in want now felt his giving to be but the giving of a straw. The gifts that he gave might stop their misery and suffering for the space of a few short hours, but the Master could give that which stopped their misery and suffering for ever. One day I heard him ask whether his giving carried with it any merit at all. The Master asked him if he gave to all who came, and he replied that he did, but that sometimes that which was given consisted only of fragments, coarse and broken grains and savoury gruel.

'It is not whether you give choice alms or coarse,' replied the Master, 'that brings merit with the giving. It is the thought that is behind the giving, whether you have consideration for the one to whom it is given, and whether you give it with your own hands and with the fragrance of loving friendship, and give it, too, with the knowledge that all is impermanent. There is virtue in the giving only when you know there is no virtue in it, for all things pass, the giver, the gift and the receiver of the gift.'

Anathapindika took to heart the Master's teaching and often I thought he seemed closer to him than other lay disciples. He killed no living thing, drank no intoxicating liquors and was blameless in his married life. Furthermore, he would go apart in silence and could still his mind and find that calmness within through which is perceived the Goal Beyond. Something of the Master's own serenity and peace seemed to emanate from him, and people who disputed would cease their arguments when he drew near. I was once with some of these wranglers of other sects when Anathapindika approached, and I heard one of them say:

'There is Anathapindika, the white-robed lay follower of the recluse Gautama approaching. He likes quietness, and perhaps if we were quiet he might think it worth while to join us, and tell us of the teaching of this Gautama.'

Their arguing ceased, and when Anathapindika came among them they asked him to explain his Master's teaching. Anathapindika replied modestly:

'Truly, I know not all the Master's teaching.'

'Will you then tell us your own views?'

'That, sirs, is no hard task,' he said. 'But would you not first tell me your views?'

Then those Wanderers began disputing in loud voices concerning whether the world had a beginning or not a beginning, and each one expressed a different view. Then at length one of them said to Anathapindika:

'Well, householder, we have all expressed our views, do you now tell us which view you favour.'

Then Anathapindika replied: 'I see all things that we know as formed of the coming together of other things, separate particles, and of thought-forms, and what has come together, must be dispersed. So all is subject to change, decay and death. But I have found the escape from the things that die, escape from being bound to them. I have found the Undying, the Immortal, the Deathless, that which is not subject to change, decay and death.

Those Wanderers listened as Anathapindika explained further and his sincerity silenced them. He spoke, not as they spoke, with clever words and fine-pointed logic, but with simplicity and directness. None disputed what he said. But after he left them he wondered if his words had been the true teaching of the Master. So he went to him, and the Master commended him for the words he had spoken. Anathapindika then unburdened himself of what had often troubled him since he first met the Master in Rajagaha.

'Is not great wealth and life in the world a hindrance to the higher life?'

'Say not so,' said the Master, 'wealth is neither good nor bad, just as life within the world with its sensual joys is neither good nor bad. It depends on the way the wealth is obtained and what is done with it, and in what spirit it is handed away. People may acquire wealth unlawfully and spend it selfishly. Truly, in either of those cases it makes no man happy. But if a man acquire wealth by lawful means and without injuring others, and is cheerful and uses it without greed or lust, and is heedful of the dangers of attachment to wealth, if he shares his wealth with others and uses it to perform good deeds, and lastly, if he is ceaselessly aware that it is not the wealth, nor the good deeds, but liberation from craving and desire, that is his goal, then, when all those things are done, truly the wealth of that man brings joys and happiness. He holds it not for himself but for all. Such a man is bound for enlightenment and may have his being within the Deathless Essence.

Chapter VII—Sources

Woodward—p. 141 (Anathapindika)

Samyutta-Nikaya—*Kindred Sayings*, I—Pali Text, vol. 7, p. 271 (Anathapindika)

Anguttara-Nikaya—*Gradual Sayings*, III—Pali Text, vol. 25. p. 158

Anguttara-Nikaya—*Gradual Sayings*, V—Pali Text, vol. 27, pp. 119 and 127

Vinaya—S. B. East, XX, p. 187 (Anathapindika)

Dhammapada Commentary—Harvard O. S., vol. 29, pp. 100 and 230 (Mallika and Pasenadi)

Fo-Sho-Tsan-King—S. B. East, XIX, p. 262 (Anathapindika)

Vinaya—*Book of Discipline*, V—S. B. Buddhists, XX, p. 222 (Anatha-pindika)

MEDITATION OR THE CALMING OF THE HEART WITHIN

DURING this first sojourn of the Master in Savatthi, I was also there, both for the rainy season and after. For some weeks I had been going for alms early and returning late, watching the villagers at their work, the bamboo-basket maker with his strips of bamboo spread out and his little pot of water; the weaver threading his loom, with infinite patience tying the threads one after the other; the roof-maker spreading the bamboo matting and then the round tiles on top; the coppersmith beating his wares into shape. And there was also the music of the village—the gentle sound of the people stirring to life at dawn, the lighting of fires for cooking and then the gradually rising tune as the men, women and children went to the day's work; also there was the singing as they worked, for the people make music of the turning of a tool, or the fashioning of a pot. And there was the sweetness of the flute as a woman stole a few moments in the midst of the rice-gathering. I loved it all, and I loved to lose myself in the villagers' certainty that this earthly life is something more than a shadow cast upon the Deathless.

When I returned from gathering alms I had recently started to undertake a greater number of the tasks that are permitted to us of the yellow robe. Especially I found that I was deft with the use of my fingers and the making of robes from rags that had been collected from rubbish heaps, and soon I found my days becoming full of the little tasks that are always there for those that seek them. At times the old turmoil would return, and I would find that I was irritated with the doings of my fellows, and sometimes, too, I looked back regretfully at those first two years when consciousness of the harmony of the Dhamma was around me everywhere. But for the most part I was finding things less difficult as I slipped back into the surface life of earth, although still wearing the yellow robe.

It was in the cool of early morning that one day I passed the Master on my way for alms. He called me to him. The expression in his eyes, which always probed to the depth of one's heart, gave me once more a glimpse of that inscrutable peace in which he ever dwelt. An aching longing for that peace swept back upon me. Between it and me I saw the surface dream of life as a murky cloud I could not pierce, that surface life which a short while ago had seemed to be enough.

'Ah! Yasa, you are busied about many things,' he said sadly.

'Yes,' I replied.

He went on softly: 'There is one who is always busy, who is clever at work. He lets the time for going apart slip by, and he applies himself not to the calming of the heart within. This is the first condition that leads to the decline of the one who is training for the monk-life. It is the same with the one who spends the day doing small things, or who passes the day in the company of others, going early for alms and returning late, and so lets the time for going apart slip by, and applies himself not to the calming of the heart within.'

I was silent. I knew that what the Master said was right. I had sought to lose myself and my own conflicts, not in Deathlessness, but in the life of the world. I had known I was losing the light that once shone, and that inner sight by which we see the Goal Beyond.

After a little while the Master went on: 'Yasa, let not the time for going apart slip by; fail not to apply yourself to the calming of the heart within.'

I was ashamed; I looked down at the ground. A poor old hen was scratching plaintively in her nest under a bush. One chick more than a day old hopped around her. In the nest there were ten eggs and no sign of another chick coming from them. She would move one of the eggs with her claws hoping that it might have cracked and a little beak show through. But she had gone wandering round the village instead of sitting on the eggs—I had seen her. The eggs had become cold and the chicks had died before they had hatched. It was a sad sight; I felt sorry for that mother bird. The Master followed my eyes to the hen and my thoughts he already knew.

'Yes,' he said. 'That hen wished much for chickens, but she did not make them come into existence, because she did not sit on the eggs. The monk wishes much for deliverance from desire and for Deathlessness, but he will not find these things by wishing for them. He must make them become by practising the Eightfold Way, by practising meditation. Things do not come by wishing. We must make them become.'

I looked from the hen to the Master. He was smiling with that love and friendship which seemed to draw you with him into the Beyond. He waved his hand towards the forest.

'There are tree-roots. There are empty spaces. Meditate.'

'Master,' I said: 'I will sit on the eggs from now on until the chickens of insight are hatched.'

He smiled approval and I went on a little hesitant:

'But tell me about the lay people who have little time for going apart for meditation. Can they, too, attain insight into the Beyond?'

'They can,' he replied. 'There was Nanda's mother. Her husband had died and her son had been killed by Rajas, yet she was singing joyfully as she worked, the song of the Way to the Beyond. Saraputta and Moggallana were coming to visit her. She perceived this with her supernormal sight, and had food ready prepared for them. They were surprised and questioned her. They found she had learned to bear with equanimity the death of those dear to her, that she had made an ending of lust and desire, and that she could still her mind at will and attain the four stages of contemplation. She was completely serene and happy, for she had her being, not in this transient world, but in the Deathless.'

'If a lay woman can find all this amid the busy life of house-mother,' I asked, 'why do we leave home and don the yellow robe?'

'Do you feel the call, Yasa, to return to the householder's life?'

'No, Master.' I realized my question had not been necessary. Do we not all know that to each is the way ordained by his nature, and that it is folly to question why the way of the householder is for some and the way of the homeless is for others.

After that the Master sat beside me in meditation, and my heart was calmed within; for a little while it was released from the pain of its desires, and I knew the bliss of Nirvana's peace.

The sun had risen high when the Master and I set forth by different ways to receive alms from the villagers. That day I lingered no longer than the white-faced monkeys which scampered from the fields with ears of stolen rice between their teeth. On the way back to the forest to meditate, I saw a deer-trapper and his friends killing the deer they had trapped. Deer-trappers are accustomed to plant crops; when the crops are grown, they remove the fences and the deer rush to eat. While they are absorbed in their feeding, the deer-trappers and their friends surround them on all sides, and then, at a given signal, they charge in upon the browsing deer and slaughter them. It was a horrible sight, that slaughter of beautiful creatures with graceful heads and fathomless limpid eyes. I knew that deer must be destroyed if the farmer's crops are to live. But I turned away hoping that no venison would be put into my bowl during the next days. The eating of meat which is slaughtered for us is forbidden, and the trade of a butcher or hunter is forbidden to any who would be disciples of the Master. But we of the homeless life must take whatever is put into our bowls and sometimes if the giver were not a lay disciple he might put meat therein. Always terrible to me had been the slaughter of animals for food, animals so like unto ourselves, and after seeing those deer it seemed more terrible than before. Yet a yellow-robed one must be possessed of neither attraction nor revulsion, I told myself as I turned miserably from the sight, and made my way into the forest to calm the mind in meditation.

The Master, too, had seen those deer being slain, and when we gathered around him to listen to Dhamma-talk after the hour of cow-dust, when the cows return along the dusty trails to their milking, he told us a parable about the deer.

'Do deer-trappers plant crops to keep the deer in good condition?' His question made the Brothers smile. 'Why do they plant them?' He looked at the younger Brothers and one of them replied:

'Deer-trappers plant crops knowing that the deer will find them more attractive than what grows within the forest, and will rush in to feed, so that the trappers will be able to kill them easily.'

'Suppose,' said the Master, 'that a second herd, seeing the fate of the first, kept away from the crops for a long time until the hot weather came, and food and water in the jungle gave out, what then?'

The same young Brother, who had been the son of a deer-trapper, replied: 'No, that second herd would also at last rush in and eat, and it, too, would be killed.'

'Would it be different if a third herd, seeing the fate of the first two, made its lair just beyond the fields?'

'Not one wit, Master.'

'Now, let us imagine a fourth herd wiser than any of the others. This herd makes its lair in the depth of the forest, and then, circumspectly, from time to time and in full mindfulness of what it is doing, it ventures forth, eats what is necessary of the crops, and returns to its lair in the depths of the forest. Would that herd escape those trappers?'

'Yes, Master, it would, but those deer would have to be human beings to be so wise that they did not rush in greedily, so wise that they remained always mindful and returned to their lair immediately they had eaten enough.'

'Now, the deer I tell you of,' went on the Master, 'are in fact human beings. They are recluses and Brahmins. The deer-trapper is Mara, the tempter, the individual self with its desires. The crops are the pleasures of the world. The depth of the forest is the stillness of the heart in meditation. The first herd are those recluses and Brahmins who think they can continue to enjoy unharmed the pleasures of the world. But none can seek two goals. Those who seek to enjoy the pleasures of the senses, cannot find the Deathless. Very soon their lusts and desires will overwhelm them, and Brahma-life will die within them.

The second herd are those recluses and Brahmins who think they can keep away from the things of the senses altogether, and repress their bodily and intellectual cravings by the power of their individual wills. But not for ever can a man live apart from the transient world around him. Sooner or later his desires and cravings will overcome him; he will rush in and his downfall will be even as the first.

The third herd are those recluses and Brahmins, who think they can make their home just outside the life of the sense objects; to wit, in the realm of intellectual speculation. They include the sophists, who argue on abstract questions as to whether the soul and body are separate or the same, whether the world has an ending or whether it exists for ever. Sooner or later they, too, are overwhelmed by the temptations of lust and craving, and their fate is the same as that of the others.

The fourth herd are those who seek the quietude of heart that is within. There is only one place where Mara, the cravings and desires, cannot enter, and that is the stillness of a heart in meditation, when all diffuseness is banished, and the being is centred in the Deathless and Eternal. That is your true home, and with that as your home you may venture unharmed in mindfulness among the objects of the senses.'

I turned over the Master's words in my mind. If Nanda's mother could make her home in the stillness of the heart, was it not folly for me, to whom there was greater opportunity, not to do so. How foolish to let the divine life die within me, how dishonest to have accepted the alms of generous villagers without pursuing the training for which they gave me alms! Then I heard one of the Brothers ask:

'Is it not enough to master the sacred sayings and runes and ponder upon the Dhamma?'

'It is not enough,' he replied. 'One may master the sayings, songs, catechisms, the marvels and the runes, but if such a one neglects to go apart for meditation and devotes himself not to the calm purpose of the Self—such a one has only heard of the Dhamma by hearsay, he lives not according to the Dhamma, he knows not the Deathless from his own experience. It is the same with the one who teaches the Dhamma to others, or ponders over the Dhamma all day long. Such ones, if they neglect to go apart for meditation know not through actual experience and inner sight, the Goal Beyond, and they live not according to the Dhamma.'

When the Master spoke thus he seemed to bring the Deathless into our presence. But I knew now this is not enough. I must make it become by the ceaseless practice of stilling the heart within.

Chapter VIII—SOURCES

Anguttara Nikaya—*Gradual Sayings*, II—Pali Text, vol. 24, p. 51

Anguttara Nikaya—*Gradual Sayings*, III, Pali Text, vol. 25, pp. 70–75, 91, 152

Anguttara Nikaya—*Gradual Sayings*, IV—Pali Text, vol. 26, p. 35 (Nanda's mother), p. 82 (hen and chicks)

Majjhima Nikaya—*Further Dialogues*, I—S. B. Buddhists, vol. 5, p. 108

Majjhima Nikaya—*Middle Length Sayings*—Pali Text, vol. 29, p. 194 (Deer-trapper)

CHAPTER IX

MORE OF BHADDIYA AND ANURUDDHA

AFTER the Master had stayed in Savatthi for some considerable time he set forth for Kosambi on the River Jumna, and he asked me if I would come as his attendant.

First we went to Anupiya, near Kapilvatthu, for Bhaddiya, formerly Raja of the Sakyan clan, dwelling in the forest near by, had been heard to murmur over and over again: 'Oh happiness! Oh happiness!' The Master visited him and questioned him concerning this.

He replied: 'I was thinking of the worries which beset me when I was Raja. I thought I had security in wealth and position, but I see now that the more a man owns and the higher his position, the more he is afraid, for he fears to lose that which he has. A prince even surrounds himself by armed guards, so fearful is he. But now that I own nothing and have no position, I have nothing to lose and therefore nothing to fear. Is not that happiness?'

The Master appeared pleased and added: 'Yes, if a man cares not if things are thus and not thus, then, provided he has no harsh thoughts, he has indeed found happiness. He has certain security for he has found freedom from grief and care. Truly, he has overcome the world.'

Meeting Bhaddiya at length convinced me that it was neither by hearing nor by not hearing the sweetness of music that I would end this craving for it, but only by taking refuge in the Dhamma like him.

When we reached Kosambi we found that knowledge of the Master's coming had travelled before him, so that there were many to wait upon him, including the young king, Udena. Although Udena did not become a devout lay disciple like King Bimbisara and King Pasenadi, he asked the Master to arrange for one of the Brothers to visit the ladies of the palace daily, that they might be instructed. The Master chose Ananda who became the teacher of those within the palace, and visited them frequently during the years that followed.

After the King departed, various mendicants waited upon the Master, thinking he would reveal to them the secrets of the universe that others had not been able to reveal. When the Master told them only of the ending of suffering through the living of the Brahma-life, they were not content, and questioned him further. I remember one moonlight night when we were gathered about him in the simsapa grove outside Kosambi, one of these asked him concerning the creation of the world. The Master took up a handful of simsapa leaves and for some time sat silently contemplating them. Then he looked up and said:

'What think you, which are more—these simsapa leaves which I hold in my hand, or the leaves remaining on all the simsapa trees in this grove?'

'The leaves which you hold in your hand, are few;' replied one, 'the leaves remaining on all the trees in this grove are very many.'

'Just so,' went on the Master, 'the things that I have told you are few. The things in the universe are very many. And why have I not told you of those others? Because those others are without profit to you. They are not necessary for living the Brahma-life; they do not lead to detachment, to the ending of lust and desire, nor to the ending of sorrow.'

'Master,' said another, 'tell us what exactly are the only things it is necessary for us to know.'

'Only those four great Truths that I have spoken of,' replied the Master, 'that suffering is, that it arises from desiring, wanting and craving and the sense of "I" and "me", that you escape from the burden of suffering when you are liberated from your self and its desires, and I have told you of the practical Eightfold Path by which this can be achieved.'

What the Master said seemed very clear, but I fear that even those that belonged to the Order did not understand. They learned the teaching of the Master like a creed or doctrine, and not as a way of life, and some would learn the Dhamma like Brahmin rules, and some would learn the Vinaya rules of discipline like the Vedas, and they continued to dispute with one another as before. I have often wondered why it was there were so many discords at Kosambi as if the gods of strife had taken up their abode in this town. Was it because all that joined the Order there had belonged to rival sects which argued with one another? Or was it because Kosambi, lying in the midst of fertile plains, is over-prosperous, and, as Bhaddiya had found, peace of mind is not easily achieved when men have great wealth. Whatever the explanation, the doings of the monks of Kosambi are sad to recount.

However, I mention things not to happen for some years. Now the Master left Kosambi and we made our way down the River Ganges towards Vesali. The river was running low at this season and the sandy banks were a white glare in the scorching sunlight, broken only by the herds of cattle taken down to the water and the groups of fishermen hauling in their nets. We travelled down the river by boat for the first part of the way. This was the only time the Master travelled by boat. Large numbers of wandering mendicants travelling without payment are a burden to boatmen, and the Master had compassion for them in their need to earn enough to maintain their wives and children. It was for the same reason that he did not travel in carts or on horses but always on foot. He would walk about fifteen miles every day, resting near villages at night and sleeping at tree roots if there were not bamboo shelters erected for wanderers.

Before entering Vesali we went north to Gosinga Wood, where the sal trees stand full of perfumed bloom on moonlight nights, and where Anuruddha, Nadiya and Kimbila were then dwelling.

It was now some time since I had been the unwilling helper of Mahanama in persuading his brother, Anuruddha, to take to the homeless life. Often I had wondered whether Anuruddha felt any of the conflict that continued within my own heart, a conflict between the clear vision of the Dhamma, and Mara ever tempting me with thirst for my old life and its music. From the little news I had heard of Anuruddha it seemed that he had already found inward peace.

We reached Gosinga Wood in the evening, and the keeper came to meet us saying: 'Do not go into that wood, Venerable Sirs; three young men are living in this forest for the sake of the Brahma-life. Do not disturb them.'

But Anuruddha, overhearing, or perhaps hearing with inward ear, came up and said: 'Good keeper, it is our Master who has come. Do not warn him off.'

The other two had followed Anuruddha, and now the three came forward to welcome the Master, taking his bowl and robe and getting water for us to wash our feet. He then inquired concerning their well-being. They told him that they were well-supplied with alms and that they lived together in perfect amity. Each would give way to the others and each would help willingly with the few necessary labours such as fetching water for drinking and washing. It seemed that they were of one mind in all things. How different, I thought to myself, from those monks in Kosambi! The Master then questioned

them further as to whether they had attained the concentration of
mind so that they could reach the four stages of rapture and trance,
and Anuruddha answered for them that they were all so able, for he had
clairvoyant sight and knew their experiences to be the same as his own.

I was greatly heartened by the meeting with these young men,
whose former lives had been so like my own. It showed me that the
discord in my heart would end and that I should find the means to
give to the Dhamma my whole heart and mind. Thereafter the darkness which descended upon me from time to time took a new form.
There was now anger with myself that the asavas[1], the delusions and
cravings, should still arise unwanted, though I was determined they
should have no place; and I worried because at one time the Spotless
Eye of Truth would show me the way clearly, and then a short while
later, when I was less mindful, Mara, who is within oneself, would
again be at my side.

It was when I was thus worrying that I again met Anuruddha.
His countenance was serene and happy, and I marvelled at the change
that had been wrought in one who had led such a life of ease.

I asked him concerning what had often passed through my mind.
'Brother, how is it that you have changed so much since I first saw you
when you were lying back on cushions and listening to sweet music?'

He replied: 'I think it was my mother who wrought the change,
though little did she intend it. It was with reluctance that I obeyed
Mahanama's wish and went to my mother to ask her permission to
join the Order. She led me to a silken couch, and gave me sweetmeats
while she ran her fingers through my hair and called me her darling
son, saying that all that life could give would be mine if I but stayed
within her care. I felt she was treating me as a child, and I jumped up
indignantly, determined to submit no more to such soft dalliance,
even though I might never gain her consent to go forth from home.
Truly, I think it was her opposition that stirred in me a determination
to change from the easy life I had led.'

'You have attained to serenity of heart very early, Brother,' I
said, adding: 'it would seem as if in you all the asavas, the cravings,
delusions and ignorance, have been utterly destroyed.'

'No, Brother,' he replied laughing, 'only a few weeks ago I was
moaning to Sariputta that I was still held within the asavas.'

'But surely,' I protested, 'you are known far and wide as one
possessing pre-eminent clairvoyant powers?'

[1]See Appendix.

'Clairvoyant powers have nothing to do with liberation from desire,' he said sadly. 'I was boasting to Sariputta that I had such powers, and also deva-sight, by which I can scan the thousand-fold world-systems. He replied with truthfulness that this statement of mine was merely conceit. I also told him that I had been so strenuous in my endeavour that I could at will centre my mind in meditation. He replied, again with truthfulness, that my assertion was merely arrogance.'

'Friend Anuruddha, you surprise me,' I said, 'although I confess I often wondered if you ever felt any stirring of inner conflict caused by a lingering thirst for the things of the world—the—', I hesitated—'the music, the rhythm, the dancing.'

'I do have such longings,' he replied solemnly; 'not for such things as these, but rather for the clean and decent food of my mother's kitchen. At times I feel a loathing for the scraps of food, sometimes food not clean, which is put into my bowl. I also sometimes have a great longing for the clean covers on the bed and its softness. I was complaining to Sariputta that I could not free myself from the asavas, and that I still had cravings and desires.'

'And what did Sariputta say?' I asked. 'For I, Brother, have cravings even more insistent for the things I knew in my mother's home.'

Anuruddha looked into the nothingness of distance and replied slowly: 'He told me that my moaning was worry, useless worry, and that instead of worrying I should focus my mind on the Deathless Essence of all, that which alone does not die.'

These words gave me fresh courage. Sariputta was wiser than any save the Master. If we could fix our minds upon that which does not perish, we should be untroubled by loss of what does.

Chapter IX—SOURCES

Majjhima-Nikaya—*Further Dialogues*, I—S. B. Buddhists, vol. 5, p. 148 (Gosinga Wood)
Majjhima-Nikaya—*Middle Length Sayings*—Pali Text No. 29, p. 257
Anguttara-Nikaya—*Gradual Sayings*, I—Pali Text, vol. 22, p. 260 (Anuruddha and Sariputta)

Samyutta-Nikaya—*Kindred Sayings*, V—Pali Text, vol. 16, p. 307
   (Simsapa leaves)
Woodward—p. 308 (Simsapa leaves)
Buddhism in Translations—Harvard O.S., vol. 3, p. 117
Udena—*Verses of Uplift*—S. B. Buddhists, vol. 8, p. 23 (Bhaddiya)
Vinaya—*Book of Discipline*, IV—S. B. Buddhists, vol. 14, p. 501
   (Anuruddha and others)
Vinaya—*Book of Discipline*, V— S. B. Buddhists, vol. XX, p. 257
   (Bhaddiya)

VESALI AND THE SISTERHOOD

THE Master had passed through Vesali on his return to Kapilavatthu the second time, but he had not lingered. He now intended to spend the rainy season there. Vesali is the capital city of the Licchavi clan of the Vajjian confederacy. The news that King Pasenadi, as well as King Bimbisara, had become his disciples, had reached the Licchavi lords, and as soon as he arrived they invited him to partake of food and teach them a message which would make for their well-being. The Master accepted and told them the basis of wise and stable government.

'As long as you hold full and frequent meetings, your lordships, and meet together in concord, just so long may you be expected to prosper and not decline. As long as you do not seek to overturn what has been beforetime appointed, but conform to the Vajjian laws and customs, and respect and reverence the elders, so long may you be expected to prosper and not decline. As long as you respect the women and maidens of the clan, and the shrines, and the saints and sages that are among you, during such time the Vajjian confederacy will have prosperity and strength.'

While the Master was speaking with these lords, the Brothers saw approaching from the north-west a large band of yellow-robed women, bare-headed and bare-footed, and stained with long travel. They wondered who these women might be. It is true there were women wanderers, especially among the Niganthas, while, among the Master's well-known yellow-robed women disciples, was Khema, the former wife of King Bimbisara of whom I have told, and also Bhadda Curly-Hair, who had previously belonged to the Niganthas.

Bhadda Curly-Hair had studied the art of debate until she found none equal to her. She then went about from town to town and village to village. At each she would set up a heap of sand and in it plant the branch of a rose-apple, telling the children, who always come to watch such folk, to let all know that any who should wish to meet her in debate should trample on that rose-apple bough. Every time she was the victor until Sariputta saw that bough. She had not before debated with a great one of the Master's disciples, and she gathered a large following to come and witness the combat. After exchange of courtesies, Sariputta asked her to put her questions first. He answered them all until she grew weary of questioning. Then he put to her one question only: 'What is that which is one?' Bhadda Curly-Hair did not reply, though why I could not understand for there are many well-known answers from Vedic lore, but it may be that she had already perceived that Sariputta could give her an answer that would make her defeat of small account. Be that as it may, she asked him to give his own answer and he told her of the Deathless and the Noble Eightfold Way that leads thereto. She listened and was convinced, and asked to become his disciple. He refused, but bade her come with him to the Master, which she did, and the Master ordained her.

Bhadda's ordination had taken place only recently and was still much talked of. But neither Bhadda, nor Khema, nor any other of the Master's ordained women disciples, nor any of the Niganthas nuns that we know of, travelled with such a large company about her as the women we now saw approaching Vesali.

Before I tell of these women, whose coming into Vesali was to mark an epoch in the development of the Order, let me say how the Master told us that, when he found enlightenment and Mara tempted him to depart alone, and as a hermit enjoy the bliss he had found, he vowed he would never cease from his labours in the world until there were ordained men and ordained women and devout lay men and lay women able to show forth the Dhamma. Up till this time there were very few ordained women, for only those women took to the homeless life, who, like Khema and Bhadda Curly-Hair, were of outstanding ability. The whole of the Master's objective had therefore not at this time been realized.

I should further mention that, when a council was called together at Rajagaha after the Master's death, no women were called to its deliberations, so that the matters reported upon, were reported only by monks, who were naturally not unbiased, and forgot about those early women yellow-robed ones and also about the Master's earnest vow. Further, little was said of how the Master made no difference between men and women in the treading of the path to enlightenment. Most of the Brothers, having at one time or another been beset by the lust of sex, regarded women as a snare set by Mara, and were always for noticing them as little as possible and keeping them humbled. They would forget that Mara is within our own hearts, our own lusts, and they would blame always womenkind and not themselves, when they felt stirrings of desire. Thus it came about that, when that Council met after the Master's death, it did not confer with the Sisters and treated them of little account, so that the report given concerning the events I am about to tell, was coloured by reason of lack of full evidence.

Having said so much, let me now return to that band of yellow-robed women approaching Vesali.

It will be remembered that, after the death of the Master's father, Suddhodana, his aunt, Pajapati, asked that she might don the yellow robes and go forth from home. The Master refused to give his permission, probably because he was mindful of the leaving of Rahula and Nanda, and because she was now the head of a large household. Pajapati sorrowfully went back to her work. But she continued to ponder over the way of renunciation the Master had taught. She knew it was renunciation, not of the things within the world, but of the desires within the heart; but, surely, she thought to herself, the giving up of the desires within the heart would be easier if the temptations of the householder's life were removed. Pondering on these matters, she organized the household that responsibility was given to others; she then gathered together various ladies of the Sakyan clan and told them what was in her mind concerning going forth from home. What she said seemed good to them, and they agreed together that they would cut off their hair, and, clad in saffron robes, walk barefooted to Vesali, whither they heard the Master had now gone. As they drew near to Vesali, they fell in with Ananda, and Pajapati told him of their travelling thither and their desire to take to the homeless life as members of the Order. In view of the Master's previous refusal of Pajapati, Ananda went before them to announce their coming, and to tell him of their sincerity as evidenced by their travelling thither, not as ladies of the nobility, but as humble mendicants living on such scraps of food as were given to them. The Master bade Ananda fetch them to him, and he ordained them as Sisters of the Order.

Pajapati then asked that, before they departed into solitude, he would teach them the Dhamma. And now, when I hear various Brothers striving to put the Master's teaching into rules and lists and categories, I think back to what he then said to Pajapati.

'What is Dhamma you alone can judge. Of whatsoever teachings you shall be conscious that they conduce to peace and not to passion, to detachment and not to bondage, to wishing for little and not to wishing for much, to solitude and not to love of society, to exercise of earnest striving and not to slothe, to contentment and not to complaining, verily, you may then bear in mind that this is the Dhamma, this is the Vinaya[1], this is the teaching of Truth-Finders of all ages.'

Now Pajapati had been the manager of a large household since she was a girl, and soon she turned to the task of organizing the Sisterhood and recommending to the Master Vinaya rules so that their outward conduct should be in all manner seemly. Those Brothers that were so able were authorized by the Order of monks to be their instructors, and within the Order, as within the world, it was taken for granted that the Sisters would look to the Brothers, who were more experienced, as they would look to elder brothers in the world. But when a man or a woman comprehends the Dhamma, all consciousness of sex departs. As long as a man or a woman takes thought of the fact that he is a man or she is a woman, just so long does Mara have power to tempt, but if a person takes thought of this no longer, then does Mara depart sad and dejected and the lute falls from his hand. Insight into the Dhamma wipes away all distinctions of sex, and some of the Master's ablest and wisest disciples, such as Khema and Uppalavanna, were women. Furthermore, Pajapati was stern to check material advantages that any of the Brothers should seek to obtain by reason of his longer standing and the veneration paid to him. Once, six of the Brothers had some of the Sisters wash, dye and comb sheep's wool for them with the result that those Sisters neglected their practice of meditation. At once Pajapati reported the matter to the Master and he made it a rule that Brothers should not request Sisters to do their work for them. At a later date, certain Brothers, who had been artisans, were given special leave to assist certain of the Sisters in the building of a monastery. But the work of each was to learn to gather in diffuseness of thought, and no other work must take them from their meditation.

Pajapati, under the Master's oversight, organized the Sisterhood so that it was separate from the Brotherhood, and thereafter the number of Sisters increased rapidly, for it was now possible for women of less outstanding character than Khema and Bhadda Curly-Hair to don the yellow robe, and many women took advantage of this, and through earnest practice became numbered among the saints. Let me tell of Patacara as an example of many others.

[1]See Chapter XV.

Before she joined the Order, Patacara had roamed the streets of Savatthi without clothing and was known as the little mad woman. Folk told me that she came of good family, but had formed an alliance with a serving-man, that she had given birth to two sons, but that husband, sons and kinsfolk were now all dead. She was a pathetic figure, but only a few had pity on her and gave her scraps of food; most drove her away when she came near them. Then it happened that the Master came to Savatthi. He was teaching a large gathering in Jeta Grove when Patacara came towards him. On seeing her, some of the congregation said: 'Suffer not the little lunatic to come hither,' and others got up and would have driven her off. But the Master said: 'Forbid her not,' and he ceased his teaching and rose, and waited for her to come near. Then he stretched out his hand towards her and his compassion seemed to envelop her like a mantle. She stopped her aimless wandering and looked at him.

'Sister,' he said with indescribable tenderness, 'recover your reason.'

As she looked at him the crazed expression on her face passed from her, and there came instead a great calm and sweetness. You could have heard a leaf drop, so great was the hush that fell upon those that saw the miracle that was taking place. Gradually she became conscious of her body and perceived that it was naked. A blush of shame spread over her face and she stooped, crouching to the ground, until the man who was nearest threw her his outer cloak, which she gathered gratefully around her. Then she came and bowed at the feet of the Master, saying:

'Master, help me. My husband is dead of a poisonous snake; one of my babes was carried off by a hawk and the other was drowned, and my parents and my brother were killed when the roof of their house fell upon them, and there is none left with whom I can take shelter.'

The Master sat down and Patacara sat at his feet, and when she was still, he said: 'Think not that this is so. There is no shelter, no refuge, in husband, children, parents or brother, nor in any blood-bond. For always death must overtake them, and ever must your tears fall when you lose dear ones to whom you are attached. For ceaseless rounds of births and deaths have tears fallen because of the loss of those that are dear. But I can show you a shelter and refuge that never fails.'

Patacara had been listening intently, but sorrowfully. Now she sat up straight and looked deep into the Master's eyes, saying:

'Is there such a shelter? Tell me of it.'

'It is the shelter of Nirvana. It is the shelter of the Dhamma, the way which leads to Nirvana. Trading that way nothing can harm you.' Then the Master told Patacara of the Eightfold Way, and she listened in rapt silence. Before he concluded, a wonderful radiance overspread her face, and we knew that she had seen with the Pure and Spotless Eye of Truth and entered the stream, which leads to Nirvana. When at length he ceased speaking, she asked if she might join the Order, and he took her to the Sisters and she was ordained.

The second time I saw Patacara was many years later and in a distant place. In the interval she had found liberation and was widely regarded as a saint. She possessed a gift for public teaching and went about the countryside preaching to the village folk, and gradually gathering a band of Sisters about her. These women had in many cases never seen the Master, and to them their own mistress, Patacara, was the Buddha, the Enlightened-One. Indeed, when I saw the beauty of compassion that illumined her face as she taught, it was as though I were in the presence of the Master himself. Many who listened had lost their own children, and they knew that she spoke as one who had suffered as they had, when she told them that such is life, a continual coming into existence, and a passing out of it, and that to cling to what passes so swiftly is like clinging to a whirling wheel, a source of ceaseless misery. They knew, too, that when she spoke of the shelter of the Dhamma, she herself dwelt in its serene calm, and because she dwelt there herself, she could show the way to its shelter to those that sought it.

Chapter X—Sources

Theragatha—*Psalms of the Sisters*—Pali Text, vol. I

Vinaya—S. B. East, vol. XX, p. 320 (Pajapati)

Vinaya—*Book of Discipline*, II—S. B. Buddhists, vol. XI, p. 94 (work for monks)

Vinaya—*Book of Discipline*, V—S. B. Buddhists, vol. XX, p. 352 (Pajapati)

Digha-Nikaya—*Dialogues of the Buddha*, vol. 2—S. B. Buddhists vol. 3, p. 78 (Vajjians)

Mrs. Rhys Davids—*Gautama the Man*, p. 130

I. B. Horner—*Women Under Primitive Buddhism*

E. J. Thomas—*Life of the Buddha as Legend and History*, p. 110

Maha Bodhi Journal—Article by Dr. Ambedkar, vol. 59, June 1951, p. 137

Anguttara-Nikaya—*Gradual Sayings*, IV—Pali Text, vol. 26, p. 10 (advice to Licchavi lords)

NOTE: The story follows the Texts but omits the reference to the supposed reluctance of the Buddha to admit women to the Order. Reasons for the omissions: (*a*) Reluctance would be a contradiction of the vow he took not to cease from his labours till there were ordained women as well as men. (*b*) The existence of nuns in the Jain Order has not prevented Jainism still being a virile religion in India today. (*c*) The derogatory passages about women are contradicted by others the opposite. (*d*) The evidence is contradictory and that which is against the recorders, who were men, must be accepted. (*e*) It is not believable that a man of the Buddha's superb wisdom could be persuaded against his own judgement.

CHAPTER XI

SUFFERING: THE FIRST GREAT TRUTH

AFTER the Master departed from Vesali on this occasion he went to Banaras and travelled among the Kasi people. But what befell him then I never rightly heard, for I did not accompany him, and soon after he left, I fell ill of a grievous sickness. I had never been ill before. Youth and good health seemed to me the natural thing. It is true that wherever I travelled I had seen the sick, the aged and the dying. But it is one thing to know with one's intellect that suffering is the first great truth of life. It is another thing to accept that suffering when it comes to oneself. I was now overwhelmed with pity for myself, and hatred of the pain, and when the weeks lengthened into months I was bowed down with anxiety lest I should never recover. When at last the pain did depart, it left me with a weakness and weariness, and a sense of despair that were almost worse than the pain.

I was thus lying one day in this depth of misery when in a vision the Master came and stood beside me, looking upon me with those wonderful eyes, the kindest eyes the world has ever seen. He recalled to my mind that happy journey from Rajagaha to Kapilavatthu to see his aged father. As we had stood watching the large boats on the River Ganges while the raft was being made, he had said to us: 'In the days before I found enlightenment I visited the Eastern Ocean. In the harbour, a seafaring vessel, rigged with masts and stays, lay stranded upon the bank. An old sailor told me that six months had that boat lain there. In the dry weather its rigging had flapped in the sun and the wind; in the rains it had been stretched taut; in the stresses and strains of those six months it had been spoiled and had easily rotted away. Just so, Brothers, a monk, who trains himself on the Ariyan Way, by the passage of time finds that the fetters are weakened and rot away of themselves. Do not fret; do not strain; do not worry.'

The vision passed, but it was as if a strong man had reached out an arm to help a weaker one. After that I slept peacefully. The vision recalled to my memory the Master's own sufferings before he found enlightenment, and when by imperceptible stages my strength came back, I used to ponder much upon those sufferings.

At long last I was again able to rise from my couch and go to the village for alms. New life and vigour came to me, and I was filled with joy and love towards all the world. I rejoiced that I seemed able to pour over everything a wonderful radiance of compassion. One day, going for alms, I heard a group of peasant girls singing as they worked. It was a well-known spinning melody they sang. Always before, it had filled me with an emotion that went to the very roots of my being. Although it was as lovely as ever, I realized with tre-mendous satisfaction that it had no longer power to stir my emotion and my desire. I listened to it, as to waves of sound, fleeting as the wind that swept across the fields. At long last, I proudly thought to myself, the fetters, the thirstings and desirings of the senses, have fallen from me like the masts from that ship. So great was the bliss I experienced, it seemed to me that I had attained to enlightenment. I looked back at the thoughts of desire and malevolence that had once stirred me, and behold: they had departed as if they had never been. I seemed at peace with all the world, and the dreariness of those weeks of suffering had turned to zest and happiness.

As I was thus walking back with free, light steps and musing with great satisfaction, upon these matters, I tripped on a stone hidden by the grass, and fell. I picked myself up, but in falling I must have twisted my back in some manner, for when I rose there was a curious feeling in it and I could not walk without a little pain. I made no account of it, however, and returned to meditation under the palm tree near my shelter. But that night my back ached badly, and during the next week it became worse, so that it sometimes prevented me from sleeping. I thought it wise to rest it completely for a few days and asked one of the Brothers if he would fetch alms for me which he gladly agreed to do. I still made little account of it, and still rejoiced that this small accident had in no wise disturbed my joy and loving kindness towards all.

But the days passed, and though I went again for alms myself, the pain did not go, and sometimes it was severe. I could walk only for a short distance and that with difficulty. Gradually the former mood of elation departed and I was swept again into gloom and despair.

I tried breathing deeply and trying to combine this with my effort to concentrate in meditation, but the black depression continued unabated, and the more fiercely I struggled to meditate, the more did my pains bear me down. All seemed hopeless and the more hopeless for the mood of elation that had gone before. "If only the Master were near me," I thought, but he was said to have left Banaras and was making his way to far-off Savatthi, many weeks' journey distant, that is, if I could walk thus far, and this I doubted. As I thought of the Master, words of his came into my mind, concerning the making of selves. There are body selves when we are attached to the lusts and desires of the body and mind-selves when we are attached to ideals and ideas. But there are subtler formless selves which we make when we take delight in our virtues. I realized that I had been making one of these subtle formless selves, and that by so-doing I had cut myself off from the Deathless Essence as effectively as the one who indulges in the grossest of sensual lusts. How subtle is Mara in creeping in under the guise of our noblest virtues and making yet another self in the place of those cruder selves we have destroyed!

Thinking thus and miserably admitting failure, I sat down to meditate once more, striving in the midst of gloom and despair to banish that formless self and find peace. But the more I strove, the more did thoughts of self creep in, and the more did I feel the misery of life would have no ending. "When the mind is sluggish," the Master's words came back to me, "or depressed and weary, that is no time for cultivating tranquillity and meditation. As well might you hope to make a fire by piling wet grass upon it." I got up and set about the little tasks of tidying the monastery and helping a young novice who had just arrived. The black mood continued, but I wasted no more energy in trying to concentrate and find peace. I let the dull pain in my back have its way and the dull misery in my mind continue.

Next morning, going for alms, I saw a certain little girl playing with the other village children. I had often seen her before and taken no notice of her. She had only one leg and hobbled on crutches. But she laughed and shouted like the other children as she helped to make mud pies. A great shame overcame me that this little girl with her far greater impediment should be bright and happy, and I so dull and despairing. Something in my mind seemed to give in and relax. I would learn from her. I had been identifying myself with my body, making a body-self. Pondering on this discovery that the body is not the Self, I recalled how Upali, the barber, had told me of the glad day when he discovered in actual experience that his intellect was not his true Self. 'It is a clever thing,' he said, 'but it overreaches itself. See that monkey making a great commotion like an earthquake in that tree. See! Now he reaches over and springs to another tree, making a great commotion there, also, and nothing does he achieve by this. And thus it is with the intellect; it overreaches everything, thinking with its absurdly insignificant brain to accomplish things, when all it can do is to bring them into difficult straits.'

Now that I had found peace from the torments of pain, a great urge came upon me to see the Master and hear about the sufferings I knew he underwent before he found enlightenment. It was only two months until the rains and a long journey to Savatthi, and I could travel only very slowly. However, I might still arrive in time; so when dawn broke, I took up my bowl and departed. Although members of the Order travel always on foot, I knew that the Master would allow one who was lame to accept transport in chariots and bullock wagons when it was offered. Travelling thus I made as rapid progress as if walking.

The usual route to Savatthi goes through Kapilavatthu, and I hoped that the Master might have lingered there on his way. On approaching this town I fell in with Sariputta who said that the Master had in fact stayed there, but had shortly departed and was by now in Savatthi. Whereupon I told him of my sickness and he, to cheer me, told me of what the Master had said to sick and aged Nakulapitar at the Crocodile Haunt outside Kapilavatthu.

Nakulapitar was sick and fretful, and sorry for himself. When the Master came to him, he said: 'I'm a broken-down old man in the last stage of life nearly ended. I am always ill and ailing. If you or some of the Elders came to see me, I might feel better. But no one comes to see me. I am miserable and always in pain.'

The Master looked upon him with that infinite compassion which knows all sorrow as its own, and said: 'True, your body is weak and ailing, but for one carrying a body about, to depend upon its health for happiness, must always bring disappointment. No one can depend upon health for a single day, can he?'

'No, I suppose not,' complained the old man.

The Master continued: 'The body is ever liable to accident and disease, and even if it escapes these, in the end it always decays and dies. To look to your body for help, is to look to that which is always failing you, always changing, always decaying. But there is an ever present help, and you can find it now.'

'I cannot see that there is anything left when health and strength have gone,' the old man continued to wail, 'what else can there be to depend upon?'

A light not of earth seemed to shine from the Master's eyes as he replied: 'If you make for yourself an island of the True Self, and take refuge in Dhamma, the Ever-Living Law which holds all, then weakness and sickness have no power to injure you. Though the body may be sick, the True Self is never sick, and you may take refuge in that, an island amid the storms of life's suffering.'

Nakulapitar listened, as all listened, not so much to the words as to the sense of eternity and security that seemed to flow from the Master. He was lifted out of his body, lifted out of the deep waters on to that island of the True Self. His illness, his weary weakness, no longer seemed important; they belonged to another world now a long way from him. He had found refuge in the Universal, Deathless Essence and was at peace. When he left the Master, his face was radiant as the Master's own.

On his way from the Crocodile Haunt he met Sariputta who at once noticed the radiant peace upon his drawn and pain-pinched face. He said: 'Surely, Nakulapitar, you must have come from the presence of the Master.'

'I have indeed, and it is as if I had been sprinkled with ambrosia.'

'Tell me what happened and what he said that your face has become so radiant.'

And Nakulapitar told Sariputta of the wonder of his meeting with the Master, and his voice had the rapt ecstasy of one who has talked with gods, but Sariputta was not wholly content; for him the Master's argument had not been carried to its logical finish, and when Nakulapitar concluded, he said:

'Did it not occur to you to question the Master further, as to how the body and the mind became sick, and how the body may be sick but the mind may be kept well?'

'No, I am afraid I did not, but if you, Venerable Sir, would tell me about these matters it would be for my well-being. Indeed, I would travel far to hear what you would say.'

'Let us sit down then,' said Sariputta, 'and I will instruct you.' They sat at the foot of a nearby tree and Sariputta continued:

'The untaught many-folk identify their bodies with their real Self, and when the body is sick they say: "I suffer" instead of "the body suffers". Or they identify their emotions and feelings with their True Self and say: "I feel miserable" when it is really only their feelings that are miserable. They are always talking about "I" and "mine". Now this is not a true way of looking at things. You are not your body, are you?'

'No,' replied Nakulapitar, still dwelling with rapture on the Master's words. 'No, I am the True Self; I merely carry the body about with me.'

'Yes, that is right,' said his instructor, still determined to make the logic of the discourse complete though it must have been clear that Nakulapitar understood very well indeed. Peradventure the logic would be remembered when the magic of the Master's presence had become dim amid the agony of pain, and Sariputta continued: 'When a person speaks of his body as if it were his real Self, then when the body is sick, the mind is sick also. But one trained on the noble Ariyan Eightfold Way says to himself, "I am not my body." He is then no longer possessed by his body and if the body gets weary or old or diseased, he feels no repugnance to pain, and he therefore no longer despairs. Such a one has a sick body but a well mind. Do you understand?'

'Yes, I do indeed,' said Nakulapitar, not thinking of Sariputta's logic, but of the Master's picture of the Island amid the sorrow and suffering of life, and of Dhamma, the Ever-Living Law, a refuge for all. He was still wrapped in ecstasy and he hardly heard as Sariputta concluded: 'Then, when you know your body is not the True Self, nor the feelings the True Self, you no more hanker after the past with its youth and strength. You are released from the graspings of your body and its desires, and you are held in bliss ineffable.'

'Yes, and you have made an Island of the True Self,' added Nakulapitar with a far-off look of rapture, 'and the body is a stormy sea which pounds upon the Island and the Island is not affected by it. Thank you, Venerable Sir. You have put things very clearly.'

Sariputta arose and blessed Nakulapitar, knowing that the Master had taken the old man into those higher realms whither logic and learning cannot follow. Sariputta told this story against himself. He was a humble man and smiled at the thought of how he had sought to help Nakulapitar, when the Master had already done so and with very few words indeed. None the less Sariputta had helped me, for I went forward to Savatthi strengthened and refreshed.

On my way to Jeta Grove at Savatthi, I met a jovial rotund Brahmin, dressed in white and riding in a white carriage drawn by white mares. He was smiling delightedly and so was I, for I was still thinking about Nakulapitar. Although we were strangers we greeted one another.

'My name is Janussoni,' he said. 'I am returning home after having visited the wanderer, Gautama,' and here his smile broadened, 'Gautama, who leaves behind the footprints of a really big elephant.' He laughed, and then went on to tell me how, when he was leaving the city, he chanced to meet the wanderer, Pilotika. This is the story of his encounter, as I remember him telling it.

'Wherefore, Venerable Pilotika, are you coming into the city thus early in the morning?' asked Janussoni.

'I am returning from visiting the Buddha, the All-Enlightened-One.'

'You mean Gautama?' questioned Janussoni. 'I have heard of him, and how Anathapindika bought Prince Jeta's park for him by spreading money all over the ground. What is your view concerning him? Has he depth of thought? Is he learned?'

'Who am I to comprehend the depth of the recluse Gautama's thought?' answered Pilotika with solemn vehemence. 'Only his peer could do that. I am but as dust compared with him.'

'It is lofty praise you accord him, Pilotika.'

'Who am I to praise him,' went on Pilotika with the same vehemence. 'Praised by the praised, is he who is foremost among gods and men.'

Janussoni was seeking for information and was willing to wait patiently until he should obtain it. So he next asked: 'Then what rich blessing did you find in Gautama to make you so ardent an adherent of his?'

Pilotika continued as before: 'It is as if to an elephant forest there should come an elephant tracker, who should see elephant footprints and draw the conclusion that there had passed a really big elephant. I saw the Master's four footprints. I recognized at once an All-Enlightened-One.'

I got to know Janussoni very well at a later date, and I can see the smile that must have been continuing to broaden over his plump features, as he tried to draw from Pilotika some facts concerning the recluse of whom he had heard much talk.

'And what, Pilotika, were his four footprints?'

'This have I seen,' said Pilotika solemnly, 'learned ones came to the recluse Gautama, sages well able to dispute on any point, split hairs and argue on anything and everything. I have seen them frame questions to put to him, calculated to confute him no matter what way he answered. Well, I've seen them go to him, listen to him, and forget to put their questions at all, let alone confute him, and then I've seen them go away completely converted and become his disciples. Say not that these are the footprints of a really big elephant?'

Janussoni was at last impressed. He alighted from his white carriage with its white mares, bowed reverently with his white gown in the dust and said: 'May it be mine to meet some day this revered Gautama and have speech with him.'

'Do so, Brahmin Janussoni and you will find things as I have said.'

Janussoni did not wait until a later date. As soon as Pilotika was fairly out of sight, he decided that his business could wait for another time and that he must approach the Master at once. He told me that he and the Master had liked each other as soon as they met. I noticed he called the Master familiarly by his surname as if he were his equal. He never became a disciple in the full sense of the word, for he could not free himself from his attachment to ritual and ceremony, and to good living and jovial company. He liked to listen to the gossip of the street corners and there were few important people in Savatthi he did not know. But he frequently sought out the Master, listening to his discourses and questioning him freely. And the Master would answer his questions and tell him things concerning his past life that he was not accustomed to tell to us.

After parting from Janussoni I went straight on to Jeta Grove. Now it had been my intention, when I met the Master there, to ask him concerning those sufferings he underwent while alone in the forest after he had gone forth from home at the age of twenty-nine. But when I met him, there seemed no need to question him. The words died upon my lips. It was enough to be near him once more. Thus it came about that it was not until some weeks later, when Janussoni visited the Master, that I heard something of what I had pondered on when I lay sick. We all knew that the Master, in going forth from home, had left his wife and his infant son and had then spent six years practising great austerities, but few of us had heard more concerning those six years. Janussoni, as I have said, loved the company of large numbers of people, and now he said to the Master:

'It must be hard, Gautama, to brave life in the depth of the forest far from the haunts of men. To live alone must be equal to death. In the days before your enlightenment, Gautama, did you never find the solitude overpowering? And what of savage beasts and robbers and supernatural beings?'

'You are right, Brahmin, I did sometimes find the solitude oppressed me. But then I was put to shame, for I remembered that others sought the forest solitudes from purely selfish motives of their salvation. If *they* were not oppressed by the solitude, how much less should *I* be, when it was from no selfish motive that I sought it, but to find liberation from sorrow for all.'

'Then you *were* frightened, Gautama?'

'For a short space, Brahmin, yes; for example, when an animal passed along or the wind rustled the fallen leaves, or a peacock knocked off a branch, I would start. Then I would realize how foolish, for I was waiting for fear and dread to come, and what we think we bring into existence. So I would say to myself: "Come as they may; just as I am they will find me, and I will overcome them without altering my posture." If walking up and down, I continued walking up and down; if sleeping or lying, I continued sleeping or lying. In a little while fear and dread would depart.'

'And why do you still go alone into the forest, Gautama?'

'It is out of compassion for all sentient beings.'

I was hoping that Janussoni would now go on to question the Master concerning those painful austerities that people said he practised for many years after he had overcome those early fears. But at this moment there came up a young girl carrying a dead baby on her hip. I had seen her when I was last in Savatthi. Her name was Kisa Gotami. She was thin of body and plain of feature, and born of a poor family. She had been treated disdainfully by all, especially by her husband's family. Then she had borne a son, and people no longer saw her ugly features, but respected her for her boy-child. That was when I had last seen her. Now the child lay dead upon her hip and she was distraught with grief. She told the Master that she had gone from door to door pleading with folk to give her medicine to restore her child to life, but they had all laughed at her. Then one kinder than the others had told her of the Master, saying that he could give her medicine for her child. And that was why she now came. She held forth the child to the Master, and the depth of agony in her eyes made her seem as one crazed. He looked upon her with deep tenderness and said:

'Sister, go enter the town and bring back a little mustard seed; but—it must come from a house where no one yet has died.'

The young girl took the dust from his feet and departed with great hope and joy. That evening she returned.

'Gotami, have you found the little mustard seed?' he asked.

'The work of the little mustard seed has been done,' she answered, and went on to tell him what had happened. She had inquired of the first house for a little mustard seed which the great Buddha had said would cure her child. The folk there were glad to give her mustard seed, for they felt pity for her. Then she added: 'But the mustard seed must be from a house where none yet has died.'

Then they of that house said softly: 'Who shall say how many have died here? Last week the house-mother died here. The dead are many; the living are few.'

'Such mustard seed will then have no virtue,' she said, and departed sorrowfully to a second house, where she was told the same thing, and then to a third, but always they of the house replied: 'The dead are many; the living are few.' By evening she knew her quest would have no ending, and the dead child grew heavy upon her hip. Suddenly it came to her that it was out of his great compassion the Master had sent her upon this quest that she might find out for herself the first great truth that all must suffer. Her eyes filled with tears that the World Honoured should seek to help her, even her, the despised and ugly one. She took the dead child and laid him in a charnel field, for she was poor and had no money for cremation.

It was late at night when the Master finished teaching Kisa Gotami. He looked across to the city where the lights flickered and were extinguished, as one by one the folk lay down to sleep. 'Even so,' he concluded, 'as little lights are the lives of men. They flicker for an instant and are gone.'

The last light in the town went out, and there were only stars. In the darkness I seemed to hear the Master taking once again the vow that is said to be taken by all Enlightened Ones out of the great compassion of their hearts, which is this: "Having found freedom from suffering, may I set free all those who are yet bound with the bonds of it. Having won peace, may I bring peace to others. Having seen the light, may I light for all sentient beings the way to the transcendance of the cycle of birth and death."

Yes, be it a light for us, but we suffer of ourselves, and each must take that light, and light it in his own heart for himself if he would tread the way that leads to the ending of suffering through the ending of self.

Samyutta-Nikaya—*Kindred Sayings*, III—Pali Text, vol. 13. pl. and p. 37 (Nakulapitar)

Majjhima-Nikaya—*Further Dialogues*, I—S. B. Buddhists, vol. 5, p. 125 (footprints of big elephant), p. 12 (braving fears)

Majjhima-Nikaya—*Middle Length Sayings*—Pali Text No. 29, pp. 21 and 220

Woodward—p. 18 (braving fears)

Theragatha—*Psalms of the Sisters*—Pali Text, vol. I, p. 106 (Kisa-Gotami)

Anguttara-Nikaya—*Gradual Sayings*, IV—Pali Text, vol. 26, p. 293 (perils of pleasures)

Samyutta-Nikaya—*Kindred Sayings*, 5—Pali Text, vol. 16, p. 40 (ships and masts)

Digha-Nikaya—*Dialogues of the Buddha*, I—S. B. Buddhists, vol. 2, p. 241 (self)

Woodward—p. 44 (self)

Majjhima-Nikaya—*Further Dialogues*, II—S. B. Buddhists, vol. VI, p. 120 (Janussoni)

Samyutta-Nikaya—*Kindred Sayings*, V—Pali Text, vol. 16, p. 95 (wet grass on a fire)

Mahavastu, I—S. B. Buddhists, vol. 16, p. 45 (Bodhisattva's vow)

NOTE: Yasa's story is his own, but all the incidents except that of the crippled child are from the Texts. The Buddha, not Upali, compared the intellect to a monkey.

CHAPTER XII

MIRACLES AND HEALING

THIS time, when the Master left Savatthi, he went to the south of Magadha, and thence north to Rajagaha passing on his way through Nalanda which lies a few miles away amid the plains.

At Nalanda he was approached by a certain young householder who said: 'This Nalanda of ours is influential and prosperous, and full of folk devoted to the Venerable Gautama. It would be well if you would give command to some Brother to perform a miracle here. Thus would this Nalanda of ours become even more devoted to the Venerable Gautama.'

The Master replied: 'It is not my custom to give commands to the Brothers to perform miracles.' He turned to go, but that young householder would not let him do so and repeated his request. Whereupon the Master said: 'There are three kinds of miracles. The first is the ability to rise in the air, pass through walls and the like. You have heard of this kind of miracle?'

'Yes, Master Gautama.'

'There is great danger in the performance of this kind of miracle;' the Master's voice rose slightly. 'Therefore I loathe, detest and am ashamed thereof.'

'Oh!' said the young man, taken aback. This was the first time he had heard a holy man speak thus. Usually sages and seers regarded the ability to perform miracles as a sign of great sanctity.

The Master went on: 'Then, householder, there is a second kind of miracle, the kind performed when one claims to read the thoughts and emotions of another. There is great danger in the performance of these miracles, also. Therefore these, too, I detest and abhor.'

'Do you then detest and abhor all miracles, Master Gautama?'

'No,' replied the Master, 'there is a third kind of miracle which I love and with which I am pleased. This is the miracle performed when a person becomes educated, that is to say, he becomes practised in the living of the Brahma-life. A man so educated comprehends the Four Truths; he has learned the means to destroy desire and craving; he is assured of final liberation and sainthood. That miracle is performed within a man's own self; it needs no charms, or prayer to any god. It is the miracle of overcoming the world, so that nothing of earth has power over such a one. That miracle is the greatest of all miracles, and that miracle I love and venerate.'

Then that young householder went away telling everyone that this Gautama would perform no miracles, but would show the way to perform the miracle of making saints and that that was a good miracle even as the others were bad.

Now, whether the report of this interview with the young house-holder travelled before the Master into Rajagaha, I cannot say. But, if so, the Treasurer there learned nothing by it, for he, too, desired to see a miracle performed. He accordingly had a valuable block of sweet-scented sandalwood fashioned into a bowl. This bowl he caused to be erected on the top of a bamboo pole, far above the reach of a man's hand. Then he had it announced that whatever holy one, Brahmin or saint, should be able to take down that bowl, to him would the bowl belong.

Many wanderers and sages came and looked at that bowl on the top of the bamboo, but none were able to raise themselves above the ground to take it down, although the power of levitation is one of the commonest of the miraculous powers to be acquired by those who practise concentration of thought. As these wanderers were looking up at that bowl, it happened that Moggallana and Pindola came into Rajagaha for alms, and saw that bamboo pole and the eyes of all around looking up to the bowl on the top of it. When they heard the purpose of the bowl being erected thus, Pindola turned to Moggallana, saying:

'You have supernormal powers, Brother Moggallana, including the power of levitation. Fetch down the bowl and it will be yours.'

'I have no wish to do so,' said Moggallana, for though he could not tell the reason, he felt it would not be fitting. 'But,' he added, 'you also have those powers, take it down yourself if you think it proper to do so.'

Then Pindola, exercising his supernormal powers, rose through the air and took down the bowl. A great burst of applause rent the air from those looking on, and the Treasurer, gazing from his house surrounded by his wife and children, bowed with clasped hands in reverent salutation, saying: 'May the Venerable One descend upon our dwelling-house.'

When Pindola, bearing the bowl, came into the Treasurer's house, the Treasurer took the bowl from his hands, filled it with costly food and presented it to him with deep reverence. Pindola then walked towards the monastery where he was lodging, and the people with shouts loud and long followed after him singing his praises, so that he returned, as it were, amid a triumphal procession.

The Master, coming into the town at this time, inquired the reason for the shouting and the procession, and on being told, he asked that Pindola should come to him, and when he did so, inquired of him the truth of what was reported. Then the Master, looking upon him sternly, said: 'This conduct is unworthy of one who has inner sight, Pindola. How can you for the sake of a miserable pot display before laymen the supernormal powers you have obtained? It is just as a woman displays her body for a miserable piece of silver. This display does not conduce to the conversion of the unconverted. Rather will it cause disgust in those not converted, and in those who are converted, a falling away.'

Then the Master called the Brothers together and forbade the display of miraculous powers before lay people. He ordered the bowl to be broken and powdered up, for sandalwood when powdered is used as an eye-ointment.

After his death, many miracles were attributed to the Master. But in fact he did not display the miraculous powers he possessed. In all the years I knew him, only once did I know him exercise these powers. This was when a certain lay-woman, who used to minister to the sick Brothers, cut off a piece of her own thigh to provide a sick monk with meat which he craved, but which she could not buy. The Master insisted that she be brought to him, and, when she was carried into his presence, her flesh was immediately healed. There may have been other miracles performed by him, but, if so, I did not witness them, nor did I hear about them. The ending of suffering is not brought about by the healing of a sick body, any more than by rising through the air, but only by the healing of a sick mind.

The Master was called the incomparable physician, but it was men's hearts and minds he healed, not their bodies. None the less, because all are one, he taught the need for compassion towards all who suffer in their bodies. The lay people who were sick and aged should be cared for by their own families and none might don the yellow robe if it meant forsaking those that needed his compassionate care. The sick Brothers and Sisters should be cared for by others of the Order, and the work of learning meditation must not come before the need for caring for the sick ones.

The Master himself set the example of caring for the sick. I was with him once when he came to a monastery from the door of which there issued a foul smell. On inquiring the cause he was informed that one of the Brothers was suffering from so filthy a disease that none would go near him. At once the Master had them bring water and clean clothes and food, and he himself went in to the sick man, and washed, clothed and fed him. After that he took away the befouled garments and cleaned them himself. In shame for their neglect some of the Brothers at length began helping him, but so overpowering was the smell of the foul disease that one of them could not restrain his nausea and vomited.

When the sick man had been made comfortable, one of the Brothers said to the Master: 'How is it, Master, that you can soil your diamond hand in this manner?'

The Master replied: 'He who sees things as they truly are is not affected by scents whether vile or pleasant. He has neither liking nor aversion. The good nurse is the one who is no more affected by the filth he removes than by the sweet-smelling ointments he uses to relieve the patient's pain.'

But the best of all nurses, the Master said more than once, is the one capable of cheering the patient and comforting him with Dhamma talk, and in this he himself was the incomparable nurse as well as the incomparable physician.

Once he was told of a certain novice of no reputation lying sick. On hearing the words "novice", "sick", "of no reputation", he at once went to him. On seeing him, the sick novice tried to get up from the couch that he might give the Master a seat, but the Master said:

'Enough, my son, stir not from your bed, I will sit here. I hope that you are bearing up.'

'No, I am not bearing up,' said the novice, very sorry for himself. 'The pains press upon me, and my head feels as if it were bound with a leathern strap, and the pains do not abate.'

The Master appeared to perceive at once the innermost cause of those pains and said: 'Have you doubt or remorse? Do you reproach yourself?'

'I have indeed doubt and remorse. I do indeed reproach myself,' said the young man.

'Is it as to morals you reproach yourself?'

'No, Master, it is not as to morals.'

'What, then, is the cause of your doubt and remorse?'

'I do not understand the purity of life as taught by you,' sighed the young man. 'I do not understand how there can be an ending of lust, desire and passion.'

'Then you do understand the Dhamma as taught by me.' The Master smiled.

'With my mind only, Master,' continued the novice with the same despair. 'But it seems that I am utterly vicious and impure.'

'But you understand that your feelings and emotions are not the true Self of you?'

'I know these things are transient and the source of sorrow.'

'And likewise your remorse and doubt.' The Master's voice became stern. 'You have heard me advise people to meditate upon their virtues. You have not heard me advise them to meditate upon their failures. And why?'

The young man thought awhile and then answered: 'What we think upon, we make become.'

The novice, who himself told me this story, said that the Master lifted his eyes from him and looked through the open door to the sunlit courtyard in which grew a Bodhi tree. Tiny squirrels, with a stripe down the middle of the back, darted about like lightning among the roots of the tree; a faint breeze stirred the branches and a few of the broad spear-pointed leaves dropped to the flagged pavement. A peace he could not understand seemed to wrap round him. He closed his eyes and slept. When he opened them, the Master was standing at the door. He turned and said:

'And now, leave your bed; go forth into the forest and take refuge in the Dhamma.'

The young man got up eagerly. 'Teach me the Dhamma, Master.'

'No,' replied the Master. 'Buddhas only show the way. You alone can find and follow it.'

Before the novice could say more, the Master had gone. He suddenly realized that the pains had departed. He put on his outer robe and set forth into the forest.

Generally, when a man was sick, he had longing to see the Master, who could lift the burden of pain, even though he might not cure him as he cured that novice. Vakkali was one of these. But he was not diffident like that novice, and had one of the Brothers go to the Master and ask him out of compassion to visit him. The Master went to him and questioned him somewhat as he had questioned the young man. But when he asked the reason for his depression, Vakkali replied:

'For a long time, Master, I have been longing to set eyes upon you.'

The Master may have smiled inwardly, but he spoke solemnly, 'Enough, Vakkali! What is there in seeing this decomposing body of mine? It is enough to see the Dhamma. He who has seen the Dhamma, has seen me. This body of mine is like all else—forever falling into decay.' Then he talked to him of the impermanence of all things within time and space and of that which lies beyond time and space.

It is true that to see the Dhamma was to see the Master, but, as we all knew, sometimes to see the Teacher in the flesh brought peace, an understanding of the Dhamma and a vision of the Beyond that many months of meditation could not bring, and no tender care by others was equal to that. And furthermore, when there is peace within the heart, the body tends to be at peace also, and its ills to be healed. It is a significant fact that until the last year of his life, the Master's body was indisposed only on three occasions that I heard of, and then only with trifling ills from which he speedily recovered.

Chapter XII—Sources

Digha-Nikaya—*Dialogues of the Buddha*, I—S. B. Buddhists, vol. 2, p. 272 (miracles)

Vinaya—S. B. East, XX, p. 78 (bowl)

Vinaya—S. B. East, XVII, p. 80 (healing)

Vinaya—*Book of Discipline*, V—S. B. Buddhists, vol. 20, p. 149 (bowl)

Vinaya—*Book of Discipline*, IV—S. B. Buddhists, vol. 14, p. 295 (healing)

Dhammapada Commentary—Harvard O. S., vol. 30, p. 35 (bowl)

Dhammapada Commentary—Chinese—S. Beale, p. 94 (foul-smelling disease)

Samyutta-Nikaya—*Kindred Sayings*, IV—Pali Text, vol. 14, p. 23 (sick novice)

Samyutta-Nikaya—*Kindred Sayings*, III—Pali Text, vol. 13, p. 101 (Vakkali)

Woodward—p. 128 (Vakkali)

'All things are transient and void of self.' Lumbini was the birthplace of the Buddha—but the pleasure gardens and fertile fields have gone. In the distance rise the Himalaya Mountains

Bullock wagon. 'Suffering follows the evil act as the wheel of the cart follows the foot of the ox that draws it'

A wandering religious medicant such as has roamed India from days before the Buddha. They take what robes, food and lodging they can get. The Buddha was a 'Wanderer'

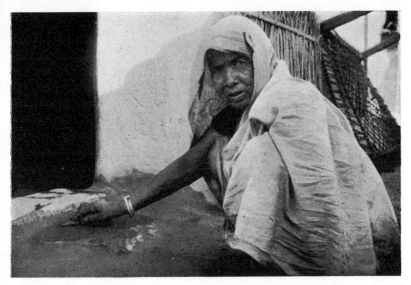

An old woman spreading fresh cow-dung on a mud floor. This type of floor polish is often mentioned in the Buddha Text

Grass huts like these are seen all over India. It was probably this type of hut that the Buddha's monks sometimes built for themselves for shelter during the rainy season

Potters making their pots on a whirling wheel from the clay of the river banks, are mentioned in Buddha's time. They ply their same trade today

When we read in the Buddhist Scriptures of 'Places from which water is fetched' we can picture it being fetched in pots like these

SONA AND EXCESS OF ZEAL

WHILE the Master was in the south of Magadha, I travelled among the people of Kosala. One day I had accepted an invitation to travel in a bullock wagon. The road was seamed with ruts and as the wagon jolted down into a particularly deep one, I was thrown out. When I picked myself up, I found that the pain in my back, to which I had grown accustomed, had apparently disappeared. I could hardly believe it, and I expected every moment that it would come back, but it did not do so. My first feeling was one of bounding joy. But sternly I put this thought from me. Not again would I make islands of the pleasures of earthly life. There is no place either for complaining or for gratitude, for nothing we have is ours, there is no permanent self which can possess anything. If health were now restored, it was restored only for the well-being of all sentient beings.

From Kosola I made my way south and eventually crossed the Ganges River and entered Magadha, intending to meet the Master once more in Rajagaha where I heard he had now gone. I also heard the strange story of Sona Kolivisa, the son of a wealthy family of Campa. It was said that he had been so delicately nurtured that down or hair had grown on the soles of his feet, and that King Bimbisara had invited him to visit Rajagaha so that he might see the soles of his feet. I was told that, while Sona Kolivisa was in Rajagaha, the Master arrived, that Sona went to listen to his teaching, was at once converted, became ordained, and was now travelling north with him. It was at the Cool Grove that I again met the Master and became acquainted with Sona. He was at once drawn to me, partly, I think, because he, too, was deeply stirred by music. I felt towards him as an elder brother on the pilgrimage to Nirvana, and in view of my recent experiences and new-found liberation from the craving for music, I regarded myself as well able to help him on that pilgrimage. There was a look of ecstasy in his eyes as he told me of his intent to depart alone into the forest to meditate strenuously until he had probed to the depths of the ultimate Beyond. I tried to restrain him, telling him it would be well for him to take a preceptor as his guide and teacher even though this was not at that time made obligatory. Sona would not do as I suggested; he was determined to work alone. He prepared to depart at once into the forest and I therefore said I would accompany him. As we walked together I reminded him of the wild beasts which ranged the forest—lions, tigers, leopards, and the eerie noises. He listened impatiently until I had done speaking and then in turn reminded me of what we all knew, that no wild beast will attack if one remains perfectly still and unafraid, and suffuses it with love. I in turn retorted by saying that, despite all this, one could not will oneself to shed fear and acquire loving-kindness for everything until one had practised for many years. And so the argument continued. I began to get heated in my persuasion and Sona began to grow irritated. Finally he said with some asperity:

'Can you not remember the joy with which you entered upon the religious life?'

'Yes, I can,' I said, 'but though there may be joy at the beginning, there can be many years of suffering afterwards before one finds liberation from desire.' I spoke with the assurance of one who had won complete emancipation. I felt immensely superior to Sona, and he knew it and resented it. The atmosphere that had been created between us was not the right one for meditation. We had now reached the grove where he intended to meditate. All was quiet and still. Sona and I chose different tree-roots and sat down to meditate, he confident that he had already almost reached the Goal Beyond, and I equally confident that he would fail in his endeavour, but still genuinely anxious to help and protect him.

For some time Sona sat as advised, breathing evenly, and letting his eyes centre until they gradually half-closed. Needless to say, I could not compose my own mind, and in a short while I heard him muttering to himself. After an hour or so he arose and began pacing up and down restlessly, getting very distraught as he did so. Finally he kicked off his shoes; it might have been because of disgust with himself or because he felt that bodily pain would enable him to concentrate his mind with greater ease. I went up to him and once again tried to soothe him, pointing out that he was striving too ardently and that the Master had said progress on the way must always be gradual. My interference only angered him. When a man is determined upon a certain course of action it is wise to let him have his way until he shall come to another state of mind, but this I did not realize. I was greatly concerned for him and feared that in taking to the forest solitudes before he was freed from the asavas, the cravings and delusions, he might easily become discouraged before he had fairly started. However, he would not listen to me, and I left him and sat down to meditate again. As might be expected, I could concentrate my mind even less than before. Soon I overheard him murmuring words about wealth and good works. I looked up and perceived that the stones on which he walked regardless of pain, were now becoming stained with the blood from his feet. Indeed, the grove looked almost like a butcher's shambles.

Then it was that the Master came into the grove, and as a strong man reaches out to help a weaker one, even so did he reach out to help Sona, who was sitting dejectedly upon a bank. He tried to rise but his feet were paining him too sorely. The Master sat down beside him, smiling a tender laughing smile in which one could see one's folly without being hurt.

'Sona,' he said, 'did not this train of thought occur to you as you went apart in solitude, "Here am I, one of the disciples of the Buddha, striving with earnest zeal. Yet is my heart not released from the asavas." And did you not then strive more earnestly than before?'

'Yes, Master,' answered Sona.

'And when all your striving brought you no success, did not then the thought occur to you, "Great possessions await me at home. That wealth I may employ to do good. How now, if I were to return to a layman's life and employ my wealth to do good deeds"?'

'Even so, Master,' replied Sona miserably.

'Now, Sona,' went on the Master cheerfully, 'formerly, when you dwelt at home, were you not skilful at playing stringed music on the lute?'

'Yes, Master, I was,' and Sona smiled a little smile of childlike pleasure and pride.

'Now, how say you, Sona, when your lute-strings were overtaut, did the lute give forth a sweet sound?'

'No, Master, it would give forth a shrieking sound. But I could tune the lute well so that its strings were neither too taut, nor too slack. And my brothers and sisters would dance to the music I made.'

'Even so, Sona, excess of zeal makes one liable to have self-exaltation and leads to failure, even as lack of zeal makes one liable to sluggishness. But there is a middle way when the strings of your endeavour are strung neither too much nor too little. Then will the music from the Beyond be heard.'

'Yes, Master,' said Sona.

The Master had been speaking to Sona, but he seemed also to speak to me. I had thought I was superior to Sona, and able to be his helper. Yet was I not also a disciple of the Buddha, striving with earnest zeal, in whom the asavas were not yet dead? The Master looked at Sona's lacerated feet and the stones dabbled with blood, and continued:

'In the monk-training, Sona, pleasure is not to be sought, but pain is not to be sought, either. You will meet many hardships in this training—heat and cold, hunger and thirst, stinging insects and stinging words. But it is folly to injure yourself needlessly. Put your shoes on your feet and since you have been delicately nurtured, it would be wise for you to wear shoes with soft linings.'

Sona did as he was bidden and I noticed that his feet had now stopped bleeding. The Master rose and in silence we followed him back. After that Sona avoided me and I went to my lodging that night sick at heart. I had tried to help him and my own serenity had been disturbed, for I had become almost angry. My pride had been injured. I thought over a score of reasons as to why I could not have done other than I did and how the Master's advice had shown that I had been right. But the fact remained that Sona, whom I loved as a brother, had taken my endeavours amiss and had turned against me. Worst of all, I could not concentrate my own thoughts, and the recently found inner peace had departed.

As I lay awake that night I remembered a conversation the Master had had with a certain Licchavi who had boasted he had won deliverance from desire. The Master had said that if such a one is puffed up with his achievement, he may well do what is not good for one whose heart is set on attaining supreme deliverance. Like that Licchavi I, too, had been puffed up with my success in putting an end to craving for music and youth and health. I had thought I was able to guide another, forgetful that even Buddhas only show the way, and that each must find the way for himself. Once again I saw how subtle is Mara in making new selves. No sooner is the cruder lusting overcome than that evil spirit within us is alert to find new ways of asserting self-importance and self-desire, and surely pride in achieving progress towards Nirvana is one of Mara's most persistent implements for our temptation. I remembered that the Master had once compared the one who boasted of success in conquering desire, to a man from whose flesh the doctor had removed a poison-arrow, and the wound of which the doctor had dressed. There seems to be no poison left behind. But such a man is not really out of danger. Therefore the doctor bids him diet himself, bathe and dress the wound, and avoid exposing it to wind and sun lest dirt get into it. If such a one neglects to do what the doctor says, the wound becomes infected once again. And so with the one whose mind is set on Nirvana. There is always danger; let him not persuade himself that the poison of self and its desires is ever wholly dissipated. Let him be ceaselessly mindful.

During the days that followed, Sona continued to avoid me. My own mind was still torn between the need to justify myself in what I had done and the truth shown by the Master in the parable of the extraction of the poisoned arrow. Truly, the farther one travels on the way to Nirvana, the smaller are the failures that cause distress, and the deeper the distress that they bring.

I struggled more than ever, but my mind still refused to become calm. We reached the River Ganges. That day I sat under a spreading neem tree, not attempting to meditate, but watching the folk of the village. Down at the river, the laundrymen were banging the washing on stones and then spreading it out on the sandy banks to dry in the hot sunlight. Two fishermen were dragging the muddy shallows with a net while a white bird looked on expectantly. I could hear the whirr of the potter's wheel as he sat on his haunches in the shade of a banyan tree, turning the pots made from the mud of the river banks. Some of the huge pots he had made were carried away by a man bearing them in a bamboo basket on his head. The grain of the recent harvest was spread out on bamboo mats beside the track through the village; a baby had crawled over and would have scattered it into the dust, had not his mother suddenly seen him and snatched him away. I was looking idly at the life that went on in that little village on the banks of the river, when all at once my mind cleared and became calm as a lake whose bottom can be seen. I saw the folly of my failure without being troubled. I ceased to turn over in my mind arguments to justify what I had done. Remorse died. And there arose instead compassion for Sona, compassion which suffers with another but does not strive to change him. Loving-kindness filled the world around me and my heart was at peace. Sona must have realized the change that had been wrought within me, for that night he avoided me no longer and I knew there was peace between us.

Chapter XIII—SOURCES

Woodward—p. 238 (Sona), p. 303 (poison arrow)

Vinaya—S. B. East, vol. XVII, p. 6 (Sona)

Majjhima-Nikaya—*Further Dialogues*, II—S. B. Buddhists, vol. 6, p. 148 (poison arrow)

Vinaya—*Book of Discipline*, IV—S. B. Buddhists, vol. 14, p. 236 (Sona)

CHAPTER XIV

SIHA AND THE EATING OF MEAT

You meet wandering ascetics wherever you go, young and old and a few women among them. Some wear saffron robes, some white, and some go completely naked. Most seek only to discuss abstract metaphysical questions, but others are earnestly seeking the Brahma life and the way to the Immortal. Some follow a particular teacher and some are alone. They take what food and clothing they can beg; sometimes they find shelter and sometimes they do not. In the Master's day the largest body of earnest mendicants, other than that of his own disciples, were the Niganthas, whose teacher was Nataputta. Non-killing and harmlessness or ahimsa was his basic doctrine, but some of his disciples would adhere to it in the letter rather than in the spirit. Often his monks would go without food sooner than touch even a tiny morsel of meat, so that they had to take great care as to the houses from which they would receive alms. In Vesali, General Siha was the best known of the lay Niganthas, though how a general of the army reconciled the profession of killing human beings, as a soldier expects to do, with the doctrine of harmlessness, non-injury, or ahimsa, I could never understand.

It was in the Gabled Hall on the outskirts of the great forest that stretches north from Vesali, that the Master stayed during the next rainy season after Sona had become a member of the Order. This hall is not far from the usual closely packed village of bamboo cottages, plastered with mud and covered with thatch, but the palms, bananas and mangoes grow particularly luxuriantly around it, while the villagers are unusually kind to the gentle mild-eyed elephants which drag the trees from the forest for main posts of large buildings like the Gabled Hall.

Since his first long stay in Vesali, the Master had become well known throughout the land, and when he came again to Vesali, it was natural that some of the younger Niganthas should see him as the leader of a sect, which was rivalling their own, the older one, and therefore endeavour to prevent their members from visiting the new Teacher.

Now, General Siha was energetic and hard-working, and the rumours that came to him concerning the Master and the things he taught, made little appeal to him. He heard that the Master enjoined men to give up all thoughts of worldly things, shutting themselves off from the activities of this life. To him, for whom work was the most important thing, this seemed absurd. Surely activity was the thing for which men were born! In this manner he reasoned with himself. Then, one day when the Licchavi nobles were assembled in the mote hall, a discussion arose concerning the Master, and many were loud in their praise of him and of his teaching. And Siha's curiosity was stirred within him to meet this sage who was called a Buddha, and who dwelt always outside the city among bamboo cottages and vegetable gardens, because he liked solitude and quietness. He thought that, even though what this Gautama taught was heretical, none the less it would be a matter of interest if he could see and hear him. Therefore he went to his own Master, and told him of his desire to visit the sage, Gautama.

'How can you, who believe in action, go and hear Gautama, who believes in non-action?' asked his Master. And Siha's desire to visit the Buddha thereupon subsided, and he told himself, it would indeed be folly to visit the sage who taught something absurd.

But in a little while further stories came to him concerning the compassion of the sage, Gautama, and also of his charm and courtesy. He went to his Master a second time, and a second time he dissuaded him and set his desires at rest. Yet a third time he conceived a wish to visit the new Teacher, and this time he decided to go without consulting any of the Niganthas. He took his chariots and servants and went to the Gabled Hall. We had often seen him in the streets of Vesali, but not before had we realized how strong were his features and how vigorous his carriage. In his blunt, outspoken way, he went straight to the point.

'I have heard that you affirm the theory of inaction and train your disciples in it. I have assumed that the persons who say these things are not misrepresenting you, or telling lies. But I have no wish to accuse you wrongly, and therefore I come to inquire of you yourself whether such report is true.'

'In one way I teach inaction,' replied the Master serenely, 'and in another I teach action.'

'How can you teach both?' asked Siha.

'I teach inaction as regards misconduct in deed, in word, and in thought. I teach action as regards good deeds, good words, good thoughts.'

We could see Siha was delighted with the reply, but he would not give in all at once. 'And what about annihilation? Folk say you are an annihilationist.'

'They are right,' replied the Master, smiling. 'I teach annihilation of lust, hatred and infatuation.'

Siha laughed. He would not have visited the Master had he not in some unknown way been drawn towards him, and before the discussion had continued much further, he asked to become his lay-disciple.

'Be not in such haste, General Siha. Do not leave your own sect without due thought. I do not seek to draw people from their former teachers, but only to show them how to find release from suffering. Make a thorough examination of yourself and of my teaching before you decide to become my disciple.'

'I have more than decided already, Master.'

'None the less, go now, and consider the matter well. Investigation is profitable in well-known people like yourself.'

Siha again protested that his mind was already made up. But the Master said: 'No, consider the matter well. And this I ask: whatever decision you make, you will not cease to give alms to the Niganthas who depend upon your bounty for their sustenance.'

These words delighted Siha more than ever, and very reluctantly he agreed to consider the matter before severing his connexion with the Niganthas. 'But will you none the less take food at my house tomorrow?' he concluded.

The Master consented and Siha departed in high spirits. He was somewhat like a young man newly fallen in love, and he went about telling everyone of his visit to the Master and that he was no longer a Nigantha. In his determination to sever himself from all he had done when with them, he prepared for this feast food as different as possible from that which he was wont to prepare for the Niganthas. He noticed that, unlike the Niganthas, the Brothers of the Master's Order questioned not the food that was put into their bowls, but ate everything even though it might be meat, and the sumptuous repast he provided included meat. Some of the Niganthas heard of this and even as we were eating, a messenger came and whispered in Siha's ear that they were going about the streets and cross-roads of Vesali, crying: 'Today a huge beast has been slain by Siha, the general, and a meal has been prepared from it for the recluse, Gautama, and the recluse, Gautama, is going to eat of the meat knowing it has been killed for him.'

Siha jumped up angrily. 'That is not true,' he cried; 'for a long time these worthies have wanted to disparage the Buddha, but they do not harm him and this is a wicked vain lying. Not by intentionally taking life, must life be maintained.'

None the less, it was certain Siha had provided meat at that meal, and many of us were disturbed, for, while we took whatever food was put into our bowls without questioning it, yet no lay-disciple of the Master would purposely provide meat at any meal for him. And it is little wonder that Siha became angry, for he must soon have realized that in his ignorance he had erred.

After the meal was over and the Master gave Dhamma-talk, he spoke of non-killing, and the aura of his compassion flowed from him like waves of light, until everything in the world around seemed drawn into the one great radiance. To injure the least of things would then have been impossible, for all were one. That any should kill a four-footed animal for food, became a dream of a dark and distant world now far away.

'All sentient beings are bound together,' the Master said, 'in suffering as well as in blood, and compassion it is that links all in one. How can a man know compassion if he knowingly slays beast or bird for food? He is no disciple of mine who follows the trade of butcher or hunter, and he who knowingly takes from the butcher or hunter that which he has slain, is even as he who slays. Not for the sake of maintenance of life may one intentionally deprive any other being of life and it were mere verbal quibbling to eat meat and say that it was slain before the invitation to partake of it was given. None the less, if any eat meat, not knowing that it has been killed or specially prepared for him, then it is no fault in him. For there is a middle way between being a party to the slaughter of beasts for food and clothing, and refusal to take of food placed in a Brother's bowl because there is meat among it. It is not by the abstinence from flesh that the heart is purified, but only by the abstinence from lust. It is not by the refusal of meat that compassion arises, but by ceaselessly pervading all quarters of the world with thoughts of loving-friendship. Suffuse all creation with widespread love, and the lust to eat flesh will die within you.'

After the occasion of Siha's feast, the Master made it a rule that

no Brother of the Order must eat the meat of a beast if he even suspected it was killed purposely for him, indeed, if he suspected it was
in any way specially prepared for him. So rapidly was the story of
Siha's feast spread through the towns that there was never again any
record of a lay-disciple providing meat for the Order. It is a fact that
when the Master commenced to turn the wheel of the excellent Law,
he being then thirty-five years of age, the killing of animals for food
was the universal custom, and the Master often likened a man burdened
with lust to a cow walking with each step nearer to the butcher's knife.
But when he passed into utter Nirvana at the age of eighty, so great
had been the influence of his compassion that fewer beasts were killed
and many were they that ate not flesh.

Chapter XIV—SOURCES

Vinaya—S. B. East, XVII, p. 108 (Siha)

Anguttara-Nikaya—*Gradual Sayings*, III—Pali Text, vol. 25, p. 31
(Siha)

Anguttara-Nikaya—*Gradual Sayings*, IV—Pali Text, vol. 26, pp. 46
and 124 (Siha)

Jennings—p. 200 (Siha)

Sutta-Nipata—Harvard O. S., vol. 37, p. 63 (meat eating)

Sutta-Nipata—*Woven Cadences*—S. B. Buddhists, vol. 15, p. 38
(meat eating)

Vinaya—*Book of Discipline* IV—S. B. Buddhists, vol. 14, p. 318 (Siha)

CHAPTER XV

HOW THE VINAYA RULES WERE MADE

BEFORE I proceed to tell of the next sojourn of the Master in Savatthi let me tell something of the Vinaya rules of discipline that were made for the regulation of the outward conduct of the Brothers and Sisters of the Order, for as the Order grew in size rules became necessary. The Master allowed much difference in the way of living of those that took to the homeless life. Some went from place to place and some stayed principally in one monastery; some taught the Dhamma, and some showed forth the Dhamma merely by living a life of renunciation; some sought the loneliness of the forest solitudes and some dwelt in huts near the homes of benefactors. Had all who joined understood the meaning of the life of wanting little and taking nothing not given, few rules would have been necessary, but as the numbers grew it was inevitable that some who joined did not understand. Very early the Master made it a rule that novices should undergo a period of probation and take a preceptor who could instruct and help them. Another important matter was the institution of Holy Days at the new moon and the full moon. King Pasenadi had suggested this, for other sects had Holy Days. Lay men and women would come to the monastery on these days both to meditate and to listen to Dhamma-talk. But for the Order, the chief purpose of these Days was to be reminded of the need of purity of living, of harmlessness towards all life, of truthfulness, of courtesy and not taking from the laity what was not given. It was made a rule that all the monks of any one district should meet together for this purpose, and the assembly was not complete if so much as one were absent. If any could not come through illness, then another must take to the meeting his assurance that he had committed no fault in outward conduct, or if he had, then his confession. By this means the faults of the Brothers were speedily brought to light. Another important rule was that during the rains members of the Order must cease from travelling and remain in one place. This rule was made because the earth then teems with life which may be destroyed by the trampling of feet, and also because then the young crops are sprouting and may be injured, and the Master would not have the labours of the lay people interfered with. At the end of the rainy season the Brothers would make up and distribute the robe materials they had received and replace those worn out during the rains. Also, before departure at the end of the rains, they would meet in concourse and speak of any offence that they suspected of having taken place. Therefore, once again there was the opportunity of bringing offences to light and checking them by confession, and in certain extreme cases by cutting off the offender from communion with the Order.

In addition to these main rules, others were made from time to time as offences were committed. For example, when certain monks were greedy and wanted more than was given to them, the Master made it a rule that when one was admitted to the Order he must be reminded that there were four requisites and no more, to wit: for food, scraps left over by other people; for dwellings, roots of trees; for robes, rags gathered from rubbish heaps; for medicine, ammonia; all else, they were to be reminded, were extras and not to be expected. Rules like these that were made from time to time aimed at showing consideration for others, especially the laity, and at removing the temptations of the six senses. But the Master recognized that what is temptation for one is not temptation for another, that circumstances are different in different places and that rules should therefore differ from individual to individual and from place to place. To indulge overmuch in the bathing of the body is pandering to bodily lusts in a place with a cool climate, but where the climate is hot it is an offence to others if the body is not frequently bathed.

Most of the ordained ones were pure and virtuous in their living, and for them few rules were necessary. If I now recount some of the stories of wrong doing that led to the making of rules, let it not be thought that such falling away was common.

It happened once during the rainy season that monks from Rajagaha made grass huts on the Isigili mountain slope. Among these was Dhaniya, the potter's son. When the rainy season was over, all the Brothers, except Dhaniya, demolished their huts and went on tour into the country. But Dhaniya did not like touring. He liked a home of his own. So he stayed in his hut after the rains departed. One day while he was away at the village getting alms, women loaded the materials of his hut on their heads and took it away for fuel. He rebuilt it. They again demolished it, for of course they never suspected that a Holy Brother might be seeking to keep a home for himself. This happened three times. Dhaniya then remembered his potter's craft, and from the red clay of the flats below he built himself a little domed hut looking for all the world like a little red ladybird on the hill-side. The Master, while passing by, saw that little red lady-bird thing from afar, and on hearing what it was, he was displeased. He sent two of the Brothers to Dhaniya to bid him demolish his hut and remind him of the insects whose lives he had destroyed in building it.

These same Brothers went as they were bidden, but either they did not find Dhaniya or they troubled not to look for him. So they themselves took down the hut. And when Dhaniya returned he found his pretty little ladybird thing was no more. He was dismayed but by no means discouraged. He remembered the timber-yard of the King, went to the overseer and asked him for sticks. The overseer was surprised at such a request, saying: 'This timber belongs to the King, and is being kept for repair purposes.'

'Then, good overseer, that is all right. The King has given this wood to the Order.'

The overseer was doubtful, but Dhaniya was a Holy Brother and as such a speaker of the truth. He therefore let him have what he wanted. Dhaniya took it away and used it to build another hut.

Now it happened that Vassakara, chief minister in Magadha, finding various repairs that were necessary, went to the timber-yard to arrange for timber required to be made available and found it was not there. On hearing what had happened he went to the King and asked him if it were true that he had given the timber to the Order. The King said it was wholly untrue and directed the overseer to be arrested. Dhaniya saw him taken away, his conscience smote him, and he went along with the arrested man. On seeing him outside the palace, the King waited upon him and asked him if it were true that the pieces of wood held for repair purposes were given to the Order.

'It is true, Your Majesty,' said Dhaniya unhesitatingly.

'We Kings are busy people and cannot remember everything. Pray remind me of the occasion on which I gave this timber.'

'Do you not remember, Your Majesty, how when you were first annointed you uttered these words: "Let recluses and Brahmins enjoy gifts of grass, wood and water"?'

The King was deeply shocked, and replied severely: 'Truly I said this, but I referred to grass, wood and water in the forest-jungle, and not such things which are owned, and this you well know. Your taking of that timber was larceny by a trick, for which a layman would be flogged, imprisoned or banished. But how can I flog, imprison or banish a Brother of the Master's Order? You are freed on account of your calling. But I am deeply grieved that you should so disgrace the Order.'

When people heard of the theft, they were angry, saying: 'These monks are shameless liars. They pretend to be followers of the Dhamma and speakers of the truth. But they are not such at all. Goodness and virtue have departed from the Order. If they deceive a King, how much more will they deceive lesser folk?' And the other Brothers who were modest, scrupulous and conscientious, were also upset because Dhaniya, the potter's son, had brought disgrace upon the Order. Finally the matter was reported to the Master, and after ascertaining the truth, he made it a rule that a Brother who committed an offence that in a layman would be punished by flogging, imprisonment or banishment, should be refused the communion of the Order. But the Master appeared sad when such rules were made, for the making of such does not mean the making of people who are pure and virtuous.

Now, on another occasion some monks were spending the rainy season on the banks of the Vaggamuda River. There was famine in the land, food was short, ration tickets were being issued and the Brothers found it difficult to get alms food. Then some of them took counsel among themselves as to how they might get more than their share of the scanty rations available. They decided to offer to manage the affairs of householders and do commissions for them, and to take it in turn to sing the praises of one another, saying that such-and-such a Brother possessed supernormal powers or great spiritual attainments. When householders heard these things, they felt it was for their gain that such unusually proficient ascetics had come to dwell in their midst, and they would go without food themselves and deprive their wives and young children of food so that they might give it to these Brothers. The result was that at the end of the rains, when other people were lean and haggard, these Brothers were plump with clear skins and good complexions.

When the rainy season was over, these Brothers packed up their bedding and taking their bowls and robes went to Vesali where the Master was residing in the Gabled Hall. Other Brothers from the neighbourhood also gathered there, and these other Brothers were lean and haggard like the lay men and lay women of the district, and they were in great contrast to the plump and well-fed Brothers. The Master asked the plump and well-fed ones concerning their sojourning during the rainy season. When they hesitated to tell the whole truth, he looked at them with that piercing glance which made you feel he saw into your very heart, and gradually the whole story was drawn from them. They stopped speaking. There was a long silence. Even before the Master said anything, I think those well-fed Brothers began to feel shame at their good condition. When he spoke it was like thunder that has no passion or human emotion behind it, and yet is utterly relentless and unsparing.

He said: 'When you joined the Order you gave up everything, your homes, the pleasures of the world, sensual delights and bodily appetites, so that by thus doing you might be able to give the greatest of all gifts, the gift of the Dhamma. In return, it was right that those to whom you gave such a gift should give to you the bare means of living. And now, for the sake of your stomachs, your bodily appetites, you court favours and say what is untruthful, and you deprive others of food.' The Master's voice rose, but it was still calm and passionless. 'I say, better it were that your bellies were cut open with a sharp butcher's knife than that you should do such things. The ripping open of your bodies would result only in the suffering and death of the body, whereas your theft, your theft, I say, will take you to the abyss of hell. There are robbers who pillage towns and destroy them. But there are worse robbers who obtain alms by flattery and by claiming supernormal powers. And this would be so even were a country prosperous and plentifully supplied with food, but to do these things among people who are starving. I say, better it were you had swallowed red-hot balls than the alms you thus extracted from famine-stricken men, women and children.'

The Master's voice was stern and the guilty Brothers quailed before him. Then his voice softened and he added: 'Yes, I know I have hurt you, but sometimes the doctor must use a knife.' His voice dropped to tenderness. 'Brothers, it was for you to set an example of men whose wants are very few, and who have renounced self utterly. Your shameless conduct will have led astray many who had taken the first steps upon the Way, and will prevent others from starting on it.'

I watched the faces of those Brothers. Some of them were weeping. All had seen their wrong doing. The sharp words of the Master were not like those of other folk. He was calm and serene as he spoke and the knife that cut also healed, for he had that compassion which could see into the hearts and minds of men and which sought only their well-being and never their hurt. His face was inscrutable in its gentleness as he rose to leave. The guilty Brothers also rose and silently went to their lodgings, and I noticed that only one of them went for alms the next day. They were too ashamed.

That might have been the end of the episode, but that some of the elders asked that a rule be made to prevent such shameful conduct again, and the Master made the rule for which they asked, that any Brother who claimed to possess miraculous powers or more than normal spiritual attainments must leave the Order. So far as I know there has been no other teaching in which a claim to miraculous or priestly powers is a grave offence and not a merit.

At Alavi there was trouble somewhat similar to that of those Brothers on the banks of the Vaggamuda River, but it was not so shameful. Certain Brothers there, at one time, decided to build themselves a monastery. Now, at Alavi there was no benefactor, and seeking to build a monastery without such, these Brothers went about asking the lay men and lay women to give them this, that and the other—a servant, an ox, a wagon, a hatchet, a knife, or a spade. And people were oppressed by the importunities of these Brothers, and when they saw a Brother approaching they would run away by another route or close the door hurriedly. It was told how once, when they saw some cows, they ran away thinking they were the yellow robes of the Brothers.

It was Kassapa himself who discovered the conduct of these Brothers. When he came to Alavi and took his bowl for alms, people ran away and no food was given to him. This was strange, for when he had visited Alavi previously, people had readily given alms. When he was told about the building of the monastery, he was most indignant, and as soon as the Master arrived in Alavi, he went straight to him and reported the offence.

The Master smiled and said: 'It is right that lay men and lay women should be the judges of whether the Brothers are living in docility to the Dhamma and whether they are worthy to receive the charity of the land. Bid those Brothers come to me.'

Kassapa was not mollified and he spoke very roughly to those Brothers when he bade them come. But the Master spoke to them gently, first ascertaining that the report of their begging was true. He said: 'It is difficult enough for householders to maintain their families without their being harassed by your begging them for carts and oxen and workmen. When you joined the Order you were reminded that you must be content with tree roots for lodgings and that you must take nothing not given voluntarily.' As we listened it seemed impossible that any should offend in such manner again, and by now those Brothers were ashamed as well as hungry. But Kassapa was not satisfied.

'Master,' he said, 'will you make it a rule that Brothers may have no monasteries unless a benefactor provides them?'

'That is too drastic a rule, Kassapa. There are times, especially during the rainy season, when it is desirable that ordained ones should build shelters for themselves if shelters or monasteries are not already there. And it may well be that there is no wealthy benefactor able and willing to provide such for them.'

'Then, Master, will you make it a rule that only grass huts be made, and these in a place authorized by the Order.'

'Ah! Kassapa, you are ever fond of the making of rules. But the mind of man is ever facile to evade rules unless the heart be willing to keep them, and then no rules need be imposed, for the man will make them for himself. However, so be it. Let no Brothers build for themselves without a benefactor a dwelling larger than a hut; and let them not build it except in a space marked out and approved by the other Brothers there, and already cleared so that no tree need be cut down.'

If Kassapa was strict to make rules for others, he was even stricter with himself. He did not ill-treat his body, but he would never give it any comfort. He was younger than the Master, but when the Master was aged, Kassapa was old also. One evening, in the Bamboo Grove, the Master looked at Kassapa's frayed robe and said:

'You are old now, Kassapa, and those frayed worn robes cannot be comfortable for your ageing body. Why do you not take some of the robes that householders would gladly give you? And would you not stay near me and sometimes accept meals which householders offer, instead of subsisting on such scraps as you obtain when you take your bowl for alms?'

Kassapa replied: 'I have been a forest-dweller all my life and I have commended solitude to others. I have always said that it was weakness to partake of meals in houses rather than accept the scraps put into one's bowl. And as for clothes, a Brother is not concerned with what is put on his perishable body. I have always worn rags and three garments only, and my added years give no reason for changing now.'

Kassapa outlived the Master and called the first Council which gathered together his words. And the reason there were so many rules gathered together along with the sermons and the talks of the Master, was because Kassapa liked rules and was strict himself in keeping them. But the greater number of rules that were recorded were not made by the Master, but later, following some incident that was told. For example, I have said how the Master made Sona wear shoes with linings because his feet had been tenderly nurtured. After the Master's death this was made the occasion for the formulation of a rule that shoes with one lining, but not two linings, might be worn. Then again, because some over-scrupulous Brothers arrived tired and hungry, having refrained from picking fruit off the ground, because that might be accounted as taking what was not given, another was made that fruit fallen might be taken but not fruit on the tree. Another precept made after the Master's death was that young boys might be ordained provided they could scare crows. This was made because Ananda reported of a certain occasion when he had recommended a lad for ordination, and had told the Master that, though young in years, he was old in a sense of responsibility, and that this was evidenced among other things by the task he had imposed upon himself of keeping the crows away from the crops. And then this was made a rule. And so was rule added to rule and precept to precept. For my part I like best to remember what I once heard the Master say:

'In the early days there were fewer precepts and a greater proportion of the Brothers and Sisters attained to sainthood. As people cease to live the true teaching, rules and precepts are made. But no rules or precepts can shape the lives of men and women. They are counterfeit teaching. It is only when men and women are reverent towards the Dhamma, and seek to mould their lives in accordance with it, that the true teaching can live and flourish.'

Chapter XV—Sources

Vinaya—*Book of Discipline*, I—S. B. Buddhists, vol. 10, pp. 64, 151, 159 and 246 (incidents of misbehaviour)

Vinaya—*Book of Discipline*, IV—S. B. Buddhists, vol. 14, p. 75 (four requisites)

Samyutta-Nikaya—*Kindred Sayings*, II—Pali Text, vol. 10, p. 131 (Kassapa)

CHAPTER XVI

THE MASTER'S MAGIC

WHEREVER we went we met what Janussoni liked to call "the footprints of the really large elephant", men and women whose lives had been completely changed since they met the Master, men and women who had forgotten how to be angry and had given up all evil ways. Yet he never tried to win converts. For him, all beliefs or modes of life were good so long as they injured not another. The Dhamma could be known and the Eightfold Path followed by all, whatever their particular belief, and the Master would take whatever belief a man already possessed and through it show the Way to the ending of suffering. If a man believed in ascetic practices, the Master would not deny the virtue of asceticism, but would show that the best asceticism was the following of the Eightfold Path; if he believed in sacrifice, that the sacrifice of self was the best of sacrifices. If it was union with Brahma that a man aspired after, he would show that such could be attained by suffusing all things with the rays of loving thoughts. If he was asked if there were lives which followed death, he would say it was enough to know this life alone; but if the one who questioned him held the belief of the many-folk in heavens and hells and rebirth and gods and devas, he would show the Way of virtue through such beliefs.

His teaching was utterly different from that of any sect, for it was not concerned with what a man could not prove for himself in his own life, and a man's beliefs were never to be disputed.

Some of us were in Savatthi gathering alms when we met such sectarians who were disputing concerning each other's beliefs, and were abusing each other with words that pierced like javelins. When we described to the Master what we had seen and heard, he compared them to blind men each seeking to describe an elephant from the part of it which he was touching, and getting angry because other blind men described it differently as their hands felt different parts.

The Master showed that, not only did people see things differently in the matter of beliefs, but also that they described even the Dhamma differently according to their different needs and temperaments. One of the novices told me how he had questioned many of the elders concerning the way in which one found the Pure and Spotless Eye of Truth. One told him it was found when one ceased taking notice of what was perceived through the six senses, another when one had grasped the Four Noble Truths, while Moggallana and Sariputta both said it was necessary to comprehend the impermanence of all things. The novice was bewildered by the diverse answers, and went to the Master, who told him that all had been right, that each had answered as the Truth seemed to him. "It is as if a man tried to describe a judas tree. Each would describe it as he had seen it. One, who had seen it blackish, would say it was like a charred stump; another, who had seen it reddish in spring, would say it was like a lump of flesh; a third might remember it with its bark stripped and compare it to an acacia; while a fourth who had sat beneath its shade in summer, would think of it as a banyan tree.'

What is true of not judging for another in the matter of his beliefs and understanding of the Dhamma, is also true as regards his mode of life. Only five trades did the Master say should not be practised because they injured others; to wit, the making of weapons for the killing of men, the making of poisons and intoxicating beverages, the trades of butcher, hunter, trapper and soldier. All other ways of livelihood were permissible to those who followed his teaching, and likewise different modes of life.

Ananda told me that Migasala, a house-mother of Savatthi, had once asked him how it could be that the Master had said of both her father, Purana, and her uncle, Isidatta, that each had seen the Death-less. 'Both were charioteers of King Pasenadi,' she said, 'but my father, Purana, lived a godly life, abstaining from carnal pleasure, while my uncle, Isidatta, continued to rejoice in the intimacy of his wife and did not abstain from carnal things.'

Ananda could not answer her questions and he sought out the Master who said: 'It is a dangerous thing, Ananda, to measure the measure of a man. Only an All-Enlightened-One can do that. A motherly woman, Migasala, with only mother-wit, cannot do so. It is not by outward actions that a man can be judged, but only by the inward heart, and only an All-Enlightened-One can know that. Two godly people, both restrained in their living, listen to the Dhamma word. One of them understands and applies it. The other is not affected by it. The first is carried forward upon the stream of Dhamma; the other is not. But who save an All-Enlightened-One can know this? In outward actions they are the same. Or there may be two others in both of whom wrath and pride are conquered, but in both of whom greed sometimes surges up. The one who understands the Dhamma with his inner being, is carried forward; the other is not. People judge from outer actions; they cannot know the inner heart. He who measures the measure of a man, digs a pit for himself, and it shall be to his hurt for many a long day. Purana might even acquire the virtues of Isidatta, but his way is not that of Isidatta; or Isidatta might acquire the virtues of Purana, but his way is not that of Purana. It is his own way that a man must tread and he may not be measured against another man.'

Other teachers went about the countryside striving to win converts, but the Master never did this. He often said he had no desire to win pupils, to cause people to forsake their own teachers or to fall away from their religious vows. All he sought was to show the way to the end of suffering. None the less, however little he encouraged them, people did become converts and confess themselves his disciples. He carried about with him an atmosphere that drew people to him, an atmosphere of peace and loving kindness. It surrounded him like an aura. You could feel him coming while he was yet a long way off, and a sense of calm and well-being would steal into the hearts of them that were open to receive it. Proud Brahmins, like Stiffneck, who deferred to none, would fall on their faces and behave with childish adulation. The Master would sternly tell them to recollect themselves, but it made little difference. It was said the only way to visit him and go away unconverted, was to stop the ears; but such folk would have felt the magic of that aura, even though they did close their ears to the magic of the words. It was little wonder that those of the various sects used to say he bewitched the people, casting spells over them to entice them from their own teachers and make them his disciples. One that had been warned the Master used incantations to win disciples, was Bhaddiya, the Licchavi. But he was interested in magic and this talk sent him at once to find out for himself.

'Folk say you are a juggler,' he said as soon as he came into the Master's presence, 'and that you know a trick of glamour by which you entice away the followers of those holding other views. Is this so?' The Brothers with him watched the Master smiling and knew that Bhaddiya himself would soon fall under that magic spell, if he were not under it already.

'Hearsay evidence is not dependable evidence,' said the Master, 'do not go on hearsay, and do not accept any teaching on hearsay.'

'No,' said Bhaddiya, 'that is why I came to find out for myself.'

'Furthermore,' continued the Master: 'no teaching should be accepted because of reverence for the teacher, or reverence for sacred sayings.'

'No,' broke in Bhaddiya. 'I should say a teaching should be accepted only if it is logical and satisfies the reason.'

'No,' continued the Master. 'No teaching should be accepted merely because it is logical, or because the teacher of it can win in argument with those holding other views.'

'Oh,' exclaimed Bhaddiya, surprised; 'then for what reason should one accept a teaching?'

'You should accept it, Bhaddiya, only if you yourself can prove out of your own experience that it makes for contentment and well-being.'

'I have not heard another teacher speak thus. Can you explain further?' Obviously, the more the Master sought to throw him back upon himself, the more he was being drawn into that magic spell.

'If a man spoke harshly to you, replied the Master, 'and you spoke harshly to him in return, answering him point by point with back-biting, what would be the outcome of such words?'

'We should both become angry,' said Bhaddiya, 'and we might end in blows.'

'You have judged rightly, Bhaddiya. Would you therefore call such speech blameworthy or praiseworthy?'

'Blameworthy, most certainly, Master. Such words would not make for the well-being of either.'

'If now, Bhaddiya, your speech were mild and charitable, returning pleasant kindly words for those which were harsh, what then would be the outcome?'

'There would be peace and concord between us, and we might even become friends. Such speech would have made for well-being.'

'You have again judged rightly, Bhaddiya. Therefore out of your own experience you have shown that a teaching which commends gentle and kindly speech, is a good teaching. Now, Bhaddiya, all worthy people teach their disciples these things.'

At this point Bhaddiya exclaimed: 'Can I become your disciple?'

The Master's smile broadened. 'Be careful, friend, how you do that. Did I ask you to become my disciple?'

'No, Master, no.'

'Remember what you were told about my being a juggler, who knows a trick of glamour. Be careful.'

'The people who told me that were right,' laughed the young man. 'You are indeed a juggler, but a goodly thing is this enticing trick of glamour of yours. I wish all my friends could be converted by this same enticement.'

Although the Master said no teaching should be accepted merely because it was logical, none the less he was very clever at answering arguments point by point in logical argument. But people are not won by clever arguments unless their minds are tending in that direction already. Those of the sects spoke more truly than they knew when they said the Master wove a spell over people. It was the spell of loving-friendship and compassion, which sought only their zeal and asked nothing in return. It was the magic of his serene joy, which healed the conflicts of their hearts, and brought peace and well-being to them that listened.

Moreover, it was a magic woven from his own knowledge of the things that trouble men. For let it not be thought that the Master knew not of the whiles of Mara, the Evil One, who is the personification of the individual self with its desires and cravings. From the time of his enlightenment until three months before his death Mara was from time to time at his side tempting him. And although those thoughts that are of Mara never gained foothold within his mind, as they do within the minds of the not-enlightened, yet those thoughts did arise; for thoughts have a life of their own, springing as they do from all-that-has-existence, and in which there can be no permanent individual self to stand aside and not know in actual experience the thoughts and feelings of others. Thus, even a Buddha, who is freed from the bondage of those thoughts and untroubled by them, is not freed from their arising.

At the time when the Master found enlightenment, thoughts of craving, discontent and passion arose before him. He sat calm and untroubled and those thoughts departed—as well might Mara's daughters have tried to cleave a mountain with a lily-stalk. Then, after he had attained enlightenment, the temptation arose within him to enjoy alone the bliss he had found, and not seek to impart it to others. He resisted that as he had resisted the first, and Mara departed sad and dejected, and the lute fell from his hand. And he who had overcome fear, none the less knew the meaning of thoughts of fear, as for example, when a great serpent raised its head beside him as he sat meditating in the rain in the dreary forest, or again when a mighty elephant stampeded through the forest breaking the branches and trampling all underfoot, or again when rocks came hurtling down beside him. But, as before, such thoughts could find no foothold and they departed then and there. Such thoughts rise only to vanish when an enlightened one recognizes them as Mara, the machinations of the imaginary individual self; but for those, who have not attained enlightenment, though they may recognize Mara for what he is, yet those thoughts do not vanish until after a long struggle. From those not enlightened, Mara does not at once depart sad and dejected, and the lute does not fall. And thoughts of worry and anxiety—the Master could help others in their distress, because he himself knew from his own experience the meaning of such thoughts—as, for example, when doubt arose as to whether his teachings were apt and suitable. And let it not be imagined that, because the Master could retire into the depths of concentration and lose the feeling of pain, that he did not know the misery of pain; when a sharp splinter of rock fell upon his foot injuring it badly, he knew full well the meaning of the misery of pain. These different thoughts that in others are the source of suffering, would arise in him only to be banished, because they could find nothing to rest upon. But they did arise, and the Master did know from his own experience the meaning of them, even though he dwelt forever within the peace of Nirvana.

Because he was one with our suffering world, and sought to ease its pain, there once arose within him the temptation to become an earthly ruler and rule as a wise King. It was when one King was planning an attack on another. He was lodging in a shepherd's hut in the Himalaya Hills; the oak trees were clad in their spring garments of ivory and coral; the blue bird was wooing its mate among the crimson rhododendrons that flamed against the azure skies and the white snows; all was happiness around. The Master knew he could stop this war, take back his abandoned wealth, and assume the kingship of these lands; he knew he could rule without killing or causing to be killed; without conquering or causing to be conquered—other Kings had so ruled in the past. Like them he, also, could rule so wisely and well that there would be plenty for all, and so that a child could leave a bag of gold in the street and none would take it. But, as soon as these thoughts arose, he knew they were of Mara, and that even though the Himalaya Mountains were turned to gold, still would man's wants remain unsatisfied. He had come to teach men, not how to satisfy their desires, but how to end desire itself.

The Master would confess to the arising of these thoughts that are of Mara, or none would have suspected them. Did he confess them to set us the example of the need of confession even for a Perfected One, or so as to show us he was one with us even in our weaknesses? I do not know. I tell but as I heard him say. And I know that whenever the Master told of these temptations, the homage of men would only increase.

Indeed, the more humble the Master made himself, and the more he withdrew, the greater would that homage become. Nigata told of the occasion the Master visited the Brahmin village of Icchanangala. The householders gathered at the entrance of the wood where he was lodging, singing hymns of praise and worship, and beseeching him to come forth and receive the quantities of food they had brought for him; Nigata urged him to do as they besought, but he replied:

'No, I have nought to do with homage and homage has nought to do with me—nor with anyone who can find at will the bliss of renunciation and inward calm. If others want homage, let them have it, but homage brings only a dunglike happiness that decays and smells. That inward peace and calm are the only true happiness. Sorrow, suffering and despair are the issue of all other kinds of so-called happiness.'

Never would the Master take seriously those that sought to worship him as more than mortal. I have already told how he teased Sariputta with merry joking, when Sariputta asserted him to be the wisest and most wonderful of all saints and sages who had ever lived or ever would live. His attitude to King Pasenadi's adulation was the same. The King had gone to see the beauty of a certain parkland. There had been rain the night before; the leaves of the trees were washed clean of dust; the air was fragrant with the scent of ripening mangoes; the green birds shone like jewels among their branches. As the King walked up and down, he was deeply stirred by the peaceful quiet of the shady woods. It was as if a spell of serenity were being woven about him; he felt himself drawn towards the Master who wove the same spell. He inquired the time of day saying how wonderful it would be to meet him before returning to the palace.

Finding it was yet early he at once went to Jeta Grove, where he handed his sword and turban to an attendant and went in alone. As soon as he saw the Master, he fell at his feet, stroking and kissing them. The Master smiled, amusedly asking why he paid such extraordinary respect to a decaying body. But of course it was not his body that the King and others venerated; it was the Dhamma that shone through his body undimmed by thoughts of "I" and "mine". It was the Dhamma that was the magic wielded by the Giver-of-Deathlessness, a magic that had freed the King from self-indulgence, from over-eating, from addiction to money and pleasure, and had shown him how to govern his people like a wise and loving father. In return for that gift of the Dhamma, the King's action of stroking and kissing the feet of the Master, may seem childish. But, I confess that, when I was newly ordained I, too, sometimes felt the same desire, especially if he showed human weakness, as when he said his back was tired and he must rest. No words can explain the feeling of veneration he aroused, nor the magnetic power which drew men and women towards him, and opened up for them a vista of joy, beside which all earthly joys appeared as tarnished tinsel.

Chapter XVI—Sources

Anguttara-Nikaya—*Gradual Sayings*, III—Pali Text, vol. 25, p. 21 (nought to do with homage)

Majjhima-Nikaya—*Further Dialogues*, II—S. B. Buddhists, vol. 6, p. 63 (Pasenadi)

Dhammapada Commentary—Harvard O. S., vol. 30, pp. 76 and 206 (Pasenadi)

Fo-Sho-Hing-Tsan-King—S. B. East, XX, p. 232 (Pasenadi)

Samyutta-Nikaya—*Kindred Sayings*, IV—Pali Text, vol. 14, p. 124 (judas tree)

Samyutta-Nikaya—*Kindred Sayings*, I—Pali Text, vol. 7, p. 128 (Mara Suttas)

Anguttara-Nikaya—*Gradual Sayings*, III—Pali Text, vol. 25, pp. 246 and 314 (Migasala)

Anguttara-Nikaya—*Gradual Sayings*, V, p. 94

Udana—*Verses of Uplift*—Minor Anthologies,   vol. II—S. B.
    Buddhists, vol. 8, p. 81 (blind men and elephant)
Anguttara-Nikaya—*Gradual Sayings*, II—Pali Text, vol. 24, p. 200
    (find out for yourself, Bhaddiya)
Samyutta-Nikaya—*Kindred Sayings*, I—Pali Text, vol. 7, p. 224
    (Pridestiff), p. 145 (Mara)
Woodward—p. 88 (not to win pupils)
Horner and Coomaraswamy, p. 85 (go not on hearsay)

CHAPTER XVII

THE MASTER AND THE LAY PEOPLE

As I have said, the Master's vow when he attained enlightenment, included lay men and women as well as ordained monks and nuns. It is therefore sad that the Council which met after his death included no lay-people, so that the words of the Master that were recorded were mainly those spoken to the ordained men. It is true that much was reported concerning Anathapindika and Visakha, the wealthy lay man and lay woman disciples, but that was chiefly because they were abundant benefactors of the Order. Indeed, to hear some of the Brothers talk you might think that lay people were on earth only to be benefactors of the ordained ones. But for the Master lay men and lay women were important for their own sake, and all steps of the Eightfold Way were equally for them. I once heard him tell Anathapindika that householders must not be content with making gifts to the Order, but that from time to time they should go apart into seclusion, like ordained ones, and find the quietude of heart that springs from the practice of meditation.

The best known of all the lay people other than Anathapindika, was the lady Visakha, who also belonged to Savatthi. The story went that when she was seven years old, the Master came to her home-town of Saketa, and that her father bade her take servants, go forth to meet him, and invite him to partake of food. Child though she was, she directed the matter fittingly, and thereafter accounted herself a disciple of the Master. When she was sixteen she was married with her own approval to the son of Migara, a banker of Savatthi, and when the marriage festivities were over, she drove into Savatthi, standing in her chariot and wearing the magnificent jewelled head-dress her father had given her, that all might see Migara's daughter-in-law came from no mean family. Behind her came her servants and the cart-loads of treasure her parents had given her as wedding dower.

Visakha's wisdom was as bright as the edge of a diamond even at the age of sixteen, but one thing she had failed to inquire about, namely, whether her father-in-law was a disciple of the Master. As King Pasenadi was a disciple, she had taken it for granted that all the noble people of his realm also paid homage to the Buddha. Great was her distress when she found that, though Migara's residence was close to Jeta Grove, yet the Master was not invited to his house and she could not so much as cast eyes upon a yellow-robed one. Therefore, she rejoiced greatly when one day her father-in-law sent a message to her that the Holy Ones had arrived and that she should do homage to them. But when she entered the hall where these so-called Holy Ones were feeding greedily from new-made bowls, she found they were none other than Naked Ascetics. She reproached her father-in-law for calling holy ones, men who were bereft of modesty. Then the Naked Ascetics in turn reproached Migara for having admitted into his household a lay-disciple of the Buddha, and urged that she be expelled. Migara told them he could not do this, for she was the daughter of a great household, and he made excuses for her. None the less, he was not pleased at what Visakha had said.

The Naked Ascetics having departed, he himself sat down to eat from a golden bowl of rich rice-porridge flavoured with honey, and he had Visakha fan him while he ate. As he was thus eating there came past a monk going his rounds for alms, and Visakha stepped aside that her father-in-law might see him and give if he thought fit. But although Migara saw the monk, he made no sign and continued eating with his head over the golden bowl. As the monk persisted in waiting, Visakha said to that monk: 'Pass on, Venerable Sir, my father-in-law is eating stale fare.'

Although Migara had resisted the importunities of the Naked Ascetics, now, when he heard Visakha say he was eating stale fare, he was angry, for he was somewhat dull of wit and understood not the meaning of her words. He stood up indignantly and called to his servants, saying: 'Expel this woman from the house.'

Visakha replied with courtesy: 'Dear father-in-law you misunderstand my words. Moreover you may not expel your daughter-in-law in such manner as this.' And she insisted that he call the eight householders appointed as her sponsors, and in their presence she explained the meaning of her words as a well-known proverb that a man did not need to acquire fresh merit by giving alms. When Visakha had satisfied her father-in-law, she said it was now proper for her to leave, and she made ready to return to her father's home. But when Migara saw she was actually departing, he repented of what he had said, and begged her to remain. Visakha replied that she would stay only provided she could minister to the Buddha and the Order, and

listen to the teaching of the Dhamma, and Migara granted her
request.

The first time she invited the Master, the Naked Ascetics would
have prevented Migara from meeting him. Eventually they agreed
that he might listen from behind a curtain. Truly, if Migara was dull
of wit, the Naked Ascetics were even duller, for did not all know the
Master's aura could penetrate walls and reach across distances, and
that each one always thought he spoke for him alone?

The banker, Migara, sitting behind the curtain, turned over in
his mind the teaching of the Master, and found that the World-
Honoured was speaking especially to him. Whereupon he came forth
from behind the curtain and kissed the bosom of his daughter-in-law,
saying: 'From henceforth you are my mother,' and thereafter she
was called "The Mother of Migara". Then he fell at the feet of the
Master, covering them with kisses, and saying that Visakha had come
into his house for his welfare and liberation.

There are many stories I could tell concerning Visakha, her great
care for the welfare of the Brothers and Sisters, her criticism of any
faults she found in them, and her wisdom generally. But let me pass
on to other lay disciples, beginning with little children who would
go fearlessly to the Master, when sometimes older people would
hesitate because of his reputation for being a World-Honoured
Teacher.

The Master was one day holding Dhamma discourse with us while
some young boys were playing outside the monastery. We could hear
their laughter and their talk and their running to and fro. It was hot
and dusty, and we heard one little lad say he was thirsty. Another said:
'But there is no well here.' 'There will be one inside the monastery,'
said the thirsty one. 'But that is the monastery of the unbeliever,
Gautama, and you know our mothers and our fathers have forbidden
us to play with the children of the unbelievers.' We heard the thirsty
one retort: 'But Gautama is not a child of an unbeliever; he will not
hurt me; I shall just go in and get a drink and come out.' A third boy
said he, too, was going in to get a drink. We then saw two dirty
faces looking round the door into the garden. When they observed
the large number of yellow-robed ones, they drew back, but only
for a moment. One of them caught the eye of the Master. They were
frightened no longer. They came straight to him without paying
attention to the rest of us.

'If you please, Venerable Sir, may we get a drink?' the leader asked.

'Come with me,' said the Master, rising, and he led them to the well which was surrounded by a low circular platform, and from which the water was drawn in a pointed bucket at the end of a rope fastened to a stick which operated as a lever. The Master loosened the stick and the boys let the bucket down. They took a long time to satisfy their thirst and seemed very loath to leave. Then one of them got a sudden idea, and he said:

'I think our playmates would like to have a drink, too.'

'By all means bring them in,' said the Master.

The boys went out and brought the others back. As they were drinking the Master told them a story about some boys in the desert who were thirsty and how they found water. And then before anyone knew what had happened, the boys were sitting round the World-Honoured Teacher while he told them stories. The one I remember best was about some tree-fairies. All our people know about the spirit-life in the trees, and some have seen the fairies. But children know more about these things than those who are grown. He told them how some tree-fairies resented the coming of monks to meditate in their forest, and at night they terrified the monks by appearing as hideous shapes, bodies without heads and heads without bodies, and making weird screaming noises. The Master told stories with extra-ordinary realism, and we saw the boys shuddering as if they saw the ghosts themselves, and then sigh with relief as he went on to tell them how the monks had gone away and returned with the weapons of goodwill and loving-kindness, and how then the fairies were glad to have them stay in their forest, and how all of them lived together thereafter in peace and happiness. Many other stories he told, and I think the boys would have stayed there all night had he not said:

'Now boys, it is time for you to go home for your evening meal. You may come again whenever you will. But be sure and tell your mothers and your fathers where you have been.'

The boys went home and next day when we went for alms we heard how the boys had behaved so well that evening, their parents had marvelled at the change in them. On hearing where their lads had spent the afternoon, they were at first shocked; then they made further inquiries, and in the end they said they would entrust their sons to none except the monk, Gautama, to train.

Those boys were small. Somewhat older were Uggaha's daughters. I met the eldest in later years, and it was she who told me of the Master's visit. There was a serene sweetness on her face, and though her features were plain, I left her with the feeling that I had seen a very beautiful woman. When she told me of the visit of the Master to her father's home, her eyes lighted with joy. This was the story as she told it to me.

.   .   .   .   .   .

'It was when I was approaching my seventeenth birthday and about to be married that my father asked the Master if he would talk with us and tell us those things, which would help us through our married lives when we should no longer have the protection of a father. We, on hearing our father's wish, got up from the floor, left our spinning wheels, and went out into the garden where the Master was walking up and down. Orange flowers were in full bloom, the walls had been recently white-washed, golden fruit was hanging on the trees and in one corner a servant and her child were plucking the black seeds from the snowy cotton. I was sad that I would soon be leaving our happy peaceful home, but when I saw the Master my sadness departed. He started by asking us how we liked the idea of getting married. My youngest sister, who was only thirteen and full of adventure, said she thought it would be wonderful to go to a strange home, and that she was good at spinning and weaving and hoped there would be plenty of work, for she liked work. The Master said:

' "That is well. If you rise early and retire late, and are nimble and deft at the home-crafts, surely you will find the new home-life is a happy one."

'But I who had heard stories of husbands who beat their wives, and who was actually to marry a man I had never seen, was afraid. When I told the Master, he said:

' "If you order all things within the house with a sweet and gentle voice, and respect what your husband respects, there will be no need for fear. The harshest and unkindest words are stilled by words that are sweet and gentle." When he said that I took heart, for never was a harsh word heard within our house, and I knew I should not find it difficult to speak as the Master said.

'Then the Master turned to my second sister, who had not spoken and asked her what she thought. And she said: "When my sister is married I shall be trained in the ordering of things in the house. I shall then know better how I feel about marriage. At present I hardly know what to think. Is there anything in the ordering of things within a household that I should specially look to?"

' "Yes," said the Master. "You should make it your business to understand your own work and the work of all the other members of the household, correcting what is amiss, dividing the food equally, and taking care of the household goods, corn as well as gold and silver." Then the Master talked to us of the joy that comes when we do not think about ourselves and our own wants. And his words have lived with me ever since. Life has brought suffering and death into my home, but I have found a happiness greater than I knew as a young girl.'

.   .   .   .   .   .

I can see Uggaha's daughter before me even as I tell what she then said. She had that sweet happiness of a middle-aged woman, who has wanted nothing from life for herself, and has found life brought her all she needed. Her husband I did not know very well, but I know that he had been a trader in weapons before he became a disciple of the Master, and that thereafter he gave up that trade, though it meant much loss of wealth to do so. It was their son, Nakula, who told me how his mother's quietness and confidence had been the strength of the family when his father lay dying. His father was fretting miserably:

'What will happen to you and the children when I have gone? There will be none to care for them.'

His wife turned to him one of her calm sweet smiles and replied: 'Fear not, dear husband. I can support the children and keep the home together. When the Master gave advice to my sisters and me before we were married, he bade us be deft and nimble in the home-crafts. And so I am, as you well know. I am deft at spinning cotton and carding the matted wool, and I can earn what is necessary to keep our children. Do not worry, dear husband; do not die fretfully. Have refuge in the Dhamma.'

Her husband seemed to take heart at her words and lay back more peacefully in his pain, and Nakula, who was then a lad of fifteen, stayed beside his mother, thinking to help her when his father died. His father seemed to feel his presence and opened his eyes once again, and once again they were filled with anxiety. His wife read his thoughts and answered them, saying:

'No, dear husband, do not fear that I shall marry again and bring a step-father to your children. Sixteen years have we two lived together the Brahma-life, and it has been good, and no second husband shall take your place.'

But the look of anxiety did not leave his face, and again his wife read his thoughts. 'Fret not, dear husband, lest I should fail to hear the teaching of the Master. Indeed, when you depart greater need will I have to listen to the Dhamma. Do not die fretfully dear husband; all will be well with me in the Dhamma-life.'

This time the husband lay back content, saying: 'You have been a good wife to me and a good mother to our children. I know that as long as Gautama has white-robed women disciples, you will be among them, one of those that keep the virtues, firm-grounded and living in the Teacher's word.'

'Yes, husband, indeed it shall be so, and I shall have calm of heart within.'

'Yes, wife, I know,' and he fell into peaceful slumber. His wife was content, for she knew he would not die fretfully. Nakula waited awhile, but her quiet strength seemed to pass into him, and he soon went out to attend to his younger brother and sister, and the work of the farm. When at length he returned, his father was half-sitting up and his mother was giving him food. It seemed as if his mother's calm and confidence had brought his father back to life.

Gradually the disease departed and Nakula's father regained his strength. As soon as he was able, he went to the Master, spinning as he walked, as the men of this hill-country are wont to do. The Master was sitting under the sacred Bodhi tree that overhung the little slab building protecting the spring. A few of the village women sat beside him and they made room for Nakula's father when he came to tell the Master all his wife had done for him.

The Master said: 'Fortunate indeed are you in having a wife so full of compassion and serving your weal as councillor and teacher. Truly, as long as there are white-robed women lay-disciples, who follow the Dhamma, she will be among them, and much have you gained from having her wisdom beside you.'

Nakula's parents lived together many years after that. They lived in peace and concord keeping the virtues, and calm in the confidence that springs from quietude of heart.

Both Uggaha and Nakula's parents were devout disciples who sought to become detached from worldly things. But there were others who made no pretence of detachment from the things of the world, and yet for them also the Master had a message. He did not tell them to forsake the things of the world, but only that attachment to them brings sorrow and suffering. I was with the Master when he visited the Brahmin village called the Bamboo Gate in Kosala, and surely there could not have been householders more worldly-minded than these. They had wives and many children, and they were men who liked Banaras sandalwood and sweet perfumes, and gold and silver and the things that gold and silver buy. When they heard that the World-Honoured-One was approaching their village, they came to welcome him and, having announced their names and families, they asked him to teach them what would be a help and guide to them.

And the Master taught them thus: 'The Dhamma is for all, and for you householders there is especially the rule of doing to others what you would have others do to you, and refraining from doing to others what you would not have others do to you. You will say to yourselves: "Here am I, fond of life and not wanting to die, fond of pleasure and averse to pain. If anyone should attempt to take my life from me, or inflict pain upon me, that would not be pleasing to me, and if I were to rob someone else of life, or inflict pain, that likewise would not be pleasing to him." Therefore you will say to yourselves: "How then could I inflict pain upon another?" As a result of such reflection you will abstain from taking life of any living thing, or inflicting pain on any living thing. And you will do the same as regards thieving, adultery, lying, idle speech, slander, harsh and uncharitable words. For you could not inflict these things upon others when you would not have them inflicted upon yourself.

I could tell of many more worthy lay people but let me conclude with Citta the householder, whom the Master pronounced foremost in expounding the Dhamma. By profession he was an overseer of new buildings, but his greatest joy was to hold Dhamma discourse, and because of this, and his delight to benefit the Order, he was glad when one of the Brothers was residing in the little hermitage near his house. At the time of which I speak Brother Sudhamma was the one residing there and Citta paid him such great veneration and respect that when he wished to invite others of the Order to have food, he would first confer with Sudhamma and ascertain whether those he proposed to invite would be welcome to him. Then it happened that a large company of elders including Sariputta and Moggallana and I —who was by this time accounted an elder—chanced to visit Citta's village; Citta forthwith invited us to eat at his house. Citta then went to Sudhamma and invited him also. But Sudhamma was deeply offended that he had not first been asked to give his permission to the invitation of the elders, and he replied curtly:

'No, householder, I do not consent to come to this meal.'

A second and third time did Citta extend the invitation, but Sudhamma continued to refuse and Citta departed, his serenity undisturbed by Sudhamma's rudeness.

However, when the meal was ready, Sudhamma, obviously out of curiosity to see what kind of food would be provided for us, did in fact come to the meal at the appointed hour. Citta was glad to see him and sat down close to him, hoping to find him recovered from his feeling of offence. But when Sudhamma opened his mouth to speak to Citta he said: 'Truly abundant is this food, householder, which you have provided, but one thing you have omitted, and that is, tilla-seed-cake.'

Citta looked upon him sadly and replied with courteous dignity: 'Much treasure is to be found in the words that fall from the lips of the All-Enlightened-One, and the reverend Brother Sudhamma is a disciple of the All-Enlightened-One, and yet the only word that Brother Sudhamma utters is "tilla-seed-cake"! There is a story told of some merchants who went to an eastern district for trading and brought back with them a hen which mated with a crow and produced a chick, and whenever the chick wanted to utter the word "crow" it said "cock-a-doodle-do", and whenever it wanted to utter the cry of a cock it uttered a crow. It could only say that which was not fitting, and similarly with this word "tilla-seed-cake" in the midst of all the wise words which might have been spoken by one who teaches the Dhamma.'

'You are reviling and abusing me,' replied Sudhamma angrily. 'This is your house and you may do in it what you please, but I, householder, shall go away.'

I marvelled at Citta's serene and kindly composure when he courteously replied: 'Nay, reverend Sudhamma, I am not abusing and reviling you. Very delightful are the wild-mango groves at this place. Pray remain among them. I will provide you with all that you require, and care for you should you become sick.'

'No,' replied Sudhamma, rising. 'You are reviling and abusing me. I depart.'

'And where will you go, reverend sir?'

'I shall go to Savatthi, to the Master.'

'Very well, reverend sir, but tell him everything that was said by you, and everything that was said by me, and I shall not be surprised if you come back again.'

Then Sudhamma, having packed away his lodging, took his bowl and robe and set forth for Savatthi. I heard later that he did in fact tell the whole truth to the Master, hiding nothing of what had been said both by Citta and himself, and in the meantime complaining bitterly that it was not the place of a layman to find fault with an ordained one. The Master was not pleased with what he reported and told him that he must return to Citta and ask his forgiveness for conduct not becoming in a recluse. But Sudhamma was not convinced by what the Master said, and it was with great reluctance that he took up his bowl and robe and started to return to the householder, Citta. When he neared the compound of Citta's house, indignation and anger overcame him and he felt ashamed that he, an ordained one, should ask pardon of a layman. He returned to Savatthi before having spoken with Citta.

In the meantime the company of elders had also returned there, and when the Master asked the Order to choose a companion as moral support to accompany Sudhamma, I was the one chosen. Right glad was Citta to see Sudhamma, and led him at once to his lodging, and I was forgotten altogether. But this was as I would have had it.

Thereafter, Sudhamma was loud in his praise of Citta and of Citta's wisdom, and he it was who told how Citta had set at rest the doubts of certain elders of the Order who had been discussing how the senses and the sense organs were the cause of suffering, and how some had said it was the six senses which were the fetters that bind man to suffering, while others said it was the objects that were perceived by the six senses.

Then Citta spoke and said: 'Venerable Sirs, it is neither. If a black ox were tied by a chain to a white ox, you would not say it was the white ox which fettered the black ox, nor the black ox which fettered the white; it is the chain that ties them together which is the fetter. Similarly, it is not the eye, nor the ear, which holds us bound to the wheel of suffering, nor is it the things perceived by the eye, or the ear. It is the desire of the one for the other that is the fetter. If the eye and the ear are not attached to things seen and heard, then there is no sorrow or suffering.' And Citta's words solved the doubts of those elders, and often thereafter they would tell of Citta's parable of the black and white oxen.

Dhammapada Commentary—Harvard O. S., vol. 29, p. 18 (fairies), p. 59 (Visakha)

Dhammapada Commentary—Harvard O. S., vol. 30, p. 197 (children)

Vinaya—S. B. East, vol. VII, pp. 359 and 367 (Citta)

Vinaya—*Book of Discipline*, V—S. B. Buddhists, vol. 20, p. 22 (Citta)

Anguttara-Nikaya—*Gradual Sayings*, III—Pali Text, vol. 25, p. 28 (Uggaha's daughter), p. 152 (householders go apart in seclusion), p. 153 (trade—weapons—humans—flesh, etc.), p. 211 (Nakula's mother)

Samyutta-Nikaya—*Kindred Sayings*, IV—Pali Text, vol. 14, p. 190 (parable of black and white oxen)

NOTE: There is no evidence in the Text that Nakula's mother was Uggaha's daughter, but it is possible.

CHAPTER XVIII

CONVERSION OF A ROBBER

THE most memorable of the occasions when I happened to meet the Master during the middle part of his ministry, was once on the way to Savatthi. As we approached the city we perceived that armed guards were posted at all the vantage points, both at the foot of the walls and at the top of them, and at many places outside the city, also. The shields of those that stood guard glinted like spangles in the sunlight, and each man had his sword by his side and his bow and arrow in his hand. When we reached Jeta Grove, the Master inquired why King Pasenadi had his city guarded with so many guards. 'Is he expecting an attack from King Bimbisara or the Licchavi lords?'

'No, Master,' replied one of the Brothers, 'all neighbouring kings and lords are friendly towards King Pasenadi. It is the robber, Angulimala, who is troubling this realm and against whom the King has need to arm.'

'Angulimala?' asked the Master; 'and who is this robber, whose name signifies a necklace of fingers?'

'Truly, Master, he is very fierce and terrible and utterly without mercy, and his hands are red with blood. Because of him, what were villages are villages no more; what were townships are townships no more; and all that remains of the people that dwelt in them is a necklace of their fingers which he wears around his neck. No one dare venture forth into the countryside now that he is near, no, not though they were a company of men all well armed.'

'And does this robber, Angulimala, have a large band of other robbers with him, that he strikes such terror into the heart of people?'

'No, Master, he is alone.'

'Alone! And where is he now dwelling?'

One of the Brothers pointed across the city, saying: 'He dwells yonder, so far as is known, for it is from there he comes to destroy the villages and slaughter the villagers.'

'Yonder will I then go and talk with him,' said the Master unconcernedly.

'No! No! Master, do not do so,' said that Brother with utmost horror. 'No one has seen that robber and returned alive, no, not though they were a battalion of armed men.'

'Master! Master!' cried another with even greater terror, 'Go not to that robber, but stay and teach those that can receive the teaching.'

The Master smiled gaily, 'But perhaps the robber, Angulimala, has need of the teaching.'

A Brother, who had not before spoken, replied drily: 'Surely he has need of it, but far more surely he would refuse to receive it.' He then altered his tone and became matter-of-fact.' See, Master, there is your sleeping-place made ready, and folk in the town are earnestly waiting to hear the teaching. Even though you take no thought for your own safety, surely with so many needing you here, you would not set forth to convert a robber, that is, if he could be converted, which we all know he could not.'

'Friend,' replied the Master in the same matter-of-fact tone, 'the robber, Angulimala, has need of the teaching and therefore I go to him.'

Another Brother made a last effort, 'Then, Master, take with you the well-armed guard which King Pasenadi has ever ready to protect you.'

The Master was almost laughing. 'The robber, Angulimala, has need only of the teaching; he has no need of an armed guard to accompany me.'

The Brother last to speak was oblivious of the Master's amusement, and replied with desperate earnestness: 'Oh! Master, can you not understand that none ever ventured into the sight of that robber and returned with his life?'

The Master appeared to be thoroughly enjoying the situation, but he now dropped his amusement and replied seriously: 'Brothers did any ever venture into the sight of Angulimala having left fear behind and carrying only compassionate love in his heart?'

'I suppose not,' admitted that Brother reluctantly.

'Then you cannot judge the outcome of the visit of one who does these things. And now, shed your own fear and have loving-friendship towards Angulimala, and tell the Brothers and the Sisters and the lay men and lay women where I have gone, and that shortly

I shall return and bring the robber, Angulimala, with me. Ask that they accord him kindness and goodwill.'

Very despondently the Brother replied: 'We shall do as you bid, Master, but sorrow is heavy within us. You have the wisdom of all Buddhas, but you know not that robber.'

I had witnessed this scene with something of the amusement of the Master. These Brothers were young and they did not yet know the power the Master wielded, nor the compassion which would be even now flowing towards Angulimala.

.   .   .   .   .   .

What happened when the Master walked towards the robber's den, I later heard from Angulimala himself. He was planning the morrow's raid on Savatthi, when he purposed to relieve King Pasenadi of his fingers. He was depending on the fact that the guards were frightened and would fall to his sword like sheep to a butcher's knife.

'Adventure!' he cried aloud in exultation. 'Adventure! Kings conquer realms! I conquer Kings! Tomorrow I raid Savatthi!'

Then he happened to glance to the right and saw the Master passing. It was a strange sight—a lonely yellow-robed monk walking right past his den. He drew his sword and shouted: 'Stop, monk!'

The Master looked up and answered quietly: '*I* have stopped. It is *you* who have not,' and he continued walking.

'I say, stop!' shouted Angulimala again and rushed towards the Master with his drawn sword.

The Master looked him in the eyes and his sword dropped to the ground. What happened he could not rightly remember, except that he stood still and gazed at this strange monk with the extraordinarily sweet smile and placid brow, and eyes that seemed to radiate peace. His mind travelled back to his childhood days, and a certain holy woman who used to come to his father's house for alms. Never since then had he seen anything remotely like the face of this monk. Terror, lust, hatred—these things were ever around him. But serene beauty and stillness were something new. His tense muscles relaxed. Unthinking, he sat down. The Master sat down, too. For a little while Angulimala remained silently watching this charming stranger. He was spellbound. At last he said weakly: 'What brings you hither?'

'You have need of me, oh Chief!'

Angulimala started, '*I* need of *you*?'

'Yes.'

Angulimala tried to break the spell he felt was being woven round him, and laughed as he went on, 'Need of your fingers only, I think, since treasure you have none.'

The Master held out his hands, saying: 'My fingers you may have willingly. But you have need of more than those from me.'

'How so?'

The Master now spoke seriously. 'You seek a greater adventure than you have yet conceived, a greater conquest than you have yet won. I have come to show you the Way.

Light began to dawn on Angulimala as he remembered the strange spell that this monk had seemed to throw around him. He said eagerly: 'You mean magic? Can you teach me magic spells? What else can be a greater adventure than raiding the city of Savatthi, or a greater conquest than the rape of the fingers of its monarch?'

The Master's tone was friendly and familiar as he replied: 'That is child's play to you, oh Chief! For the guards are afraid and the King trembles at your name.'

'I know,' said Angulimala proudly.

'I have come to show you the way to a conquest worthy of a man, worthy of one who knows no fear.'

Angulimala pondered a moment or two and then said thoughtfully: 'You are one who knows no fear. You speak as one who has known adventures and conquered. Yet you are only a yellow-robed monk. But magic!' He paused. 'Yes, magic would give me a greater power than ever. All my other conquests would be only child's play. Is it magic, oh monk?'

'It is magic and it is not magic,' answered the Master.

'I have learned all there is to learn of the ways of rapine and robbery,' Angulimala spoke thoughtfully. 'You open up new fields for conquest. I would learn the art of magic. I know not why, but I feel I can trust you.'

'Beware, my friend, how you trust me,' replied the Master sternly, 'I shall lead you into ways you know not of.'

Angulimala rose to the challenge, 'I am not afraid.' Then he added half to himself: 'You called me "friend". None has called me that since the days my teacher drove me forth because the other students disliked me. I would have a friend, one who stays beside me and yet who is not afraid of me. And now, oh monk, what is this adventure greater than I have yet conceived—this conquest worthy of man?'

'It is the adventure of the Eightfold Path that leads to conquest of your self.'

'Of myself?' asked Angulimala indignantly. 'But all the world is afraid of me—except you. Why should I want to conquer myself?'

'Because you, friend, are the slave of your lusts, your lusts for power and domination. You can no more stop your desire for further conquests than you can stop the grey hairs which gather upon your brow.'

'But all men bow before me and do my will,' protested Angulimala.

'And you, friend, bow before the lusts which sweep through your mind and do *their* will, as helpless as the rice which bows before the wind. As a craven slave you permit your passions to be your master. But I shall show you the way to be free, the way to become the master of yourself.'

Angulimala gazed across the patch-work of the rice-fields and the feathery neem trees overhanging the thatched roofs of the mud cottages whose inhabitants had fled because of him, and far beyond, to the high turrets of the city walls whose King was afraid because of him. Two monkeys with red faces and red behinds swung into the tree opposite and looked at him dubiously, but he did not see them until they sprang away. He murmured to himself, 'Adventure! Power!'

'Yes,' replied the Master, recalling him to the present. 'But this adventure will bring you pain and suffering.'

'I have never feared pain and suffering,' said Angulimala, again rising to the challenge.

'It will take long and the way will be arduous.'

'I have always had patience and hard work has been my delight,' retorted Angulimala.

'And you will learn the meaning of fear.'

'I, who have never known fear?'

'You, who have never known fear.'

'What is it I shall fear?' asked Angulimala, but there was no hesitancy in his tone.

'The evil deeds you have done,' the Master spoke very gently.

'I do not understand. But I know that I can trust you, and that you hold before me the challenge of the greatest of all adventures.

Master, I follow you.' He paused and added: 'But tell me one thing. What did you mean when you first spoke and said *you* had stopped, but *I* had not?'

The Master smiled, 'I meant that I had stopped doing harm to all beings, but you had not.'

'But you, Master, are going to teach me how.'

'Yes, are you ready for this greatest of all adventures?'

'I am.'

The Master rose and Angulimala followed him through the deserted village towards Savatthi. The doors were open; monkeys and birds had eaten the food prepared and only empty bowls remained. In the fields the cows were unmilked and the oxen, still yoked, trailed the wooden plough behind them.

.   .   .   .   .   .

Meanwhile, in Jeta Grove, the Brothers waited anxiously. I told them of the power the Master wielded because of his all-embracing love, and that, if he had any preference left, it was to suffuse with loving friendship the worst and vilest of people, as a strong archer would prefer a bow difficult to bend. But they took no notice of my words. And when King Pasenadi arrived to wait upon the Master, they could hardly delay to pay their respects before they told of the horror that was in their hearts. I reported to the King how the Master had said that Angulimala had need of him, but the King had no more faith, no, nor sense of humour, than had those young Brothers.

Then I said: 'If the Master returns bringing with him that robber, Angulimala, what will Your Majesty do?'

The King replied fiercely: 'I should have him executed with the least possible delay.'

At that moment I saw in the distance the Master returning with another yellow-robed one, and I said: 'Suppose, Your Majesty, the Master returns, bringing with him the robber, Angulimala, dressed in yellow robes, humble and lowly of mien, a man who kills not, steals not, a man who leads the Brahma-life in virtue and goodness as a Brother of the Order?'

The King replied despondently that in such an event he would have no alternative but to extend to him the protection and defence he extended to all members of the Order. Then he added cheerfully: 'But how could virtue ever hold sway over one so depraved?'

I replied: 'I do not know; but see, Your Majesty!' and I pointed to the Master and that other yellow-robed one whose face bore the marks of violence. The King turned in the direction I pointed; he began to tremble with terror and the hairs of his body stood on end. At length he gasped: 'No, it cannot be he.'

As I expected, on entering, the Master introduced that other yellow-robed one as Brother Angulimala. The King tried to control himself, but still trembling he asked for proof that this was indeed the robber. Angulimala then gave the names of his father and mother and the King had to believe. Very reluctantly and still in fear and trembling, he formally extended to him the protection and benefit he extended to all of the Order. Then he added fiercely: 'But fortunate will you be if the villagers and townspeople extend to you the same protection and benefit.'

Angulimala answered with gentleness and sorrow: 'I know, oh King, I know. If only that were all. Stones and javelins I do not fear, for I must reap as I have sown. But what I do fear is that the evil deeds of my past life will never be wiped out.' He turned to the Master, saying: 'Shall I ever atone for my evil deeds and find the inner peace of which you tell? Truly, now myself and my evil deeds seem a foul stinking lump which can never be dissolved away.'

The Master replied: 'As a man has sown so must he reap. You must go forth and meet the karma of your evil deeds and gather in the harvest they will bear. But not exactly as a man sows does he reap, for the waters of the Universal and Imperishable are vast. If you seek virtue and centre your thoughts in the Imperishable, your evil deeds will be expiated here and now. They will be washed away as would a lump of salt thrown into the River Ganges, the same lump of salt which would make a small cup of water undrinkable.'

Angulimala took the dust from the Master's feet, saying: 'I take my refuge in you as my Master. I go to meet the villagers—and my evil deeds.'

The King was deeply affected, as indeed were we all, at the scene we had witnessed, and he now turned to the Master, saying: 'It is wonderful indeed how you are a tamer of the savage and a calmer of the violent. Here is one whom I could not subdue with sword and cudgel, but you have subdued him without either.'

'Ah! Your Majesty, compassionate, loving friendship is stronger than the sword or cudgel. Can you not see that love is everything?'

The King shook his head, 'I confess I cannot. Some day, perhaps

—I may find the secret of the magic which you seem to wield. But the time is not yet, and now, Master, the duties of kingship summon me.'

'Do as seems fit to you,' replied the Master and the King departed.

I had been puzzling over what the Master had said to Angulimala and now I asked: 'I do not understand how what a man reaps accords with what he has sown, and how, none the less, his evil deeds may be wiped away. Could you explain, Master?'

'Evil deeds are not always wiped away; they do not always ripen and fall off. Whether they do, depends on whether the evil-doer has found his being in the Beyond. He who has, and who follows the path of virtue, pays for his evil deeds here and now, and though the penalty may seem grievous, his evil deeds are wiped away and have no aftermath, for he is drawn into the peace of the Beyond. The waters of the Universal are vast and sweet, and are greater than the waters of the Ganges.'

That evening, when the Brothers were again gathered about the Master, Angulimala returned from the village. His head streamed with blood and one of his eyes had been struck out. The Brothers came forward to tend him as he sank down exhausted.

'The King was right,' he said, 'the villagers did not extend to me the kindness and protection of their lord. They flung stones and knives at me. I reap as I sowed.'

'And are you content?' asked the Master.

There was peace and gladness in his voice as Angulimala replied: 'I am content. Yes, a thousand times, yes. For even as the villagers struck me and my head seemed to split, it was as if the great ocean of the Imperishable opened before me, and that for a little while I was drawn into the peace of Nirvana.'

'All is well with you, friend,' said the Master with great tenderness. 'Continue thus through the suffering you will yet meet, and you will be drawn ever deeper into the peace which you then knew.'

'It is the greatest of all adventures,' exclaimed Angulimala triumphantly, and as he spoke I understood how what a man reaps does not always accord with what he has sown, for if it did it would leave out of account the Brahma-life, and the waters of the Immortal which are vast beyond measure, and in which evil may be lost even as a lump of salt is lost within the River Ganges.

Angulimala, striving earnestly, in no long time found enlightenment and was numbered among the saints.

Majjhima-Nikaya—*Further Dialogues*, II—S. B. Buddhists, vol. 6, p. 50 (Angulimala)

Anguttara-Nikaya—*Gradual Sayings*, I—Pali Text, vol. 22, p. 227 (grain of salt)

Anguttara-Nikaya—*Buddhism in Translation*—Harvard O.S., vol. 3, p. 218 (grain of salt)

Anguttara-Nikaya—Grimm—*The Doctrine of the Buddha*, p. 255 (grain of salt)

Dhammapada Commentary—*Buddhist Legends*—Harvard O. S., vol. 30, p. 6 (Angulimala)

Theragatha—*Psalms of the Brethren*—Pali Text, vol. 4, p. 318 (Angulimala)

NOTE: The story is somewhat elaborated but does not add substantially to the Texts.

CHAPTER XIX

DEVADATTA'S SCHISM

I HAVE said little concerning Devadatta, the cousin of the Master and his junior by five or six years. He was regarded as one of the elders of the Order and respected by many because of his supernormal powers and his eloquence in teaching the Dhamma, on account of which latter he had been appointed instructor of the Sisters. He was one towards whom I had often found it difficult to cherish thoughts of kindliness, for he was a hard man who had little pity for any that failed in austerity. I heard tell that in his youth he despised his quiet cousin, Prince Siddhartha, who had learned the manly sport of shooting and sword-play only because such things were expected of a prince, and not because he took pleasure in them. But when Siddhartha had become renowned as a Buddha and one drawing great crowds to him, Devadatta came like others to listen to him, and found in him all that appealed to the best in himself. Thus it was that when Prince Bhaddiya joined the Order, Devadatta joined also.

He possessed great talents and could achieve anything to which he turned his mind. He used to sit day after day in a small cave at the foot of the hills near Rajagaha, practising meditation, and very soon he acquired complete proficiency in concentration, being able at will to direct his thought wherever he wished and hold it there. But there is both right and wrong meditation. The Master often told us that we should commence meditation with thoughts of loving friendship, first directed towards our own minds and bodies, so that we do not injure them with thoughts of worry, lust, malevolence or anger, then directed towards the circle of our near acquaintances, suffusing them with the selfless love of a mother for her only son. Finally, he said, we should suffuse the whole wide world with thoughts of all-embracing love above, below, around. Then, and not until then, should we start to direct our thoughts towards the subject suited to our temperament. Now Devadatta cannot have commenced his meditation practice with thoughts of loving friendship. Further, the Master often warned us that concentration of thought may lead to the acquirement of supernormal powers, but that the exercise of such powers might be dangerous, and in itself did not lead to compassion and liberation. But Devadatta rejoiced when these super-normal powers came to him, and instead of ignoring them, he cultivated them until he could perform what most people consider miracles, but which are merely the application of little known laws of nature. He took no heed of the Master's warning but continued in greater and greater measure to gain and display such powers.

Now, while the Master in his seventieth year was staying in Ghosita Wood near Kosambi, it is said that the thought came to Devadatta, when seated in meditation: "Whom now can I bring under my power so that, being well pleased with me, such one may bring gain and honour to me?" Then the further thought came to him that Prince Ajatazattu, the son of King Bimbisara, would be such a one. Devadatta therefore took up his bowl and robe and set forth from Kosambi to Rajagaha. It would seem that there still hung over Kosambi those dark forces of discord, which stirred the quarrelsome monks many years before, and that they had now taken hold of Devadatta's mind.

Devadatta took a boat down the Ganges River and soon arrived at Rajagaha, where he went straight into the presence of Prince Ajatazattu, and performed before him a miracle of great wonder. The Prince was very pleased with Devadatta, and to show his pleasure he arranged that every morning and evening chariots laden with food should come to Devadatta and his disciples. Thus it was that Devadatta's fame spread throughout the city and hospitality was extended to him by the leading citizens. Such gains and favours unbalanced his mind, and it is said that there arose within him the new thought, "It is I, and not Gautama, who should lead the Order." But no sooner had this thought arisen than his power to perform miracles disappeared. None the less, his fame still spread and people continued to shower hospitality and favours upon him.

Moggallana, who was dwelling at Kosambi with the Master, with his supernormal inner sight, perceived what was taking place in Devadatta's mind, and he went to the Master and told him. The Master said: 'Keep that saying secret, Moggallana. If there be within him so much as a prick end of a horse's hair of virtue, it will be possible to save him from his folly. But alas! too soon, I fear, will that foolish man make himself known. He thinks he will be protected by his disciples, but the teacher whose conduct and heart are pure, does not need the protection of anyone.'

Soon after this, the Master left Kosambi and travelled to Rajagaha.

Unlike Devadatta he travelled on foot. He went by the north bank
of the River Ganges, and despite his age he still walked ten miles and
more every day, teaching as he travelled. At Rajagaha he took up his
abode in Veluvana Pleasance, the Bamboo Grove, which, it will be
remembered, had been given to the Order by King Bimbisara on the
occasion of his first visit there, now some thirty-five years ago. As
soon as he arrived, we came and reported to him how Prince Ajatazattu
was going morning and evening to wait upon Devadatta with carts
laden with food and laying it before him in many dishes. The Master
said:

'Envy not the hospitality and favour shown to Devadatta. Gains
and favours make it difficult for growth of virtue. So long as Prince
Ajatazattu waits upon Devadatta and gives him alms in this manner,
so long, alas! will Devadatta decline in virtuous qualities, just as a
gall-bladder burst in front of the nose of a fierce dog would make him
fiercer still. To his own hurt has this gain come to Devadatta.' There
was great sadness in the Master's voice.

That evening King Bimbisara and his retinue, as well as a great
multitude of townspeople, came to the Bamboo Grove to listen to the
Master teach the Dhamma. In the midst of the discourse Devadatta
rose from his seat, and arranging his upper robe over one shoulder,
stretched out his joined palms to the Master, saying:

'Master, you have now grown aged and stricken in years. You
have accomplished a long journey and the span of your life has nearly
run. It is time that you dwelt at ease in enjoyment of that happiness
which is reached even in this world. Let the Exalted One give up the
direction of the Order to me. I will be its leader.' Devadatta was an
accomplished speaker with clear enunciation, and the beauty of his
voice captivated people. But even so a murmur of dissent ran through
those that heard him.

The Master looked upon him with great sorrow and said quietly:
'You have said enough, Devadatta. Desire not to be the leader of the
Order.'

But Mara hardened the heart of Devadatta and a second time he
made the same request. A second time did the Master reply as before.
Yet a third time did Devadatta ask. This time the Master said, with
the same quietness but also firmness: 'Devadatta, I would not give
up the leadership of the Order to Sariputta and Moggellana. How
much less would I give it up to you, who speak over-hastily and
value talk too much?'

Deeply mortified, Devadatta rose and passed out.

This was the first attempt that Devadatta made to overthrow the Master.

After he had departed and the assembled people had dispersed, the Master called Sariputta to him and said: 'Let it be proclaimed throughout Rajagaha that whatsoever Devadatta shall do either in action or word, in nothing shall the Buddha or the Dhamma be recognized, but only Devadatta.'

'But, Master,' protested Sariputta, 'in former times I sang the praises of Devadatta, saying that great supernormal powers were his. How then can I make this proclamation against him?'

'Was it not true, what you spoke, Sariputta, when you sang his praises?'

'Yes, Master.'

'Even so, Sariputta, again speaking the truth, do you proclaim throughout Rajagaha that Devadatta's nature has now changed.'

'So be it, Master,' said Sariputta reluctantly.

To most of us this seemed to be no sentence at all against Devadatta. To create a schism in the Order was considered the most serious of offences, and in the rare cases of it having been attempted, the extreme penalty had been imposed, that of refraining from converse with the guilty Brother, forbidding him communion with the Order and attendance at its assemblies. But the Master did not order the extreme penalty against Devadatta, probably because he had still hope that there might be a hair's breadth of virtue within him, by which he might be pulled out of the mire of evil into which he had fallen. Thus Devadatta remained within the Order and could attend its meetings.

When Sariputta entered Rajagaha and made proclamation as had been asked of him, those people who were unbelievers and without insight, said to one another: 'These followers of Gautama, the Sakyan, are jealous.' But those who were believers and with insight said to one another: 'It can be no ordinary affair that causes the Master to have Devadatta proclaimed throughout the city as no longer representing the Dhamma.'

Devadatta, hearing the proclamation, thought within himself that the only way by which he might gain his end was to take the life of the Master. He accordingly went to Ajatazattu, the Prince, and said to him, 'In former times, sire, people were long-lived. Your father belongs to these former times. But in these days the term of a man's life is short, and you, sire, belong to these present times. It may well be, therefore, that you will die before your father, and before you have become King.'

'Yes, Venerable Sir,' said the Prince, probably remembering that his father was still in robust health, and that his own hair was beginning to grey. 'I have counted the years until I should become King, but what you say is true. I may die while I am yet only a Prince.'

'You could hasten your father's end, sire,' said Devadatta.

'Would that be lawful, Venerable Sir?' asked the Prince doubtfully. 'You are possessed of great supernormal powers, and surely you will know?'

'It would be lawful, sire,' replied Devadatta without hesitation. When a man lives beyond the allotted span, he is no longer suited to hold power, and if he does not retire from office of his own accord, his retirement from this life should be made easier for him.'

'I have confidence in you, Venerable Sir. What do you suggest?'

Devadatta answered in the same unhesitating manner as those speak who hold authority. 'You must be brave, sire, you must take his life with your own hand.'

'I shall do what you tell me is right,' answered Ajatazattu, but not without some doubt.

'And I, sire,' said Devadatta, 'shall take the life of Gautama, who has also passed the allotted span. Then I in turn shall assume the office of the Buddha.'

Such was the influence of Devadatta, that Prince Ajatazattu, in spite of a certain affection for his father, none the less fastened a dagger against his thigh, and fearful, anxious and excited, went into the royal apartments at an unseasonable hour. The ministers who waited upon the King in his bedchamber at once suspected that he had come with no good intent. They seized him, and on searching him found the dagger and asked what he purposed to do with it. Ajatazattu was not clever. He was ambitious, but he had not liked the plan from the beginning. He now blurted out the truth, telling those ministers the whole of his conversation with Devadatta.

The ministers were shocked and horrified. Some were for having Prince Ajatazattu, and Devadatta and all the Brothers put to death. But those that understood the teaching of the Master said that none should be slain, not even Ajatazattu, but that the King should be informed. The counsel of these prevailed, and they took the Prince with them and went in to the King, and told him all. The King looked upon his son, hardly comprehending what was said to him, for the King loved his son, and always there had been friendliness between them.

'Why did you want to kill me?' he asked.

'I wanted the kingdom, sire,' his son replied.

'Ah! my son,' said the King sadly, 'the life of a King is not an easy one, but since you desire to possess the kingdom, let the kingdom be yours. A good life it will be for me to be able to hand over the duties of kingship and retire from the world to meditate upon the holy matters the Buddha teaches.'

One of the ministers then spoke, saying: 'Are your subjects to be allowed to plot your death?' He then told the King of the debate they had had concerning the killing of the Prince, and Devadatta and the Brothers.

The King was deeply shocked that some of his ministers had thought it right to slay those that had plotted against him. 'Does not the Master teach goodwill towards all, even those that do us ill?' he asked. Then he ordered that the ministers who had opposed the slaying of the wrongdoers should be promoted to high places.

Next day King Bimbisara had it proclaimed throughout Magadha that Ajatazattu was now the King.

As soon as Ajatazattu knew that he was truly King, he commanded all his men to obey the commands of Devadatta, and at once Devadatta availed himself of his power to compass the death of the Master. He called one of the King's soldiers to him, and said:

'Gautama, the Buddha, is staying at the shrine in the Bamboo Grove; go to him, kill him and return by this path.' Then he called two other soldiers, saying to them: 'Whatever man you see coming along that path, kill him and return by this other path.' On this other path he placed four further soldiers with the same instructions, and so on until he had arranged for fifteen men to kill their fellows.

Had I not been in Rajagaha at the time, I should not have believed it possible for Devadatta to sink to such iniquity. For Devadatta had a noble side to his nature. But who shall say to what depths a man may not sink, when great homage is paid to him before he has abandoned all thoughts of self and before the asavas have died within him?

The first soldier took his sword and shield and hung his bow and quiver at his back, and went towards the place where the Master was seated. The Master saw him coming and trembling at the thought of the great evil he was about to commit, and he called to him: 'Come hither, friend, do not be afraid.' That man told me afterwards how the Blessed One's words took the great terror from him and how he went forward unafraid, and fell at his feet, weeping with relief and gladness. He told him what he had consented to do, and asked forgiveness. The Master readily accepted his confession and talked to him of the way of gentleness and loving-kindness, and the man became a disciple. When he rose to go, the Master bade him depart by a different path through the bamboos than the one he had been told.

Now, the second two men, who had been commanded to kill the first, finding that no man came along the path, proceeded along it themselves, and they, too, came upon the Master seated as before. To them also he talked of gentleness and loving-kindness, and they likewise became his disciples. And when they in turn rose to leave, the Master showed them a different path by which they should return.

The same thing happened to the next four and to the last eight men.

The first man, he who had been commanded to slay the Master, returned to Devadatta and said to him: 'I cannot deprive the Blessed One of his life. He has a power not of this world. Great is the might of the Blessed One.'

Then Devadatta knew that, if the Master was to be killed, he alone would be able to do the deed. With this object in view he climbed a crack on Vultures' Peak, and stood on the edge of it. And when the Master paced to and fro in meditation along the path beneath, Devadatta hurled down a mighty rock. But it struck a projecting piece of the mountain-side and only a small splinter of it hit his foot, making it bleed. The Master looked up sadly, saying: 'Oh foolish one! Great is the demerit you are bringing upon yourself.'

When the Brothers heard that Devadatta was compassing the Master's death, they thought to protect him by walking round the quarters where he was staying, chanting sacred sayings in loud voices. On hearing them and on ascertaining from Ananda what they were doing, he called them to him and said: 'A truth-finder needs no protection, a truth-finder cannot be deprived of his life by attack. Go therefore each to your own quarters and make no more noise.'

Devadatta, having failed in this third attempt to supplant the Master, now went to the keepers of the fierce elephant, Nalagiri, a man-slayer, and said: 'As you know, I am the King's confidential adviser and also I can arrange increase in food rations and in pay for men who do my bidding.'

'Yes, Venerable Sir,' they replied, knowing that what he said was true. 'Whatever are your orders shall be carried out by us.'

Devadatta continued: 'When the sage, Gautama, passes down this road, let loose the elephant, Nalagiri.'

'It shall be as you say, Venerable Sir,' they replied.

Early in the morning the Master and several of the Brothers entered Rajagaha for alms and went along this narrow road whose houses opened right on to it. The elephant-keepers loosed Nalagiri, as they had been commanded. When the Brothers saw that man-slaying elephant in the distance, walking by itself on the road, they pleaded with the Master to turn back, but once again he told them there was nothing to fear, and that a Truth-finder could not be deprived of his life by attack. The people on the road, seeing the elephant, were filled with terror and climbed in panic upon the roofs of the houses, so that the street became deserted, save for the Master and the Brothers who would not leave him. Those that had climbed upon the roofs turned to one another, some saying: 'The countenance of the Happy One is beautiful, but none the less that elephant will do him great harm.' Others of them that were disciples of the Master said: 'That elephant will not be able to fight with him who is the elephant among men.' None the less you could see that even these looked on with great anxiety as the elephant drew nearer to the Master.

As the people were speaking, the Master was putting forth his power of loving friendship and suffusing Nalagiri with loving heart. Before he reached the Master, the elephant put down his trunk and went quietly up. The Master stroked his forehead and spoke to him. Then Nalagiri, the elephant, took the dust from the feet of the Blessed One and went back to the elephant stables, turning round from time to time to look at the Master, and to those that saw, it seemed that the elephant's eyes were filled with the same love as the Master's. From that time Nalagiri was tame and docile, and people said: 'Elephants can be tamed with sticks and goads, but the great elephant among men tamed Nalagiri without any of these things.'

As a result of Nalagiri being loosed, people became angry and indignant with Devadatta, and those that had formerly bestowed favours upon him, ceased to bestow them. But Devadatta's determination to overthrow the Master only increased. In all the years I knew the Master, I never knew of any case in which his power of loving friendship failed to win, save only with Devadatta.

Devadatta now thought of another way in which he might overcome the Master. If he appeared more strenuous in austerity of living and in ascetism, he considered that he would thereby create a division within the Order, and that the more zealous of the Brothers would follow him. He imparted his designs to four who were his closest associates. One of them tried to dissuade him, saying that the Master was powerful and that it was a foolish thing he planned. None the less Devadatta persisted, and eventually they went with him to the Master.

Devadatta said: 'Master, you have declared that it is great advantage when a man is easy to satisfy in the matter of food and support, and who has eradicated evil and quelled his passions. Now the following five things would conduce to such conditions. Let rules be made: first, that the Brothers should always dwell within the forest and never reside in villages; second, that the Brothers must always accept alms from door to door and refuse invitations to partake of meals in people's houses; third, that Brothers should clothe themselves only in rags from rubbish heaps and refuse gifts of robes from householders; fourth, that Brothers should have no shelter save roots of trees; fifth, that the Brothers should abstain from the eating of fish and meat.'

We could feel the Master's loving thoughts suffusing Devadatta, as he replied patiently: 'No, Devadatta, whoever wishes to do so, let him reside in the forest; whoever wishes to do so, let him receive only alms from door to door, wear only rags and refuse invitations to meals and gifts of clothes. But none must be compelled to these things. Sleeping under the trees during the dry weather is permitted, but during the rains the Brothers should seek sufficient shelter. Eating of fish and meat put into the bowl and not suspected of having been caught or prepared especially for him, is also permitted.'

Devadatta was delighted at the Master's refusal of his five rules. He went into Rajagaha, telling all that he and his disciples lived lives of greater austerity than did the Master, and that the Master dwelt in luxury and sought abundance of food and clothing. Some of those lay people that heard, and likewise some of the younger Brothers, were inclined to believe and follow Devadatta.

When the Master next came upon Devadatta, he asked him the truth of the report, and whether he was striving to cause a schism within the Order. And Devadatta admitted that this was so.

'You have gone far enough, Devadatta,' said the Master sadly.

He who breaks up the Order when it is at peace, gives birth to a fault which cannot easily be atoned. Blessed is he who makes peace and harmony.'

But Devadatta's heart was again hardened. Next day, when he met Ananda, he told him he would carry out the formal proceedings of the Order without the Master. When the Master heard this, he said sorrowfully: 'Easy is a good act to him who is good, but hard indeed is a good act to him who is wicked.' But the Master did not do anything to prevent Devadatta's action.

Now, when the Upasatha Day, the day of confession and purification, came, Devadatta rose from his seat and gave out the voting papers, saying that those who approved of the Five Points he advocated concerning the matter of austere living, should hand in the papers of a certain colour. It happened that there were present many newly ordained Brothers who did not know the matter in hand, and they voted for the rules of greater austerity, thinking that they were harder and therefore of more benefit, and not knowing the division within the Order that their voting would bring about. After the voting was over, Devadatta took those newly ordained ones who had voted for the Five Points of greater austerity, and also those who had followed him before, and went to the hill of Gaya-sisa.

Sariputta and Moggallana, seeing what Devadatta had done, sought out the Master and told him of it. The Master said to them: 'Suffuse those young Brothers newly ordained with feelings of great loving-kindness and goodwill, and before they have fallen into entire destruction, go to them, both of you. But there must be a feeling of great loving-kindness and goodwill towards them.'

'Even so, Master,' said Sariputta and Moggallana, understanding perfectly. They departed and went to the hill of Gaya-sisa where they found Devadatta preaching to the young Brothers seated around him. When he saw Sariputta and Moggallana approaching, his heart leapt for joy and he said: 'Behold! Brothers, how well preached is my doctrine. See, there are the two chief disciples of Gautama, even Sariputta and Moggallana coming to join me, because they are pleased with my teaching.'

But Devadatta's chief disciple, Kolalika, who had warned him against attempting to create a schism, said: 'Venerable Sir, trust not Sariputta and Moggallana. They have evil designs.'

Devadatta was so puffed up with pride that he would not hearken to this warning and replied: 'No, my friend, they take pleasure in my teaching. Let us bid them welcome.' He turned to Sariputta, inviting him to take the best seat. But Sariputta took a lesser seat and likewise Moggallana, and they listened to Devadatta, as he preached to those young men far into the night.

Those young Brothers, who abounded in good health and intellectual alertness, did not weary as they listened. But, as the night wore on, Devadatta, who was over the age of sixty years, himself became weary of preaching, and he turned to Sariputta, saying: 'This assembly, friend, is still alert and sleepless, will you, pray, give them further religious discourse. My back is tired and I would rest myself a little.'

Sariputta consented, and Devadatta folded his robe and lay down on his right side, and was soon wrapped in slumber.

Then Sariputta and Moggallana, suffusing those young Brothers with great love and kindness, showed them the true doctrine, to wit the Fourfold Truth and the Eightfold Way. As they listened, there arose within them the Pure and Spotless Eye of Truth. When Sariputta and Moggallana perceived this, they concluded their discourse and invited such of those young men as would, to return to the Master. With one accord they rose and followed these two chief disciples down the hill-side and back to the Bamboo Grove, where the Master was lodging.

Kolalika, like Devadatta, had been sleeping, but when those young Brothers arose, he heard them and awoke. As soon as he perceived what had happened, he stirred Devadatta from his slumber, saying: 'Arise, friend, Moggallana and Sariputta have led away all your disciples. When they came, said I not they planned evil?'

Devadatta roused himself from his sleep, but he could not at once comprehend what Kolalika was saying. When he did, he rose in haste, but he was dazed by the shock he had received, and it was a little while before he was able to set forth after the young men. He was weary from the strain of many weeks of evil-doing, and striving to make things go the way he wanted. He said he suddenly felt very old and weary and that the night seemed very dark. When they reached the lake at the foot of the hill, he felt faint, and said he must sit down and rest awhile. He had worked so hard and now all had been frustrated. After a while, telling Kolalika he needed to drink, he went down to the shores of the lake. Kolalika was looking down the fields at the eastern sky which was starting to brighten with the dawn, and was wondering to himself why Devadatta should have plotted against the Master whose strength could not be assailed, and who was so very kind and gentle, when suddenly he heard Devadatta give a great shout of terror and cry for help. Looking down to the lake, he saw him standing ankle-deep in the mud of the shore and struggling frantically to get one of his feet up. At first Kolalika thought that a snake must have bitten him. Then with unspeakable horror the truth flashed upon him; Devadatta was caught in quicksand, on which a man can no more walk than on water, unless he have supernormal powers and these Devadatta had lost. Kolalika sprang to his feet and ran to the nearest tree to procure a stick. But the nearest tree was some way off and when he reached it and looked around, the legs of Devadatta had disappeared completely. In frenzied terror he was struggling alternately to sit down, to lie down and to crawl, but with each movement he only sank deeper. As Kolalika at length wrenched off the branch of the tree, Devadatta's cries ceased. He rushed to the lake. Devadatta had ceased to struggle, but only his bust could now be seen. He cried out: 'My end has come. Tell the Master that before I died I repented. He would have saved me with his love and friendship, but Mara was too strong for him.' As he spoke the last word, sand filled his mouth, and Kolalika did not know whether he heard the words of assurance he tried to utter. A moment later and only a few hairs fluttered in the morning breeze. And then nothing was left to show where Devadatta had gone down to the lake to drink.

When folk heard of his end, they said he had passed down to the deepest and most terrible of all the hells and would remain there for many a kalpa. But before he died, he had regained that virtue equal in size to the prick end of a horse's hair, having which, the Master had said, he must in the end be drawn out of the cesspool of iniquity.

Chapter XIX—Sources

Vinaya—S. B. East, vol. XX, p. 233
Vinaya—*Book of Discipline*, V—S. B. Buddhists, vol. 20, p. 260
Vinaya—*Book of Discipline*, I—S. B. Buddhists, vol. 10, pp. 296 and 304

Jennings—p. 377
Woodward—p. 271
Bigandet, vol. I, Ch. XII, p. 261
Anguttara-Nikaya—*Gradual Sayings*, III—Pali Text, vol. 25, p. 287
(prick end of horse's hair)
NOTE: The Texts say Devadatta was swallowed up by the earth.
Perhaps the expression is symbolical, but there may well have been
quicksands in the lakes below the hot springs at Rajagaha.

CHAPTER XX

DEATH AND NIRVANA

DEVADATTA's attempted schism was only one of the many sorrows that clouded the last years of the Master's life. And yet they did not cloud it. He continued to carry about with him the same serene peace and unperturbable happiness. Folk said he enjoyed life; and so he did: he enjoyed it with a zest that can never be known by those who are attached to it. When people questioned him, he admitted that he was among the truly happy, truly happy because he dwelt apart from earthly things. He was in the world, mixing with the joys and sorrows of people, and understanding those joys and sorrows as if they were his own. Yet he was not of the world. He was of That-Which-Does-Not-Die, which does not belong to time and space.

Sariputta and Moggallana had attained something of the same detached joy and calm. One day Ananda questioned Sariputta concerning the reason for this. He answered: 'It must be because I am no longer attached to anything of earth, and in extinction there is bliss. Only today, as I was seated in meditation, I asked myself if there was anything at all in this whole world, whose coming into existence, or whose changing or passing away, would cause me grief. I realized that there was at last nothing at all. I can truthfully say that if anything I know were taken from me, it would bring me neither sorrow nor regret.'

'You cannot mean that, Sariputta,' said Ananda unbelievingly. 'If the Master were to die, surely that would bring sorrow to you?'

Sariputta answered solemnly: 'No, Ananda. Even if the Master were to pass away, his passing would cause no grief to me. Nevertheless, out of love for the world, I hope that the Master, who is so gifted and so wonderful, will not be taken from us, and that he may live awhile longer for the weal and happiness of gods and men. But for my own sake I have no such wish.'

Ananda replied, 'For a long time, friend Sariputta, all notions of "I" and "mine" and all insiduous conceits have been rooted out from you. And truly rooted out they must have been if you can say the passing of the Master would cause no grief to you.'

Moggallana had the same serene countenance as Sariputta, and these two friends would cheer and encourage each other, for if Sariputta had greater wisdom, Moggallana had clairvoyant sight and could meet and converse with the Master though he were at a great distance.

A short while after this conversation with Ananda, it happened that Sariputta travelled with the Master and various of the Brothers to Savatthi. Some of them went ahead and chose suitable sleeping-quarters for themselves. Sariputta, being old and feeble, was the last to arrive. He found all sleeping-quarters occupied. That did not trouble him and he chose the root of a tree. But it was winter and when the chill of early morning came, he began to cough. He rose. The Master had also risen early, and discovered him because of his coughing. The Master was concerned when he heard the reason why Sariputta had not been provided with a proper sleeping-place. He called the Brothers together and asked if they had given thought as to who should be allotted the best seat, the best sleeping-place and the best food. Some said that the best should be given to those who had belonged to the Brahmin class or the nobility, when in the world. Others said, those who could expound the Dhamma. Others again would give the best to those who could attain the four jnanas or stages of meditation, or to those who could exercise supernormal powers.

'No,' said the Master, 'none of these things merit the best, but old age alone. Long ago there was a great banyan tree on the lower slopes of the Himalayan range. Near it dwelt three friends, a partridge, a monkey and an elephant. As they desired to live together in peace and concord, they decided to give preference and greatest respect not to the one who was cleverest or wisest, but to the one who was oldest. Because he was of the greater size, they first asked the elephant how far he could remember back. He looked at the branches of the great banyan tree above them and said:

"When I was small, I used to walk over this banyan tree, and the topmost twig touched my belly."

'Next they questioned the monkey and he replied: "When I was small, sitting upon the ground I gnawed the topmost twig of this banyan tree."

'Lastly the partridge spoke: "When I was small, there was no banyan tree in this place, but there was one growing in the open space over there. One day I ate of its fruit, and I voided the seed of it in this place, and from that seed grew this banyan tree."

'Whereupon the elephant and the monkey said to the partridge: "You are the oldest. Henceforth we shall honour and reverence you; we shall support you and abide by your counsels."

'Thereafter those three dwelt together in mutual respect, confidence and courtesy. If animals know the rules of courtesy, how much more should you, who have left the world. Those who are oldest should receive the best sleeping-quarters, and the best food, and be treated with respect.'

On the occasion of this visit to Savatthi, Sariputta had reason to visit Anathapindika, the friend of the orphan and destitute, to whom the Master often talked upon the deeper matters of life and death. When I hear certain of the Brothers asserting that they of the homeless life have attained further than lay people, I think of the goodness and purity of Anathapindika, and of the many failings of the Brothers, and I know that they are wrong. The homeless life and the householder's life are different ways, and none may say that the one is better than the other, but only that far more should be expected of those who have not the trials and tribulations of a householder's life. It is harder for the householder to find the peace of Nirvana, but it is not impossible, and the homeless one should be very humble in the presence of those whose way is more difficult. The greatest joys of Anathapindika had been the giving of alms without stint, and since he met the Master, giving without thought of the praise or thanks of men and without expectation of merit in any life to come.

When Sariputta visited him on this occasion, he lay sick of a dire disease and borne down by pains that burned like fire. Sariputta spoke to him of the Dhamma in manner such as only the truly enlightened can understand. Anathapindika was gladdened and passed into deep peace and thence into death. Legend says he was reborn among the devas. But the Master proclaimed him as among those who had seen Deathlessness.

Before the Master's teaching spread abroad, there were few that did not believe the highest happiness a man could attain was to be born after death into one of the heavens, where devas dwell, and where men reap the karma of the good deeds they have done upon earth. It was with this object that men laid up the merit of good works. But the Master showed that the devas are held in the bondage of impermanence, even as are human beings. His teaching was not a teaching for the laying up of merit in a deva-heaven of delight. It was a teaching for liberation from the asavas, from the fetters of lust and malevolence, and the delusion of separateness. Once those bonds are cast off, a man is no longer imprisoned within the cycle of birth, decay, death and rebirth, either here or hereafter, for he has found his being within the Immortal.

But few disputed that such deva-heavens existed and that those who had done good works but had not cast off these fetters, would be reborn in such heavens. Moreover the Master's teaching was for such as had been so reborn as well as for those that dwell on earth. Hence it was that he was called the Teacher of gods and men. It is fitting that I should record one of those devas who sought out the Master to learn wisdom from him. His name was Rohitassa. He came, seeking to know what he had not discovered when living as a human being.

He said: 'Is it possible, Master, by knowledge and investigation of the external world to pass beyond time and space?'

'No, it is not possible, Rohitassa,' replied the Master.

'In former days, Master, when I lived as a human being, I was a great sage and had acquired much knowledge. I had studied the Laws of Nature little known to man, I had learned the means whereby I could fly through the air with a speed greater than that of an arrow loosed from the bow. I thought to pass beyond the end of this world and reach infinity. But though I flew beyond the confines of the eastern ocean and of the western ocean, I did not pass beyond space and find infinity. I found, too, the means whereby I could live without exercise of the bodily functions, and I extended the span of my life far beyond what is thought possible. I thought thereby to pass beyond time and find eternity. But when I died, I had not found eternity.'

'And this will always be so, Rohitassa,' said the Master. 'Knowledge and going forth will not show the way to the end of this world, nor will they show the way to eternity. Yet without finding the end of the world, you cannot find the ending of suffering. Within this fathom-long body was the means whereby time and space first came into your consciousness, and within this fathom-long body is the means whereby you can pass beyond time and space and find the end of the world and Deathlessness. For, friend, these things are not without you; they are within.'

Rohitassa was only one of many devas who came to the Master to learn that which neither great knowledge nor good works could show them. For my part I had not the faculty for perceiving devas, and this being so, I shall tell no more about them, but only about the Master's other disciples, who were men and women of flesh and blood.

It was soon after Anathapindika's death that Sariputta reached the sum of his own years. He was residing outside Savatthi, and Cunda, the novice, was his attendant. He passed away quietly in his sleep one night, and when Cunda came to wait upon him in the morning, he found his body cold. Deeply sorrowful, Cunda arranged for the cremation, and then took up Sariputta's bowl and robe, and went to Jeta Grove to inform the Master. Ananda, hearing the news, broke down and wept bitterly, saying that his prop and stay had been taken from him. The Master took the bowl and robe and said to Ananda:

'Did Sariputta take away from the world the things that make up the Brahma-life—loving-kindness, mindfulness, truth and peace?'

'No, Master, no, but I cannot remember these things now that he, who explained them to me, has gone.'

'Did you think, Ananda, that he would be with us always?'

'No, Master, but it is as if some mighty tree had had a great limb torn from it.'

'And yet the tree still stands,' smiled the Master, 'the Order still stands. All things that are dear must die. There is only one friend that does not die. Make for yourself a refuge in the True Self and in that alone, Ananda.'

Moggallana met his death a fortnight after Sariputta, but his end was not as peaceful. He was killed by robbers urged on, so it was said, by certain Naked Ascetics. Folks also said he met his end in this manner because of evil deeds done by him in a previous life. This may be so, but perhaps it was rather because he depended too much on the exercise of supernormal powers. He himself once confessed that the Master had bidden him be more diligent in the practice of the Aryan silence when all power and thought is laid aside. Did he at last look to those supernormal powers, rather than to the power of an all-embracing compassion, to overcome those robbers?

However these things may be, there is no doubt that in the passing of Sariputta and Moggallana the Master lost the disciples who meant most to him. I remember, how he was sitting with us in silence in a grove outside a certain village in the land of the Vajjians. He cast his eyes over the assembly and said: 'Verily, Brothers, this gathering seems empty for me since I find not among it Sariputta and

Moggallana.' He paused and added thoughtfully: 'Yet there is no yearning that their places should be filled.'

When those weighty ones passed beyond the bourne of earthly life, I realized why it was that the Master often bade us meditate upon death, and how the weaver's young daughter had found this meditation alone sufficient. Death appears unlovely only to those attached to earthly things. For those that have already found the reality of Deathlessness, the death of the body is but the consummation of a more abundant life already found on earth.

I am an old man now. I have known in my youth the lusts and desires of the senses and the sorrow that springs from them. I have known the pain and anguish that come when one sees the Goal Beyond and seeks to shake off those lusts and desires of self, the foul lump that ever stands in the way of the Goal Beyond, a lump that is none other than one's self, or those many selves we create from our desires of body and mind. I have found the gradually increasing calm and peace that come as one finds one's being more and more within the Deathless Essence, and like a prisoner escapes from the bondage of one's desires. Yes, escapes, I rejoice in that term, even as a prisoner would rejoice in it were he to escape from his prison house into the world beyond— to escape from the misery of feelings of hatred and malevolence, to escape from the depression of being overwhelmed by every outward event. But make no mistake, this escape is not from the living of life on earth. On the contrary, it can be found only when all eight steps of the Eightfold Way are trodden, and all except the last of these are concerned with life on earth here and now.

I have found that this life is a ceaseless becoming, a ceaseless passing on to something else. And that if we are to live it in happiness we cannot stand still and clutch at that which passes, but like all else we must go always onward—always onward through time till we find Nirvana and Deathlessness.

And what is Nirvana? The Master seldom talked to us of Nirvana. He had no need to do so, for all that met him knew that he already dwelt in it, and that the utter Nirvana that comes with death would be for him only the completion of a state he already knew. Furthermore, how can Nirvana be described in words when it resembles nothing of earth? All things of earth are composed of different parts or of other things; and they depend for their existence upon each other and upon other things. When they are dissolved, they are separated only to come together, a ceaseless cycle of birth, life, death and rebirth. Our knowledge of them is gained through our five senses and our intellect which is the sixth sense. Nirvana is not composed of other things, and does not depend upon other things. It is not subject to death or to rebirth. It cannot be known through the six senses but only with inner sight. It can only be described as "not this" and "not that". If a turtle were to leave the ocean and climb upon dry land and then return to the ocean and seek to describe to a fish the nature of dry land, how should he do it? He would say that dry land is not transparent, neither is it moist nor salty. And yet dry land is, and Nirvana also is. The Master showed us the Way to Nirvana. Yet Nirvana is around us and everything, and in us and everything. It is within this fathom-long body of ours. But we cannot know it in actual experience until we give up the delusion of being separate selves. Only when the self is extinguished can the True Self be known. This is Nirvana, the going-out of all things of earth, that Amata, the Deathless, may be known.

Chapter XX—Sources

Samyutta-Nikaya—*Kindred Sayings*, II—Pali Text, vol. 10, p. 185 (Sariputta's non-attachment)

Samyutta-Nikaya—*Kindred Sayings*, II—Pali Text, vol. 10, p. 184 (Moggallana—Aryan silence)

Samyutta-Nikaya—*Kindred Sayings*, V—Pali Text, vol. 16, p. 140 (Sariputta's death)

Jennings—p. 375 (not yearning for chief disciples)

Vinaya—S. B. East, vol. XX, p. 191 (respect for old age)

Vinaya—*Book of Discipline*, V—S. B. Buddhists, vol. 20, p. 224 (respect for old age)

Woodward—p. 156 (respect for old age)

Majjhima-Nikaya—*Further Dialogues*, II—S. B. Buddhists, vol. 6, p. 303 (Anathapindika's death)

Dhammapada Commentary—Harvard O. S., vol. 29, p. 304 (Moggallana's death)

Coomaraswamy and Horner—*Living Thoughts*, Ch. VI (11 and 12) pp. 213 and 216 (Nirvana—Deathless)

Woodward—Ch. XVII, p. 319 (Nirvana)

Silacara—*The Four Noble Truths*, p. 51 (Nirvana)

Sutta-Nipata—Ch. V—various translations—e.g. Harvard O. S., vol. 37, p. 209—*Woven Cadences*—S. B. Buddhists, vol. 15, p. 143

Woodward—p. 224 (fathom-long body)

Samyutta-Nikaya—*Kindred Sayings*, I—Pali Text, vol. 7, p. 85 (fathom-long body)

NOTE: It is assumed that this story, of respect for old age, is put out of place in the Vinaya, for if it were in the correct sequence Sariputta would not then have been an old man and the story would have no point.

CHAPTER XXI

SACCAKA THE CONTROVERSIALIST

AFTER the death of Sariputta and Moggallana, the Master made his way through the land of the Vajjians to Vesali where he stayed as usual in the Gabled Hall on the outskirts of the Great Forest. Some weeks later I also came to Vesali. When I arrived, I found there a wanderer named Saccaka, a great controversialist, who went about the town boasting that he could confound in argument anyone at all even though he might be a Wholly-Enlightened-One. I heard him say: 'If I take anyone in hand, point by point, he will fall trembling and quaking with the sweat pouring from his armpits. Why, even if I took an inanimate post in hand, it would fall trembling and quaking before me.'

A few days after I arrived, Assaji, who was also staying at the Gabled Hall, returned from collecting alms and informed me that this Saccaka had stood in his path, saying:

'How now, Assaji, what does your Teacher teach? Under what headings does he place his main divisions?'

Assaji, who as a young man had hesitated to try and expound the Master's teaching even to a sincere seeker like Sariputta, had no desire at all for controversy. As briefly as he had replied to Sariputta on that memorable occasion forty years ago, he told Saccaka that all things we know on earth—shapes, feelings, perceptions, consciousness itself—are all impermanent, that there is no lasting self that can be perceived in any of these things.

Saccaka broke in sarcastically: 'I am sorry to hear your Teacher, Gautama, holds such erroneous views. Sometime, perhaps, I may meet your worthy Gautama and have speech with him.'

Assaji made no comment and proceeded to leave. At that moment a number of the Licchavi lords, who had been gathered in the nearby moot house, came out. Saccaka went up to them and Assaji heard him saying:

'Come along with me, worthy lords, I am going to have a talk with the recluse, Gautama. If he teaches what his well-known follower,

Assaji, says he does, why, I will shake him to and fro point by point, as a lusty brewer shakes his crate to and fro in a pool, or as an elephant splashes the water about when he has what is termed a "merry washing day". Even so will I amuse myself with the sage, Gautama. Good sport I promise if you will come with me.'

Assaji then heard the Licchavi lords discussing the matter. Before he was out of hearing, some had said Saccaka was sure to win, and others that the Master would triumph over this inflated man. 'But I think the lords will come with Saccaka, whatever their opinion,' Assaji added, as he went into the wood to meditate.

Assaji was right. In a short time Saccaka came to the Gabled Hall with a large number of the lords behind him.

'Where is the recluse, Gautama?' he asked of a young novice. 'We would have speech with him,' he added arrogantly.

The young novice replied that he was seated at the foot of a tree meditating during the heat of the day. The novice pointed in the direction the Master had taken, adding: 'But it would be better to approach him at a more seasonable hour.'

Saccaka took no notice of the hint, but went in the direction indicated, with the Licchavi lords behind him. The novice and I and two others, who overheard this conversation, followed after the lords. Saccaka and the lords found the Master in the direction indicated, introduced themselves and sat down.

'There is a small matter on which I should like to question your reverence,' said Saccaka with the opposite of reverence in his voice.

'Ask whatever you will,' said the Master gently.

'What do you teach your disciples? Under what divisions do you place your teaching?'

As we expected, the Master had perceived with his inward ear that Saccaka had questioned Assaji, and he replied exactly as Assaji had done. Saccaka broke in:

'A comparison occurs to me, Gautama.'

'Pray let us hear it, Saccaka,' the Master spoke to Saccaka with that perfect courtesy he used to all alike.

'Every seed,' said Saccaka, 'depends upon the earth. Similarly everything depends upon the individual's material self.'

Although the Master regarded metaphysical arguments as a realm very close to Mara's dwelling-place, it often seemed to us that beneath his calm composure there was something that almost enjoyed refuting these arguments—if anyone so detached from all mundane things could ever be said to enjoy or not to enjoy. We noticed a faint flicker of a smile as he replied:

'Do you then affirm that your body—or your feelings or your consciousness—are your True Self, the Self that controls and governs?'

'Yes, that is exactly what I do affirm—and so does this great gathering,' he waved his arms over the assembled lords. Saccaka was obviously not accustomed to have his attacks met with calmness and composure, and was losing his self-assurance.

The Master's smile slightly broadened but his courtesy did not alter as he replied: 'This great gathering has nothing to do with the argument. Let us keep to the point.'

'As you please,' continued Saccaka. 'I agree that the things you mention are the True Self on which all depends and which controls and governs.'

'And now,' said the Master, 'would you in turn answer a question for me?'

'Certainly, Gautama,' Saccaka's self-assurance was returning.

'Would a King like Pasenadi or Ajatazattu have power to exile a criminal or put him to death?'

'Certainly, Gautama,' replied Saccaka pompously, 'even clans can do that. How much more a King! A King has such power and he ought to have it.'

'That being so, Saccaka, this material body—or these feelings or this consciousness—which is the True Self, the governing and controlling Self—would it have power to make any particular state of consciousness, say a feeling of pain, cease to be?'

Three times the Master courteously, but firmly, asked the same question. Finally Saccaka answered in the negative.

The Master continued: 'That being so, your body, your feelings and your consciousness, cannot be your True Self which controls and governs. To search for a permanent Self among these things is as if a forester, in search of sound timber, were to cut down a banana tree; he would find only sheaf after sheaf, and having peeled them all off, he would find nothing—no timber, neither good nor bad. To search for a permanent Self with your five senses or your sixth sense, your thinking organ, is to search in vain.'

The Master ceased speaking and there was silence. Saccaka did not attempt to reply. Finally one of the Licchavi lords spoke: 'Saccaka is like a crab whose shell has been broken by village boys and girls, and which cannot crawl back to the river.'

Saccaka turned angrily and told that lord he was conferring with Gautama and no one else. Perhaps he now wished he had not brought that "great gathering" with him. He looked at the Master, saying: 'Then let us regard what I and many others have said as so much idle chatter. Tell me now what is the fruit of your teaching.'

The Master's logic melted into gentle patience as he answered: 'The one who has ceased to search for a permanent Self among things that are transient, is no longer a slave to his desires. He has found the means of controlling those clamouring transient selves. He has won deliverance from them. He has found the peace of Nirvana.'

Saccaka was to some extent mollified by the Master's gentleness. He admitted it had been presumptuous for him to imagine he could cope with Gautama. He said: 'A man might perhaps face with impunity a rutting elephant, but not the Venerable Gautama, whom I beg will bring the Brothers and take his meal with me tomorrow.'

When the Master consented, Saccaka turned to the Licchavi lords, saying: 'These lords will provide the meal.' At this, some of the lords were indignant that Saccaka would expect them to provide the food and he obtain the merit of the giving. But in the end they agreed.

Next day the Licchavi lords provided an excellent repast, and Saccaka actually waited upon the Order himself. After the meal he stood up and said almost graciously: 'May the merit of giving this meal bring welfare to the donors,' referring by gesture to the lords.

The Master looked at him a little sadly and said: 'Alas! Saccaka, to them you can give only the little merit which can accrue to the one who is not free from passion, malevolence and delusion.' He paused and then added: 'If it is possible for you to receive it, I give to you the merit that accrues to the one who is free from passion, malevolence and delusion.'

As I had watched Saccaka humbly serving us, I thought that this would be an instance of the "footprints of a really big elephant".

But the next time Saccaka came to the Gabled Hall he was still seeking to discredit the Master. He said: 'There are some recluses who school their minds but not their bodies. My belief is that your disciples are of the latter type.'

'And what have you heard about recluses who school their bodies?' asked the Master.

'Well,' replied Saccaka, 'some recluses who school their bodies go naked, lick their hands after eating instead of washing them, refuse food from a pregnant woman, refuse food from two people eating together, and so on and so forth.'

'And what have you heard about recluses who school their minds?' asked the Master mildly amused.

Saccaka did not answer, and after a little while the Master went on: 'That schooling of the body to which you referred is not really schooling at all. Shall I tell you how the body as well as the mind may be schooled?'

'If you will,' said Saccaka without committing himself.

The Master went on: 'If a person has so trained himself that pleasant things do not take possession of him then both his body and his mind are schooled.'

At this point, Saccaka broke in sarcastically: 'I suppose, Gautama, you are schooled both in body and mind.'

The Master replied gently: 'Your remark is a little offensive, but it is true that since the day I shaved my hair and put on rags, neither pleasant nor unpleasant things have taken possession of my mind.'

'Perhaps,' said Saccaka even more offensively, 'you never knew the meaning of pleasant or unpleasant things. Perhaps you were born cold-blooded like a fish.'

The young novice who had been listening was getting more and more angry that the Master should be so insulted. He now got up and started walking up and down and clenching his hands to relieve his indignation. The Master cast a soothing glance in his direction, but he was too upset to notice it. The Master turned again to Saccaka and answered even more gently if that were possible.

'In the days before I found enlightenment and my hair was black and unstreaked with grey, and I was young, how could I have been without the feelings of the many-folk? Let me tell you, Saccaka, how I learned the way to school the mind and body.

'I thought that to school my body I needed to torture it. I set my teeth and pressed my palate with my tongue seeking to force my mind under the control of my will. I struggled so hard, Saccaka, that the sweat burst from my armpits. I did indeed thereby establish control of mind, but my body was not controlled; it was overpowered by the stress of pain, so that soon I again lost control of my mind. Next I tried meditation with suppression of breath. I stopped my nose and mouth, and in my ears there arose a roaring like a smith's bellows being blown. Once again control of mind was established, but I was so overpowered by the stress of pain that it happened as before, and again I lost control of my mind, also. And I thought that perhaps I was not struggling hard enough. So next time I tried to stop my ears also. Then it was as if a strong man with a sharp-pointed sword should crash into the brain. It happened exactly as before. I tried this method again and again, each time more strenuously than before, and in the end my struggles left me as one dead, with my object not yet achieved. I had not found the way to school either my body or my mind.

'Then I tried abstinence from food. Devas came and offered me heavenly food, but I refused it, for that would have been a fraud in me. I reduced my food until I was taking only occasionally a little juice of beans or vetch or lentil. My body reached a state of utter exhaustion. Like knot-grass did my joints become, like a bison's hoof my hinder parts, like a row of reed-knots my backbone, like rafters of a roof my ribs, while my eyes became sunk in their sockets like waters in the depths of a well, and my skin shrivelled like a gourd that is cut before it is ripe. Seeking to ease myself, I stumbled and fell down as though dead.

'Then the thought arose within me—all the feelings that recluses and sages in times past have felt—surely these pains of mine are worse! Yet by all this bitter woeful way I do not achieve control of body and mind, nor inner sight, nor wisdom.

'I was nearly in despair when suddenly there came into my mind the memory of one day when my father, the Sakyan lord, was ploughing his fields, and I, then only a youth, was sitting in the cool shade of a rose-apple tree. Sensual desires fell away from me and I entered into meditation with thought centred and sustained in the one direction. I realized that on that occasion I had come nearer to finding the way to wisdom than through all the self-tortures I had undergone. I asked myself why I was now afraid of that state of ease, why I should not take some proper food. I did so. I had with me five disciples of whom Assaji was one; they had admired me greatly because I had carried bodily mortification to such lengths. Now, when I ate proper food, they said I had returned to a state of luxury, and they left me.

'After eating food, Saccaka, I got back my strength, and alone in the forest I sat in meditation, and knew the bliss when wandering thoughts are gathered in to one point. Then with thoughts banished entirely I rose to the higher states of meditation. But the bliss I experienced did not lay hold of my mind and control it. In that night, in the last watch, knowledge arose and light arose, as they will always rise from him who strives earnestly to find them. Thus it was, Saccaka, that I learned the way to school the body and the mind. In the bliss that I then found, I now dwell unceasingly.'

The young novice, who had risen with indignation at Saccaka's insulting language, had sat down and listened in rapt attention as the Master unfolded the story of those sufferings he had undergone in his quest for finding for all sentient beings the Way to the ending of suffering. It was the first time those present had heard of these things. And so deeply were we affected that many of us now began to sink into that Ariyan silence of meditation. We were rudely brought back to earth by Saccaka's voice.

'Admitting that Gautama is an All-Enlightened-One, does he admit that he ever sleeps in the day-time?' It was as if a rude band of men had disturbed a herd of lovely wild creatures peacefully drinking from a lake at eventide. The Master looked at Saccaka and the very air seemed to pulsate with his loving friendship as he replied:

'In the last month of the hot season when I return from gathering alms, I fold my cloak, lie down, and in full mindfulness pass into slumber.'

'Some sages would call that stupor,' said Saccaka. He was insufferable. Difficult indeed it was to suffuse him with the rays of loving thought unless one knew the meaning of compassion. That young Brother was not one of these, and we could almost hear the clenching of his fists and the gritting of his teeth to keep down the rising anger.

'Stupor is neither present nor absent,' answered the Master smilingly. 'The man who has put away all cravings has passed beyond stupor, for he has put off the fetters of self.'

As on the occasion of the first visit, Saccaka did at last melt under the rays of the Master's loving friendship, but he still tried to keep that petty self of his which was causing him so much unhappiness if he had only known it. Why do people love so well the fetters that make them slaves to their passions? He now said: 'Thank you,

Gautama, thank you. You have indeed shown me things worthy to
think upon. It is wonderful, Gautama, to see how, though you were
spoken to offensively, you have not changed colour nor has your
countenance altered. I have taken in hand all the leading sages of the
day and they have either turned the conversation or got annoyed, or
bad-tempered or resentful. You are indeed quite like a saint, an All-
Enlightened-One. And now I ought to go for I have much to attend
to.'

'At your good pleasure,' smiled the Master, still seriously
courteous.

No, we had not seen the footprints of the really big elephant.
Saccaka was impressed but he was not converted, and he never became
a disciple of the Master.

After Saccaka left, the Master turned to the angry novice, who
was again striding up and down. I could feel exactly what was passing
in his mind—the conflict between his longing to throw Saccaka out
either by physical or mental violence, and his knowledge that the
Master taught kindness in thought and speech. The Master's voice
was almost mirthful when he spoke to him.

'With what are you so angry, young friend? Is it the hair of his
head or of his body? Or perhaps his teeth? Or is it one of the four
elements of which he is composed—earth, air, fire, water? Or maybe
his organs of perception?'

The Master's mirth was contagious. The novice laughed.

'If you analyze him,' continued the Master, 'strip him off, sheaf
by sheaf as you would a banana tree, you will find there is nothing
left with which to be angry, nothing for your anger to rest upon any
more than mustard on the point of a needle.'

'I know, Master, in theory—but how can I learn?'

'By practice,' replied the Master. 'If a man gives a gift to a friend,
and the friend refuses to take it, to whom does the gift belong?'

'To the man who sought to give it, Master.'

'Yes, and if a man offers you anger and malice, and you refuse to
accept it, to whom does it continue to belong?'

'To the angry man, Master.'

The Master left it at that, and the young Brother went away,
satisfied and calmed. But as I see it, unless one finds that compassion
which can enter the heart of another, it is hard indeed to strip off the
banana leaves one by one until one finds there is nothing on which
one's anger can rest.

Chapter XXI—Sources

Majjhima-Nikaya—*Further Dialogues*, I, S. B. Buddhists, vol. 5, pp. 162 and 172 (Saccaka)

Majjhima-Nikaya—*Middle Length Sayings*, I—Pali Text, vol. 29, p. 280.

Jennings—pp. 33, 203 and 212

Woodward—p. 19 (self-tortures)

NOTE: The young novice is an elaboration on the Text.

CHAPTER XXII

PEACE IN THE MANGO GROVE

AFTER a year in Vesali, the Master crossed the Ganges to travel again through the kingdom of Magadha, where Ajatazattu was now the reigning monarch. Ajatazattu had not permitted his father, Bimbisara, to retire in peace as he had desired to do, because, although his father was no longer officially King, none the less people continued to look to him with love and veneration and still sought his counsel. His son grew jealous and had his father's apartments made into a prison that none might enter, so that Bimbisara gradually starved to death. Then, in order further to assert himself, Ajatazattu built a new walled city to the north of the old, and outside its circle of hills. In doing so, he ruthlessly destroyed the little village there and its grove of mango trees, and cut down many of the giant bamboos and palm trees that had made Veluvana Pleasance a secluded parkland for the Order, although within easy reach of both the city and this village.

On account of this spoliation of Veluvana Pleasance, the Master did not take up his abode there when he visited Rajagaha this time, but went towards the hill which is crowned by Vultures' Peak and lodged in the Mango Grove of Jivaka, the doctor. Jivaka had been the son of a courtesan, but had become world-renowned as the greatest of physicians and surgeons. He had been a disciple of the Master ever since the time Ananda had asked him to visit him on account of some drowsiness of the bowels, which he had cured by putting the Master on to a diet of the juices of fruits. It was from Jivaka that I heard thus:

·　　·　　·　　·　　·　　·

On the festival of the White Water Lily, the full moon of the fourth month, Ajatazattu, the King, was seated on an upper terrace of his house, surrounded by his ministers. Many years had passed since he had been the friend of Devadatta and his tool in seeking to destroy the life of the Master. In those days he had been ambitious and knew not the sorrow he would reap when he plotted the death of his father, the good King, Bimbisara. Now he had been King for some time and the glory of kingship had been tarnished, and pain followed his evil act as the wheel of the cart follows the foot of the ox that draws it. Yet there were depths within him that longed for goodness, and which the evil influence of Devadatta had not been able to destroy completely. Now, as the full moon hung pure and perfect in a cloudless sky, a longing for goodness flooded his heart, and he sang a song of joy and thanksgiving for the beauty of the moonlight and the sacred day. Then the old feeling of emptiness swept back upon him. In the background was that sense of discord, a thirst for power warring with the knowledge that there was something better, and farther back still the gnawing memory of his father whom he had starved to death that he might hold the throne a little more securely. The moonlight had brought him a temporary sense of quietness and peace, but now it had gone. Underneath there was again that ferment he could not still. He yearned for a lasting peace that would end the discord for ever. Peace! Peace, such as the moonlight brought to the earth after the heat and discord of the day!

He turned his eyes from the moonlit landscape to his ministers, saying: 'What recluse or Brahmin is there whom we might call upon tonight and who would still our heart and bring us peace, peace in keeping with this tranquil moon?'

One of his ministers replied: 'There is Purana Kassapa, sire, well known and of great repute as a sophist, who can argue upon any subject that you place before him. Let Your Majesty pay a visit to him, and it may well be that in calling upon him your heart, sire, shall find peace.'

The King did not appear to think that this sage would bring him the peace he desired. Whereupon the other ministers spoke, recommending in turn the seer who dwelt in a cow-pen, the one who wore a garment of matted hair, and several more. But none did the King think would bring him that which he sought, and he turned to Jivaka, saying: 'You, friend Jivaka, why do you say nothing?'

'Sire,' replied Jivaka, 'the Buddha, the Blessed One, with a large company of the Brothers, has recently arrived in Rajagaha, and is even now lodging in our mango grove. He is abounding in wisdom, goodness and happiness. Let Your Majesty wait upon him, and it may well be, sire, that your heart shall find peace.'

The King could remember that vital aura of gentleness and peace that seemed to emanate from the Master, and without hesitation he agreed, telling Jivaka to have the riding elephants got ready, and to arrange for his Queens and other female attendants to accompany him. Only when he was the centre of admiration could he forget awhile the devils of discord that gnawed at his heart. Jivaka was sad that the King should desire to set forth in royal pomp, for how with such pomp could he find peace. But he understood the King's yearning and from compassion desired to help him. So he had the riding elephants got ready. The women were mounted on the she-elephants and the King on the royal elephant, and they set forth, accompanied by attendants bearing torches. The King took the lead; the moonlight glinted on the jewels of his headdress and he held his head high, secure in the admiration of those that followed behind. Before they reached the mango grove, the road ended, and the King had perforce to dismount and go on foot with Jivaka, leaving the women behind and likewise the attendants.

Soon the tittering of the women died away in the distance. He was alone with Jivaka and the eeriness of the noises of the night and the silence of the forest. There was no sign of the company of monks that was said to be lodging in the mango grove. In the shadowy moonlit darkness the King became frightened. He fancied he saw men lurking in those shadows. In what trap was Jivaka leading him? Was there a band of his enemies behind those trees? He now remembered that Gautama, the Buddha, had been the friend of his dead father, the father he had allowed to die. He remembered, too, others whom he had treated ill, some whom he had betrayed, others whom he had killed. When he came close upon the mango grove, he was seized with sudden terror and consternation, and the hairs of his body stood on end. 'Jivaka, where are you taking me?' he cried in panic. 'Are you deceiving me? Are you betraying me to my foes? How can it be that there should be no sound at all, not a sneeze, not a cough, in so large an assembly of the Brothers?'

'Fear not, oh King! I play no tricks, neither deceive you; nor would I betray you to any foe. Go on, oh King. And see! There in the pavilion hall, the lamps are burning, and sitting against the midmost pillar with his face towards the east is the Master himself.'

The King stood still with awe. Not a face turned towards them. All were silent, silent as the moonlight, still as statues, completely merged in that which is universal and imperishable. A peace which could not be described seemed to radiate outward from that silent gathering, growing and increasing in power until the King felt himself drawn into it—drawn into that immeasurable oneness of all, when there is peace—peace that passes comprehension.

For a long time he stood thus, all his thirst for power forgotten, and his craving for admiration as if he had never known it. He gazed upon that silent assembly, calm as a translucent lake, and he knew that this was what he had been seeking.

When at last he found words, he said: 'Would that my son, the boy Prince, might have such calm as has this assembly of Brothers.'

'Your thoughts turn where your love guides them?' asked Jivaka.

'Yes,' replied the King, 'I love the boy, and wish that he might enjoy this great peace.'

When the time was fitting, the King bowed before the Master, asked if he might put a question to him, and when he assented, the King said:

'The people who follow ordinary crafts,' the King mentioned all the people whose occupations minister to the royal household, such as horsemen, cooks, garland-makers, and accountants, 'enjoy in this very life the visible fruits of their crafts. They maintain themselves and their parents and children. Is there any such immediate fruit in the life of one who belongs to the Order?'

The Master smiled at the King's subterfuge to escape facing the lesson that had been shown to him by the serene peace of the Brothers seated in meditation. He asked: 'If a man, formerly the King's horseman or garland-maker, were to forsake all pleasures of sense, and dwell content with mere food and shelter, wanting nothing, would that man desire to become your horseman or garland-maker again?'

'No, Master Gautama, for all would then greet him with respect and reverence, whereas formerly he was but a servitor.'

'And if, oh King! instead of being a servitor, he were a free man, a householder or farmer who cultivates his own land, and only pays taxes to assist the King. What then? If such a one gave up everything, including his honourable position in the clan, and took to the homeless life, would he wish to return to his former occupation?'

'No, Master Gautama, he would not. For the same considerations would apply to him. He would be treated with greater respect and reverence. But can you show any other fruit of this life of a monk—sweeter and higher than respect,' he hesitated, 'this—peace?'

'Yes, oh King! there is a sweeter and higher fruit. It is the fruit that ripens when a man is content with very little, lusting and striving for nothing, renouncing his individual self utterly.'

'Tell me the way to find that fruit, Master,' said the King eagerly.

'Then listen, oh King! The man, who has followed violence, first puts away violence and the killing of things. He lays aside sword and cudgel, and dwells compassionate towards all creatures that have life.' Then the Master went on to tell the King of all the steps upon the Way and of the four stages of meditation and rapture.

The King listened. The veil of his thirst for power and admiration, the shadows of his old misdeeds, began to part, and he caught a glimpse of the clear light of the void, which is not a void but the fulness of all things; and as the Master concluded, he was lifted out of himself, so that the words that came to him seemed to come from a world beyond.

'The one who is liberated,' said the Master, 'is like a lotus lily, resting at peace upon the water, saturated through and through from the tips of its petals to the ends of its roots—drenched, impregnated. And, as a lotus lily may be red, white or blue, even so, he who has his being in Deathlessness, whatever his outward form and character, rests at peace upon the waters of all being, draws his life from the living waters of life, is saturated through and through with that which flows through all.

'The one who has renounced all, is like a mountain pool, which is fed by neither stream nor rain, but by a never-failing spring which lies beneath. Its waters are ever pure and sweet, ever renewed by that hidden spring. Even so the one who is liberated is forever renewed by the living waters of the Deathless Essence. That, oh King, is the fruit that ripens for the one who has renounced his desires, and been liberated from self.'

The King had listened intently. This was the peace he was seeking. He could feel it around him, transforming him as the silver moonlight transformed the mango trees. Then the memory of his past life rose before him.

'Master, I would like to become your disciple. But my sins have been black. Weak and foolish and wrong I was in that, for the sake of sovereignty, I put to death my father, that righteous King. I acknowledge my sin to the end that in the future I may restrain myself——' He suddenly stopped. Did it perhaps occur to him that a life of self-renunciation meant giving up everything he held dear?

The Master encouraged him to continue, saying: 'In as much as you have seen your sin and confessed, your confession is accepted. To none is the way closed. And he who rightfully confesses, shall attain to self-restraint in the future.' The Master looked upon him with love and compassion; but there was a hindrance. The Way, the Light just eluded that unhappy man. The question the Brothers were waiting for expectantly never came. The King hung his head, clutched his robe nervously, and at length, with feeble words concerning being busy and having work to do, he excused himself and departed with Jivaka down the moonlit forest-path.

The Master turned sadly to his disciples, saying: 'That King was deeply affected; he was touched to the heart. But he still had within him that lust for power which caused him to put to death that righteous man, his father. If he had not, then would the Clear and Spotless Eye of Truth have arisen within him, even as he sat there, and he would have entered the stream that leads to Nirvana. But he is still imprisoned in the karma of that deed.'

Chapter XXII—Sources

Woodward—p. 91
Digha-Nikaya—*Dialogues of the Buddha*, I—S. B. Buddhists, vol. 2, p. 65.

CHAPTER XXIII

LAST YEARS OF THE MASTER'S LIFE

ONE day, when the Master was nearing the age of eighty years, I walked to the top of the crag that forms the summit of Vulture's Peak. The old city lay below me. I could pick out the prison where Bimbisara had been starved to death and the gap in the hills to the south through which I had entered Rajagaha that first time and been so greatly impressed by its opulence. But the dust haze of the dry winter months lay over everything, so that I could only dimly discern the rectangular fields outside the circle of hills and the imposing walls of Ajatazattu's new town. I sighed to think of the change in the government of Rajagaha. Then I cast my mind over the length and breadth of the Land of the Rose Apple, and I suddenly realized that a very different and a far greater change had been brought about by the Master's long ministry among its people. "The Happy One" was the name by which he was now most often called, and as the ripples of a boat widen over the surface of a lake, so did his happiness spread through the land, carrying loving-kindness with it. I remembered that it was now many years since I had been the unwilling witness of the sacrifice of animals in religious rites. I realized, too, that women were now treated with a respect I had not seen in the days of my youth, and that compassion for the lower orders was evidenced by the increasing number of those that ate not flesh, and who venerated especially the gentle cow which fills the pail with life-giving milk. In these ways the Master had opened up the old paths of ahimsa or harmlessness, known to the rishis of old, but long since overgrown and forgotten.

I was little with the Master during the last years of his life, and what now transpired I shall let Ananda tell, for Ananda had been the constant attendant of the Master during the latter part of his ministry. Therefore let Ananda now speak in his own words.

•　　•　　•　　•　　•　　•

The Master travelled a last time through Magadha before his death and then we crossed the Ganges and travelled north to Vesali, the capital of the Licchavi. At that time, the most admired of the dwellers in Vesali was Ambapali, nicknamed the Mango-girl, because she was the daughter of a fruit-seller. So beautiful and charming was she that many of the lords had sought to have her for their wife. As they could not all have her for their wife, they had appointed her courtesan and men came from far and wide to visit her, so that because of her the city of Vesali became exceedingly prosperous. Ambapali was not only beautiful and wealthy, but she was popular with all, including her own servants, and it was from one of them that I heard how she came to visit the Master. It seemed that for many months she had been seized with uneasiness and unrest. Her attendant, who was also her confidante and friend, sought to persuade her that her restlessness was merely a passing indisposition. But Ambapali knew otherwise.

'No, Nurse,' she said, 'that is not so. This feeling of dissatisfaction has come over me very often of late. It is not a passing indisposition. I cannot understand it. I feel as if I were a prisoner and need to be freed.'

'But you are the loveliest and wealthiest of all the women of the city,' protested her attendant, 'and you know that men seek your company, not only for the joy of your body, but also for the wit and charm of your mind, and you are beloved by all, for you are kind.'

'I know all that,' replied Ambapali fretfully, 'but I sometimes wonder if the ordinary wife with a difficult husband and sickly children is not to be envied.'

'You know not what you say, mistress,' replied her attendant solemnly.' Woman's lot is hard for all except the admired courtesan. The ordinary woman is first a slave in her father's home. Then she goes to her husband's home and she is a slave there also. But you are free.'

'Am I? Then there must be something else, some other freedom which I seek, something that beauty and wealth, husband and children, cannot bring. Oh, Nurse! I would give all I possess to find that freedom, to find the ending of this aching longing for something, I know not what.'

It was at this moment that a young maid brought in the morning meal; as she turned to leave, she said:

'Did you know, madam, that the Venerable Gautama, the All-Enlightened Buddha, arrived last night with some of his monks, and is staying in your mango-grove?'

'Gautama, the Buddha!' exclaimed Ambapali. 'Have my carriage got ready at once. I must see him immediately.'

'But, mistress,' she protested, 'folk say he is not interested in the beauty and charm of women, and furthermore, he is now an old man, a very old man.'

'I know, girl, I know. That is why I must see him. Cannot you understand? Beauty and charm will pass. There is something else. Gautama, the Buddha, knows about it. I must find out. Tell them to hasten and get the carriage ready while I take off these useless ornaments and put on a plain gown.'

Reluctantly the maid took up the tray and left. Ambapali turned to her attendant, saying: 'It is the answer to my longing. Come!'

While Ambapali was thus talking with her servants, the Master was holding Dhamma discourses with us, warning us to be ceaselessly mindful of the bodily and mental feelings as they arise, examining them as wave follows wave conditioned by what has gone before, so that we did not become overwhelmed by them. 'A Brother should always have full presence of mind in whatever he may do—in going out, or coming in, in looking with the eyes, in bending or stretching an arm, in wearing his robes, and carrying his bowl. In eating, drinking, standing or sleeping, in talking or being silent—whatever he is doing, let him be always conscious of it.'

One of the young Brothers then said: 'Do you especially tell us of these things, Master, because this is the mango grove of the courtesan, Ambapali, who is said to be the loveliest woman in the world, and so that thoughts of sensuality may not possess us?'

'Yes, my son, and also this is the city of the Licchavi lords, who take pride in the splendour of their adornment and their rich array of horses and carriages. If you are ceaselessly mindful, then thoughts of neither sensuality nor covetousness will possess you.'

'Master,' continued the young man, 'in spite of being mindful, thoughts do seem to wander to sensuality and covetousness. Sometimes I despair of ever being freed from these things.'

'My son, you cannot force your thoughts and feelings, nor all at once achieve the end. But by ceaseless practise, by following the rules of discipline, such as avoidance of tempting sights and sounds and meals at unseasonable hours, by contemplation of the Dhamma, by meditation, you will find your thoughts and feelings do gradually come under your control.' The Master pointed to a farmer we could see from the mango grove, planting his fields with rice seed. 'Yesterday, when we arrived, that farmer was getting his field ploughed and harrowed very quickly. Today he is putting in the seed very quickly. Tomorrow he will turn the water into the irrigation channels very quickly, and as soon as he can, he will turn it off. But that farmer has no magic power or authority to declare: "Today let my crops spring up; tomorrow let them ear and on the third day ripen." What is it that makes those crops sprout, ear and ripen?'

'It is just the due season, Master. When the due season has come, those crops will sprout, ear and ripen.'

'And so it is with the monk who undertakes the training in the higher morality, the higher thought and the higher insight. He has no magic power or authority to say: "Let my mind be released from the asavas, the graspings, today; let it be released tomorrow; let it be released on the third day." No, it is the due season that releases him, not himself. It is his to undergo the training; but the time when he will find release is not for him to declare.'

It was while the Master was thus speaking, that Ambapali and her attendant approached. She was plainly dressed in white like a lay disciple, and she bowed low before him. The young Brother, who had been speaking, withdrew modestly and kept his eyes upon the ground, for had not the Master said that, until at will one can prevent thoughts of sensuality arising at the sight of a beautiful woman, it is wise not to look her way.

'Venerable Master,' said Ambapali, her voice trembling with eager emotion, 'I have tasted to the full the sensual pleasures of this world. I have desired and have obtained all that the world thinks good, and it has brought only aching, longing and emptiness. I see nothing before me but the life of one who plays a part in the foolish drama of lustfulness, and sinks down to decay and death. I would be free from the chains that bind me to the misery of life.'

'Daughter,' said the Master with that depth of compassion and understanding which always seemed to open the door of the Dhamma to the Beyond, 'make for yourself an island of refuge in the Dhamma. Take no other refuge. In the Dhamma is the freedom you seek.'

'Is there a way to find this, Master, a way that I, even I, can follow?' Her voice was tearful in its sincerity, and even the modest young Brother lost his fear of a beautiful woman and saw her only as an elder sister in need of help.

'Yes, daughter, there is. It is the way of self-renunciation, of loving-kindness and of truth.' Then the Master taught her of the four Great Truths and the Noble Eightfold Way. And Ambapali listened and understood; when he had concluded, she asked if he would honour her by taking tomorrow's meal at her house, and he silently assented. She then took the dust from his feet and departed.

The Master was so widely honoured in these days that not only Ambapali, but all others in Vesali knew of his coming soon after he arrived. When the Licchavi lords heard of the matter, they ordered their magnificent carriages to be got ready, mounted them and proceeded with their train to Ambapali's mango grove. They were even more splendidly dressed than usual and their clothes were designed to suit their natural colouring—the dark ones wearing dark-coloured clothes and flashing jewels, the fair ones light clothes and ornaments, and the ruddy ones red clothes with crimson rubies. They were indeed a dazzling sight.

Just outside the mango grove they met Ambapali driving away. She stood proudly in her carriage and bade the driver continue along the middle of the road, so that she drove against the carriages of the Licchavi lords, axle to axle, wheel to wheel and yoke to yoke. The leader of the lords said to her:

'How is it, Ambapali, that you drive up against us like this?'

'My lords,' she replied with a peal of glad excitement, 'I have invited the Blessed One, the Buddha, and his company of monks to tomorrow's meal. And he is coming! He is coming!'

The lords did not take seriously what Ambapali said, and one of them exclaimed laughingly: 'Ambapali, give up this meal to us and we will give you a hundred thousand. He belongs to our class; he is nobly born. It were fitting he should dine with us.'

'My lords,' she replied gaily: 'though you were to give up all Vesali and its subject territory, I would not give up so honourable a feast.'

Then the Licchavi lords cast up their hands in mock despair, 'We are outdone by this mango-girl! We are out-reached by this mango-girl!'

Ambapali proceeded to her house to prepare the meal, and the Licchavi lords entered the mango grove; as they entered, the Master said to us:

'If any of you have never seen brightly adorned gods and devas, look on these young lords. But remember the need for ceaseless mindfulness that thoughts of covetousness do not overwhelm you.'

They bowed respectfully and the Master asked them if they abided by his advice concerning the principles of good government, and it appeared that they had followed his teaching in all things. He then gladdened them with further Dhamma discourse. When he concluded, they asked if he would take tomorrow's meal with them.

'Tomorrow, my lords, I have promised to dine with the courtesan, Ambapali.'

'But this is not serious, Venerable Sir,' said one of them. 'You were a Prince like ourselves; you must dine with us. Ambapali is only a courtesan.'

'Within the Dhamma, there is neither Prince nor courtesan; neither man nor woman. Tomorrow I partake of food with Ambapali, both I and the Brothers.'

The Licchavi lords again cast up their hands in mock despair, exclaiming: 'So we are really outdone by this mango-girl! So this mango-girl has really forestalled us!' They then thanked the Master and departed.

I heard later that Ambapali could not sleep that night for thought of the great honour that was to be hers on the morrow and that, before the night was over, she rose and with her own hands prepared sweet rice and cakes. When we arrived, she served us herself, and, after the meal was finished, she brought a low stool and sat down at the Master's side while he talked of the way from sensual cravings and clinging to the things of earth that are forever passing into decay. Before we left, she presented her mango grove to the Master for the Order, and thereafter she strove earnestly to follow the Dhamma. But, as you may have heard, it was not until after the Master's death and on listening to her own son preach, that she joined the Sisterhood, and, studying the law of impermanence in her own decaying body, attained to inner sight.

.   .   .   .   .   .

Yasa, that meeting with Ambapali and the Licchavi lords was the last joyful time I was to know before the Master's death.

.   .   .   .   .   .

From Ambapali's mango grove we travelled in company with some of the Brothers to Beluva, a little village on the slope at the foot of the hills near Vesali. The rainy season was then approaching, and the Master told the Brothers that, instead of dwelling in retreat in a monastery, each should go to his own friends, while he himself and I stayed in the village.

Soon after the rainy season commenced, there fell upon him a dire sickness and sharp pains, bringing him near to death. Mindful and self-possessed, he bore them without complaint, while I ministered to him as a mother ministers to her child, and said nothing to him of the thoughts that were heavy within me. One day he seemed better and I was rejoicing, when he said to me:

'Amid the sharp pains of the body, Ananda, there arose within me the vision of utter Nirvana, the great peace when the last bond of the body is broken, and it was great temptation for me to die, but I thought to myself that it would not be right for me to pass out of existence without taking farewell of my disciples and giving a last discourse on the Brahma-faring life. So, by a strong effort of will, Ananda, I bent down the sickness and the sickness abated.'

The Master spoke in a matter-of-fact way. But, Yasa, have you ever considered what it would mean to the earth if it knew the sun would set, never to rise again—unending darkness, death, but death without oblivion? It was thus with me as the Master spoke those words.

The next day he was well enough to go outside and I spread a cover for him in the shade of the dwelling-house. I said to him: 'Master, I have beheld you in health, and now I have beheld how you have had to suffer, and at the sight of your sickness my body became weak as a creeper and the horizon of my mind became dim. The one thing that upheld me was, that you would not pass away from existence until you had left full instructions concerning the Order.'

His voice was weak as he replied: 'Does the Order expect this of me? If there is anyone who thinks he can lead the Brotherhood, or that the Brotherhood is dependent on him, it is for him to lay down instructions.' His voice strengthened as he went on. 'But I have no thought that it is I who should lead the Brotherhood or that the Brotherhood is dependent on me. I have taught the Truth without making any distinction between exoteric and esoteric doctrine. I have not the closed fist of a teacher who keeps something back from all except the chosen few. I have no secrets to be passed down from teacher to disciple. The Truth is open for all who can understand. You must be lamps unto your Selves. You must depend upon no external refuge, depend on no leader, depend on no teacher. Look within. You are Buddha!'

'Oh! Master, leave us not,' I pleaded.

'Ananda,' he smiled with his accustomed quiet humour, 'I am now grown old and full of years. My journey is drawing to a close. I am turning eighty years of age. I have reached the sum of my days. And just as yonder worn-out cart can only with much additional care be made to move along, so my body, I think, can only be kept going with much additional care.' He pointed whimsically to an ancient cart tied together with creepers which was jolting along the road, but I could see no amusement in the simile.

'Master, do not joke; do not leave us yet!'

'Ananda,' he said a little more seriously, 'do you not realize that it is only when I cease to attend to outward things and am plunged into the depths of concentration that my body is at ease? Would you want a body thus ill at ease to live longer?'

'No, Master, but who will teach us when you have gone?'

'Oh! Ananda, have I taught you so long that you do not understand what I have so often said, that you must be lamps to your Selves? Make of your Self a refuge, the Self which is within, within this fathom-long body, as I have many times said. Seek for no external refuge. Hold fast to the Dhamma as to a lamp; search not for any other lamp. What is Dhamma, you must find for yourself.'

'But how, Master, can I who am so stupid, find that refuge, that lamp within myself?' How childish was my question—I who had been known as a preacher of the Dhamma—but how childish are the excuses we make when selfish affections possess us!'

The Master, disregarding my words, replied: 'For you, Ananda, what is needful is mindfulness. Not to you need I say, as to others, that your thoughts and words and deeds should be charitable and kindly, for I think, Ananda, that never has unkindly word been upon your lips, nor unloving thought within your mind, and truth and selfless endeavour have been ever before you. But, Ananda, if you would overcome that grief that arises from your sensations and affections, you must learn to be mindful always, conscious of when a thought or feeling arises. Stand apart from it and examine it, and you will find that such thought or feeling is due to attachments of the individual self, and is not the Deathless Self. Make for yourself a refuge of the Self, Ananda, not of me, nor of affection for this decaying body and mind of me.

'It is nothing strange, Ananda, that a human being should die. You have often asked me about the after-life of those who have passed on. Such questions are wearisome and bootless. For I have taught you the way by which death is overcome, and whereby the cycle of birth and death is transcended both here and hereafter. And following that way one can predict of a certainty that he will find release from this unending cycle. Such a one is not curious as to what happens after life on earth has ended.'

'Can I really reach those heights of bliss and find Nirvana?'

'Yes, Ananda, everyone can attain to this, so long as he is a lamp unto the Self. And this is so whether I still live or whether I am dead. Whoever shall be a lamp for the Self and takes himself to no external refuge, he shall reach the summit, but he must truly seek to learn.'

Chapter XXIII—Sources

Digha-Nikaya—*Book of the Great Decease*—S. B. East, vol. XI, p. 1

Digha-Nikaya—*Dialogues of the Buddha,* 11—S. B. Buddhists, vol. 3, p. 78

Bigandet, vol. 11, p. 1

Fo-Sho-Hing-Tsan-King—S. B. East, vol. XIX, p. 257

Vinaya—*Book of Discipline*, IV—S. B. Buddhists, vol. 14, p. 315 (Ambapali)

Therigatha—*Psalms of the Sisters*—Pali Text, vol. 1, p. 120 (Ambapali)

Anguttara-Nikaya—*Gradual Sayings*, I—Pali Text, vol. 22, p. 219 (no magic power)

NOTE: Ambapali's state of mind and conversation with the nurse are not in the Texts.

CHAPTER XXIV

THE MASTER'S PASSING

(Ananda's Story Continued)

THE next day we went onward to the shrine of Kapala. Here we sat a while overlooking the broad landscape, where the peasants were moving about in the patchwork of the rice-fields broken from time to time by a patch of yellow mustard and the blue flowers of the oil-plant. The tiny villages were picked out by the green rosettes of the mango groves. Occasional little streams wandered at the feet of stately palm trees, for the weather had not yet turned to heat. White birds fished in lingering muddy pools and green birds hopped among the branches of the mangoes, where the young fruit was beginning to form. Cows and oxen munched contentedly beneath giant bamboos, and huge gourds, like inflated skins, draped the mud walls of the cottages.

'How delightful a spot is Vesali!' mused the Master. 'And the shrines of Udena and Gotamaka—very beautiful is this world of Maya! Some seers, who have attained supernormal powers, have extended their life-span in this world beyond what is usual. But this is folly!'

I was dazed with grief because of the Master's oncoming death. Later, when I realized, I was shaken with horror that he had suggested the possibility of extending his life's span, and that I had not at once begged him to do so.

After a while, he spoke again, saying: 'Leave me a while, Ananda. I would meditate alone.'

When I again met him, he told me that during that time alone Mara had come and tempted him, Mara, the desires of the individual self, who now and again during the forty-five years of his ministry had tempted him, now visited him yet one time more.

'My body was weak and in pain, Ananda, and Mara reminded me of what I had vowed when I attained enlightenment under the Nigroda tree on the banks of the River Nerangara. Very great had been the bliss of finding enlightenment, and Mara had urged me to depart

198

alone, and as a hermit dwelling in solitude enjoy the bliss I had found. I told Mara that I would not depart alone, nor cease from striving to bring to others the same happiness, until there were ordained Brothers and Sisters and devout lay men and lay women, living according to the Dhamma and able to vanquish vain teachings leading mankind from happiness. As I meditated a while ago, Mara pointed out that now these conditions were fulfilled and therefore the time had now come when I should die. I told Mara that not yet would I go, that three months would I yet live, but that he might make himself happy, for at the end of three months, he could depend on me to pass hence.'

The Master spoke with the same quiet humour and serene detachment, but for me his words were the end of hope. I spoke almost frantically: 'Master, will you not vouchsafe to remain on earth longer than the usual span,' and I added as an afterthought: 'for the happiness of the great multitudes; out of compassion for the world; for the good of gods and men?'

'Enough, Ananda,' he said kindly but firmly, 'the time for making such a request is past. In full mindfulness and without thought for my own desires, I have chosen the time that I should pass hence.'

A second time I begged him, and he said: 'Have you faith in the wisdom of a Truthfinder?'

'Oh, Master! You know I have faith.'

'Then why do you beseech me a second time, Ananda?'

'My love for you is deep, Master, and from your own lips I have heard you say that one who has supernormal powers can extend his life's span beyond what is usual for a man.'

'Often have I told you, Ananda, that it is possible for one who has attained supernormal powers to extend his life's span. But, Ananda, have I not also told you that it is in the very nature of things near and dear to us, that we must be divided from them? Everything contains within itself the inherent necessity for dissolution. How then could it be possible for such a being not to be dissolved, even though his span of life be a little extended? I have made the decision, Ananda, question it not. At the end of three months from this time, I shall die.'

I could not accept the Master's decision, and I continued to blame myself for the missed opportunity when the Master had looked over the fair beauty of the shrines of the countryside and spoken of the possibility of extending life's span. As I brooded over what I thought was an opportunity I had allowed to slip, I wove into the remembrance more and more blame for myself, until in the end I imagined that the Master, too, had found fault with me.

After that, we went to many other places, the Master teaching the Brothers and Sisters and the lay men and lay women. Then we came to Pava. Cunda, the worker in metals, lived in this place. He had been a devotee of Brahmin purifying rites and a hunter, until he learned from the Master the way to purification by the Dhamma, and the sacredness of all life. The Master lodged now in Cunda's mango grove, and Cunda forthwith invited him and the Brothers there to partake of food. I did not accompany the Master to Cunda's house, for he had sent me on some business or other, and afterwards I heard various stories as to what had happened. Some said that Cunda caught and killed a young pig; others that he offered fried boar's flesh, but neither of these things would be likely, because Cunda for many years had been a lay disciple and therefore almost certainly did not eat flesh. Others said he gave the Master truffles, a fungus much liked by pigs, but rich and not easily digested by men. I heard that the Master knew that the food, other than the rice and sweet cakes, was not good food and that he would not let the Brothers eat it, but, tender for the feelings of Cunda, ate it himself. However this may be, one thing is certain, that after eating that meal, the Master fell sick of dysentery. Again I nursed him through the sharp pains that came upon him, pains so sharp that it seemed he must have died, but that the three months he had set before him had not yet come to an end. There was joy in tending him, but that joy was mingled with a, fierce resentment at the fate that would so soon take him from me even though I knew it would mean the ending of his pain and weariness.

As soon as he was able to rise, we proceeded towards Kusinara. The weather was intensely hot. The baked mud was now cracked in huge fissures; the little streams were dry, and the larger ones ran only sluggishly. The Master needed often to rest, and then I would fan him to keep away the flies which buzzed around us in myriads. Surely the great heat, if nothing else, should have made me wish for him the cool of Nirvana, but it did not. Once when I spread a robe for him to rest upon, a great thirst overcame him, and he bade me fetch water. I protested.

'The nearby streamlet, Master, has only now been crossed by many carts and oxen and the water flows foul and turbid. A short way farther is the River Kakuttha, which is clear and pleasant, and where you may both drink and cool your limbs.'

But he merely said again: 'Fetch me some water from the streamlet, for I am thirsty.'

I went to the streamlet, and behold! in spite of the many carts and oxen that had passed over, its waters ran clear and bright, and free from any foulness. The clear running of the water seemed a miracle. But I think it must have been running more strongly than I had imagined. The Master could exercise great supernormal powers if he thought fit, but he seldom did think fit, for it is not through the exercise of such powers that the way to Nirvana is found.

After crossing the streamlet, we were met by a young Mallian named Pukkusa, who said how he had often marvelled that those who entered the depths of meditation could rest at peace unmindful of the noises around them.

'That is so,' agreed the Master, 'even though the noise be of storm, lightning and thunder, but greater than this, they also remain at peace amid the storms of sorrow and suffering.'

Now, Pukkusa, seeking to honour the Happy One, brought him new robes of lustrous golden colour, and the Master divided them with me. When the Master put on his robe, his whole body shone with such radiance that the golden robe seemed pale beside it. His eyes blazed with celestial light, and I could not bear to gaze upon him, so exceedingly bright was the glory that shone from him.

I asked: 'Master, why does your whole being shine with radiance surpassing that of earthly splendour?'

He replied: 'This night in the sal-tree grove of the Mallians, the Truthfinder will pass into utter Nirvana. Let us now go to the River Kakuttha.'

The Master spoke as of any natural happening of no moment. But I was like a man around whom a great storm has been raging, and whom now the lightning has struck. I was numbed, powerless even to serve him. When we reached the river, we were met by others of the Order, and Kandaka assumed the position of attendant to the Master. At the river, the Master drank and bathed. On the other side it was Kandaka, not I, who spread a robe for him to rest upon. He lay on his right side in lion posture, and meditated calm and possessed. When the time for his arising came, he called me to him, saying:

'It may happen, Ananda, that someone should blame Cunda, the worker in metals, because it was after I had eaten at his house that

I died. Now, Ananda, after I pass away, go to Cunda and tell him that it was gain to him that he gave me the last meal after which I passed into utter Nirvana. Tell him that from my own lips you heard it, that there have been two meals of equal merit and profit to the giver—the offering of food, after I had partaken of which I attained supreme and perfect insight, and the offering of food, after I had partaken of which I passed away by that passing away of which nothing of the transient earth remains. Tell Cunda that, in providing the last meal, he laid up karma redounding to inheritance in heaven.'

Something, well-nigh like hatred surged up within me. 'Master, I cannot, but for Cunda you might have lived.'

The Master looked into my eyes with inscrutable tenderness. Gradually a wave of great compassion for Cunda spread over me. Of course I could not let him be hurt. I answered very softly: 'Master, I will.'

When the Master was rested, we proceeded to the sal-grove of the Mallians of Kusinara which lies in a bend of the river. I made a couch for him between twin sal trees with its head to the north, and he lay in lion posture and meditated. Devas strewed flowers upon him and heavenly music sounded in the air. The stately sal trees were flowering out of season; the hot air was heavy with their perfume and some of their blooms fell upon him. One of the Brothers said the sal trees wished to do honour to him.

'Maybe,' said the Master, 'but it is not thus that I am honoured. I am honoured by the Brother and the Sister, and the devout lay man and lay woman, who walks according to the precepts and venerates the Dhamma.'

When they realized that the Master's end was very near, those of the Brothers who had not attained liberation, wept bitterly, saying: 'Too soon, too soon will the Light of the world vanish away.'

The weeping of those Brothers unbalanced me again, and I said like a stupid child: 'What shall we do with your remains when you pass onward? In what manner can we fittingly honour them?'

He looked at the Brothers who wept and said: 'Do not trouble yourselves about honouring my remains. There are many nobles and wealthy people who will dispose of my ashes. Trouble not yourselves concerning them.' Then he turned to me, 'Be zealous, Ananda, in treading the Path, intent on enlightenment and release: that is the way to honour my remains.'

But the weeping of those Brothers was infectious. I went away and, leaning against the lintel of a doorway, I, too, wept, telling myself I was but a learner, that I had still to learn the way to Nirvana, and that the Master was about to pass away, he was so kind. He missed me and, calling me to him, said gently and patiently:

'Do not weep, Ananda; have I not told you many times that it is in the very nature of things most near and dear, that we must be divided from them? For a long time, Ananda, you have been very near to me in acts of love, never varying. And you have been very near to me in words and thoughts of love, kind and good beyond all measure. All you have done has been well done, Ananda. Be earnest in effort and you will soon be freed from the illusion of a separate self.' Then the Master turned to the Brothers, saying: 'He is a wise man, is Ananda. He knows when it is the right time to visit me, and for others to visit me. Always he knows those that are ready to receive the Dhamma. Have you noticed, also, how Brothers and Sisters and the lay men and lay women are filled with joy when they see Ananda and hear him teach the Dhamma, and how they are sad when he remains silent?'

But I still could not rise above my selfish misery and now I pleaded: 'Master, do not die in this little bamboo and daub town. There are great cities, such as Rajagaha, Savatthi, Kosambi and Banaras, where there are wealthy nobles and Brahmins to honour your remains.' Foolish man! How could I have thought of such trivial matters at such a time? Did I think to prolong his life if he travelled a little farther?

He smiled patiently and said: 'Say not so, Ananda; in times past this was a great city, and in times to come the great cities of today will be as dust.' His voice changed to one of command—I think he was determined to wipe the dust of ignorance from my eyes before he passed from earth. He said: 'Ananda, the Mallians may feel sad if a Truthfinder dies in their midst and they do not know. Go, therefore, and tell them that in the last watch of the night the Truthfinder will pass away, and that they may come hither before the last watch has gone.'

Here was a last service I could do for the Master and a kindness for the Mallians. I took up my selfish grief, and cast it from me, as a climber might cast away the burden of useless stones he had carried up the steep hill-side. I set forth with one Brother as my attendant, entered Kusinara and spoke to the Mallians as the Master had bidden. The full moon was rising behind the sal trees when they arrived with their wives and young men and maidens. I realized that if they came singly, one by one, into the Master's presence, the night would have brightened into dawn and he would have passed into the peace of Nirvana, before all had seen him. I therefore organized them into their families and introduced them in groups, the women first, and when only the first watch of the night had gone, they had all seen him and received his blessing.

Now, at that time, there was dwelling in Kusinara a mendicant named Subhadda. He was not a disciple of the Master, but when he heard that a Buddha was lying in the sal grove and would die that very night, he came to me, saying how he had heard from fellow mendicants of great age and wisdom that seldom do Buddhas appear in the world, that a certain feeling of uncertainty had sprung up in his mind, and that a Buddha would be able to rid him of it. He therefore asked that even at this late hour he might speak with the Master.

'The Master is weary, trouble him not,' I replied.

Twice Subhadda made the same request and twice I refused him. But the Master, overhearing, called me, saying: 'Forbid him not, Ananda. He asks because he truly seeks to know. He does not ask out of idle curiosity. He will quickly understand; let him come.' Shame overcame me that I could ever have thought of my own sorrow when the Master, even on his death-bed, thought not of his own comfort but of the need of another.

I brought Subhadda to the Master and Subhadda said: 'Sages and Brahmins, founders of schools of doctrine and good men esteemed by the multitude, such as Purana Kassapa, Makkhali of the cattle-pen, Ajita of the hair-garment, Nataputta the Nigantha, and many others, have all, according to their own assertion, thoroughly understood things. Now, what I seek to know is, have they or have they not, or have some of them and not others, understood things?'

'Subhadda,' replied the Master, 'what these people assert, concerning their doctrines, is not material. In whatever doctrine or discipline the Noble Eightfold Way is found in its entirety, there will also be found liberated persons of true saintliness. In whatsoever doctrine and discipline there is not found the Noble Eightfold Way in its entirety, there cannot be found true saintliness.'

'Tell me of that Eightfold Way, Master.'

Then the Master taught Subhadda the Way and Subhadda was convinced, and the Master himself admitted him into the Order. He was the last of many thousands to whom the Master had shown the way of liberation.

After Subhadda had been admitted to the Order, the Master said: 'Ananda, if the Order think fit, let it abolish the lesser and minor precepts.' Then he turned to the Brothers, 'If there is any who has doubts or misgivings, let him speak now.' The Brothers remained silent, and the Master continued: 'It may be that you fear to speak out of reverence for me as your teacher. If that is so, then speak to me as my friends.' But still the Brothers remained silent.

A great joy filled me and I said: 'Is it not wonderful, Master, that in this whole assembly there is not one Brother who has doubt or misgiving as to the Way and the Truth?'

'Out of the fullness of your faith you have spoken, Ananda, but what you say is true, for I can see into their inmost hearts and I know that even the most backward of these has entered the stream and will find Nirvana.'

Very quiet was the grove as the Master lay upon his couch between the twin sal trees, with his head to the north and the full moon in the south now hanging high above them in a cloudless sky. The great heat of the day had gone, and the night was faintly cool, cool like Nirvana. As he looked with loving-friendship upon his disciples, his eyes filled with the same unearthly radiance I had beheld before. It spread over his face and then over his whole body, so that none could look upon him, but cast the eyes downwards, while a light not of the moon flooded the grove. The Master opened his lips a last time, 'All things individual die—strive earnestly—to find liberation——' his last faint words mingled and were lost in the breeze that stirred the sal trees.

After the Master closed his eyes, the Brothers remained bowed in silence and the light gradually faded. Then Anuruddha arose, saying: 'The Master has laid aside his fleeting individuality. He has triumphed over pain and death and entered into the peace and bliss of utter Nirvana.'

Whereupon those of the Brothers, that were not yet freed from earthly attachments, wept in anguish. But those of the Brothers, who had their being within the Deathless, did not weep. Anuruddha turned to those that wept, saying: 'Do not lament. Has not the Master declared to us that that which is born must die, and that that, which is near and dear to us, must be divided from us?'

I was not among those that wept. A strange peace seemed to wrap round me. The Master's body was dead, but the Deathless Essence was not dead. And it was the Deathless, not his body, that had made him the Light of the world, and the Light of the world had not vanished away. I withdrew into the shadow of the moonlit trees. Anuruddha followed me, and we spent the remainder of the night in softly talking together on these things. When we cling to that which is of earth, it must often pass away from us before we can find Nirvana, the going-out of the things of earth. If he had lived longer, I think the Master would have sent me from him that I might find Nirvana.

When morning came, on Anuruddha's suggestion, I set forth to inform the Mallians of the death of the Master. They came to the grove of the sal trees, weeping with bitter lamentation, to do honour to the remains of the Happy One, the Awakened One, the All-Enlightened One, and to embalm his body until the day of the cremation. For they did not perform the cremation this day, nor the next. They still continued their rites of reverence. It was not until the seventh day that they had built the funeral pyre and placed the body of the Happy One upon it.

END OF ANANDA'S STORY

Chapter XXIV—Sources

Digha-Nikaya—*Book of the Great Decease*—S. B. East, vol. X, p. 70
Digha-Nikaya—*Dialogues of the Buddha*, II—S. B. Buddhists, vol. 3, p. 110
Anguttara-Nikaya—*Gradual Sayings*, II—Pali Text, vol. 24, p. 88 (last words)
Jennings—p. 423 (last words)
Woodward—p. 333
Note: Ananda's reactions are an elaboration on the Texts.

CHAPTER XXV

EPILOGUE

AFTER THE MASTER'S PASSING

THAT is the end of the story of the Master's last years as I heard it from the lips of Ananda who was closest to him. What followed, I myself witnessed, for it happened that, before the funeral pyre was lighted, Maha Kassapa and various of the Brothers of whom I was one, arrived in Kusinara, having heard on the way of the passing of the Master. After we had done reverence to his body, the pyre burst into flames of itself and consumed the earthly remains of him who was · the Light of the world.

When King Ajatazattu heard that the Master had died, he straight-way asked that he might have the relics to erect a magnificent cairn above them. After him, others also came, claiming the right to have the relics, and the Mallians began to become angry, saying that as the Master had died in their midst, to them belonged the relics. Then it was that Dana, the Brahmin, arose, saying: 'Forbearance was what the Master taught. It is therefore unseemly that strife should arise concerning the disposal of his remains. Let us unite in friendly harmony and divide the relics among all.'

Dana's words seemed good to them, and they gave to him the task of dividing the relics. Thus it came about that throughout the land many sacred cairns were erected in honour of the Master. But the only cairns that would have given him joy were lives well lived in the Dhamma, and it is of these that I would say something before I end. First, however, I must tell of the calling of Kassapa's council, and the collecting of the Vinaya rules and the principles of the Dhamma as understood by the Elders of the Order.

On our way to Kusinara, after hearing of the Master's passing, we had met a certain Subhadda, who had been received into the Order in his old age and who must not be confused with Subhadda, the last to be ordained. He was a surly old man, and when he observed that many of the Brothers were still weeping miserably at the thought of the Master's death, he became impatient and said:

'Friends, weep not. The Master forbade lamentation and grief over the death of what is beloved. Indeed, we are well rid of the Teacher who was always saying what was allowable and what was not. Now we can use our own judgement as to what is proper for us.'

Subhadda had twisted the Master's words around and for that reason I think it unlikely he had ever met him. The Master was not always telling us what was allowable and what was not. On the contrary, he said, not only to Pajapati but to many others, that what is Dhamma and what is Vinaya each must find out for himself. What leads to wanting little and to inner peace and contentment, that, he said, was Dhamma, that was Vinaya. For example, some Brothers were once watching an elephant-trainer at his work. One of those Brothers had himself been an elephant-trainer in former days and he noticed a mistake in the technique of the elephant-trainer they were watching. He spoke up and pointed out the mistake, and the elephant-trainer took heed and successfully trained that elephant. When the Master heard of this, he said that Brother should not give instructions to those in the world in the doing of their work. For why? Such practice would distract a Brother from his own work of stilling the heart and attaining knowledge of the Eternal. Even had the Master not said this, that Brother would have found this out for himself. If a man sought to acquire skill in the playing of the lute, would not his fingers lose their delicate touch if he used them to fashion clay for the making of pots? The work of the ordained ones is likewise a work of a particular skill.

During the days that followed, Kassapa brooded over Subhadda's words until they took on an altogether sinister meaning and filled him with dark foreboding for the future of the Order. Therefore, as soon as the cremation was over, he brought the Brothers together and urged that a council be called to collect and chant together the words of the Master, before that which was not Dhamma and Vinaya be spread abroad. This seemed good to those that were assembled, and they asked Kassapa to choose from their midst such of the Brothers as were qualified for that purpose. Kassapa chose a large number of the elders of whom I was one. But he did not choose Ananda. The Brothers were surprised, for had not Ananda been the closest companion of the Master and had not the Master immediately before his death praised Ananda before all the disciples? Moreover he was loved by all because of his goodness, noble simplicity and modesty.

'Ananda is not qualified,' said Kassapa, 'to be of such an assembly, because, as he himself admits, he has not attained complete liberation. Did he not weep bitterly when the Master died, thereby showing that he is still attached to things dear and delightful?'

It was many years now since I thought I had attained to detachment from things both pleasant and unpleasant, and had realized the oneness of all sentient beings. But as Kassapa spoke, a shadow seemed to fall across the light of that realization. Who shall say what man or woman has attained to liberation and sainthood? Surely none save oneself, and if a person should so assert, then surely such a person has not so attained, for he would not be liberated from the sense of "I" and "mine". Ananda was modest and never boasted of his attainments. It is true that no one wholly liberated would have wept with such bitterness at the thought of the Master's passing, but because a man does not weep that is no sign he is liberated from the asavas. It may be merely a sign that he lacks compassion.

The delusion of individuality, which had arisen within me, lasted but a moment, and when I rose to speak it was with gentleness. 'None the less, Venerable Sir,' I said, 'Ananda was closer than any other to the Master, and he is incapable of falling into error through partiality, malice, stupidity or fear. More than any has he learned the Dhamma from the Master himself. Therefore let the Venerable one choose Ananda, also.'

A general murmur of agreement ran through the assembly, and Kassapa, seeing that all wanted Ananda to be of the Council, wisely gave in.

Afterwards Kassapa reported that Ananda strove and attained enlightenment. But I am of opinion that Ananda so attained after he held religious discourse with Anuruddha following the death of the Master. Even now, as I think of the simple goodness and sincerity of Ananda, and his modesty, Mara tempts me to feel unkindly towards Kassapa; but there was none except he who could have called that council to preserve the words of the Master.

The members of that Council for chanting the Master's words having been chosen, there remained only the selection of the place, and Rajagaha seemed suitable because of the abundance of alms and lodging-places to be had there. It was also decided that no other monks should then resort there, for had they done so, the assembly would not have been complete had they not attended also, and it was desired to keep the assembly exclusively to those chosen by Kassapa.

When we arrived at Rajagaha, we found that many of the lodging-places were in bad repair. Kassapa reminded us that the Master had always spoken in favour of the repair of dilapidations and during the first month we devoted ourselves to the work necessary to put such places in repair, and King Ajatazattu lent all aid in this matter, being exceedingly anxious to do honour to the Master's memory, even as he had been tardy to venerate him while he was yet alive.

The repairs having been completed, we met together in the large cave on the western hill, and Kassapa conducted the meeting thus. He called upon one after the other to give his report. First he called upon Upali, who knew most concerning the Vinaya rules of discipline. Kassapa asked, where a certain rule was promulgated? Upali told him. Concerning what? Again Upali told him. And then that rule became established as part of the Vinaya not to be departed from, and many minor rules concerning washing-places and food were included among those of great moment. So dry and methodical was the procedure that I marvelled Kassapa did not order everything to be written down, as merchants write down their accounts and prices. But Kassapa had been a Brahmin, and sacred sayings were always recited, and never written, lest those outside the Brahmin caste became possessed of them. And Kassapa carried on in the Brahmin way even though he knew no teaching of the Master was secret. To some, the procedure seemed unnecessary. One of the Council told of a certain Vajjian Brother who had come to the Master in Vesali, saying: 'I have recited two hundred and fifty rules twice a month, and I can't stand such a training,' and how the Master had smiled and said: 'Can you practise the higher morality, the higher thought, the higher insight?' and how, when the young man said he could, the Master had replied: 'Very well, that is all that is necessary. Do that, and you will find that lust, malice, and delusion will be abandoned by you and that you will do no evil deed. Rules are designed only for this object; if the object can be attained without them, no rules are necessary.'

As no rule was embodied in this story, Kassapa passed it by, and went on to question the next person. At length he came to Ananda and questioned him concerning the Dhamma. Ananda replied to many questions. Then he said, 'Concerning the precepts, just before his passing, the Master spoke: saying "When I am gone, Ananda, let the Order, if it should so wish, revoke the lesser and minor precepts!'

'Did you then, Venerable Ananda, ask the Master which were the lesser and minor precepts?' asked Kassapa.

'No, Venerable Sir, I did not,' replied Ananda, 'for which are major and which minor precepts must surely be easy to determine.'

But it was not easy to determine by that Council, for there followed a long discussion, some saying one thing and some another, and none remembering that only an hour before he died, the Master had told Subhadda that the Noble Eightfold Path was all that was necessary. Kassapa was well able to lead a Council like this. He let them talk on until it was plain no agreement could be reached and then he said:

'There are certain of our precepts which relate to matters in which lay people are concerned. Now the lay people know that such and such things are expected from the Brothers. If we were to revoke the minor rules, the lay people would say we kept the precepts only until the smoke of the Master's funeral pyre should arise. Let us therefore retain all the precepts, both major and minor.' He paused. No one spoke, though I know many did not agree with this overruling of the Master's last words to Ananda. Kassapa went on: 'The assembly keeps silent. Therefore it is agreed.'

But the Brothers were not satisfied and some turned to Ananda, saying: 'It was ill done by you that you did not ask the Master which were the lesser precepts.'

Kassapa took up this reproof and said: 'Confess your fault, Venerable Ananda.'

'I see no fault therein,' replied Ananda. 'None the less, such faith have I in this assembly that I confess it to have been a fault.'

Kassapa then brought up many other matters in which he accused Ananda of being at fault, such as stepping on the Master's rainy season garment when sewing it, permitting the body of the Master to be saluted by women before men, failing to ask the Master to remain on earth for more than the allotted span, asking that women be admitted to the Order. To each Ananda replied as before, that he saw no fault, but that such was his faith in the Order, that he admitted it to be a fault if they so required. When the monks at Kosambi had quarrelled, had not the Master said that, even though a thing appears no fault, yet if others find it such, then it should be admitted as a fault? Never would Ananda cause discord and schism within the Order. He was one who brought about reconciliation and delighted in peace. But because of his silence, rule after rule was added, regardless of the circumstances in which the Master had spoken concerning it. Thus did that Council seek to make permanent and inflexible rules in a world where all things are impermanent and subject to ceaseless change. And be it noted that the rules made concerning the Sisters were very stringent. No Sister was present. Kassapa hesitated when some of these rules were urged, for he still remembered the worth of his former wife, Bhadda, who had remained his friend even after they both donned the yellow robes. But too strong for him were the feelings of the greater number, whose passions had run hot in their youth so that they were fearful of women, unlike Kassapa, who had been able on his marriage night to sleep with a garland of flowers between him and his bride.

When the Council had finished its work of collecting and chanting the major and minor precepts, the Vinaya and the Dhamma as they were understood, there arrived at Rajagaha the Venerable Brother Purana, the Old One, who had been wandering through the southern hills with various others of the Order. When he came in, he was told how the Vinaya and the Dhamma had been collected and recited, and he was bidden listen to them and likewise learn them by heart. Purana listened and then replied:

'The Dhamma and the Vinaya have been learned and chanted over by you. But not in the manner I heard them from the Master. I myself shall bear in my memory what I have learned from the mouth of the Master himself, and not what I have heard from you.' And he arose and departed.

I also rose and started to follow Purana. What folly had been ours to strive to place within a permanent cage the words of the living Truth with which the Master had flooded this world of impermanence, the Truth which, with his deep inner sight, he applied in changing ways to changing circumstances and different individual needs! I remembered Sona, whose feet were delicate and whom he bade wear shoes with linings. Then there was the time when he said the custom of shaving the head should not be made the occasion of wasting energy, but that the hair might be allowed to grow up to two inches long; or when hungry monks had left fallen fruit on the ground and he had spoken of the unwisdom of this obedience to the letter of the rule instead of the spirit of not taking what is not given. Then there were themes for meditation which the Brothers were now striving to put into lists and categories. I remembered the inner sight of the Master by which he knew the right theme for each.

There was the weaver's young daughter whom he knew was about to die, and her he bade meditate on death; there was the rejected Brother to whom he gave the snow-white napkin to meditate upon, while the Brother, whose body was stirred by sensual passions, he sent to a charnel field to contemplate decay. Who were we who knew not the mind of others as he did, to crystallize in forms and categories? Even Buddhas only point the way. The guide and the power to respond to that guidance are within. And yet, here we were striving to make a Lamp and a Higher Power without, and to make unchangeable that which is subject to ceaseless change and decay.

I had risen to follow Purana, but I sat down again. I was an old man. Surely the fact of impermanence would break through this hard cage we had made. Surely I could help it best by letting the light of the Dhamma shine through me to the world. Furthermore, whatever way we did things, errors would arise. Without strict rules of discipline, the lives of the Brothers and Sisters of the Order would become lax, and scandals would arise. Without the creeds and dogmas and the lists and categories, the words of the Master might have been lost for ever. And if a man or woman were truly bent on finding liberation, no rules and regulations, no creeds and dogmas, could prevent.

I went out into the forest and sat at the foot of a tree. The shadow of conflict passed from me. Great was the Truth and all would be well. A thousand years—what were they in the span of human lives? In the end, impermanence would sweep away all these precepts and lists and dogmas, and the light of Truth shine forth again. I sank into Ariyan silence, and Purana's warning faded into nothingness.

But lest any should be misled, let me make it clear that the Master said that the Eightfold Way contained all that was necessary to find freedom from sorrow and to find Deathlessness, to wit: right views, the fact of suffering, the arising of suffering, the ending of suffering, and the way to the ending of suffering, right aim, the mind set on selflessness, right speech, right action, right living, right effort, right mindfulness, and right contemplation or meditation. But in the end, what is Dhamma and what is Vinaya, each must find out for himself. 'Go not on hearsay,' said the Master, 'nor on what is handed down by tradition. Even as gold is tested by fire and by rubbing, so must my words be tested each for himself.'

And now let me turn from the making of creeds and precepts to the spreading of the light of the Dhamma in other ways, the Master's best memorials are not the cairns erected above his ashes, but lives well lived in the Dhamma. Anuruddha's was one of these, but he died soon after the Master. Of the other elders still living, Ananda was the one who more than any other trod faithfully in the footsteps of the Master. When he finally found enlightenment, he understood the Dhamma in its fullness. Feelings of malevolence and anger had never been known to him, and to such an extent had pride of self died within him, that he erred on the side of humility, and perhaps it would have been better had he assumed the leadership of the Order. But after Kassapa took this role, Ananda sought to serve him as his attendant, even as he had served the Master, and likewise to show him the people whom, out of compassion, he should visit.

It was to this intent that he asked Kassapa to visit the Sisters, as he passed through Savatthi, and give them Dhamma-discourse, as the Master would have done. Kassapa had no wish to visit the Sisters, but eventually he consented, and the following day, Ananda walking behind him as his attendant, he went to the Sisters' monastery and gave them religious instruction. Sister Fat-Tissa was not pleased, for all loved Ananda and hoped he would deliver the sermon. After the discourse was over, she said:

'How can the elder, Kassapa, deem he can speak the teaching of the Master in the presence of the elder, Ananda? It was as if a needle-pedlar were to deem he could sell needles to a needle-maker!'

Sister Fat-Tissa perhaps spoke truly, but not charitably, and Kassapa was not pleased, for he had had no wish to visit the Sisters in the first instance. Ananda tried to mollify him but he would not be mollified. He boasted how he could attain the four stages of meditation, and that the Master had made this proclamation concerning him, but not concerning Ananda. Ananda hastily disclaimed any such attainment, and did not retort, as he might have done, that Devadatta had also so attained. Instead, he again tried to smooth Kassapa's ruffled feelings. Kassapa was a strange contradiction. The long periods he spent alone in the forest and his proficiency in meditation usually gave him serenity. But meditation is only one section of the Eightfold Way, and it cannot be called "right meditation", unless all the other seven sections are mastered. Few indeed are they who master all and no longer have thoughts of "I" and "me", so that no harsh words escape their lips. At that time Kassapa was not one of those few.

Sister Fat-Tissa, disregarding her own rudeness, was shocked at the rudeness of him who now claimed to be the leader of the Order. But that was not the end.

Ananda, the universally beloved, had gathered about him a band of young men, who were not yet ripe for the homeless life, and eventually they returned to the life of the world. Ananda went back to Rajagaha without them. When Kassapa next met Ananda, he reproved him for touring the countryside with a group of young men whose senses were unguarded, and called him "corn-trampler", "despoiler of families" and a mere "boy". Ananda smiled good-naturedly and without resentment asked whether his grey hairs justified him being called a "boy". Kassapa's usual serenity departed and he repeated his harsh and uncharitable speech. Ananda continued to cherish only thoughts of kindness and gave him no retort.

Now it happened that Sister Fat-Tissa heard of this incident, for news travels quickly even from Rajagaha to Savatthi. She exclaimed:

'What next? Does the elder, Kassapa, who was once a teacher in another sect, deem he can chide the elder, Ananda, who knew the Master's teaching better than any? How can he presume to call the elder, Ananda, a mere "boy"?'

After that, she gathered the Sisters around her and said that, with Kassapa as the head of the Order, the homeless life was not for her, and that she would be better able to follow the precepts of the Master within the life of the world where there were many who were humble and sincere.

Ananda's humility had caused him to refrain from playing the leading role with the Sisters at Savatthi when it would have been better had he done so. But it did not prevent him from taking upon himself the difficult and disagreeable task of visiting Brother Khanna in Kosambi. Brother Khanna had in former days been a servant in the household of the Raja Suddhodana, and passionately devoted to the young Prince, Siddhartha. When he joined the Order, he could not control his personal affection, and even worship, of the Master, and he was wont to go around the countryside, disputing concerning the Teaching and boasting proudly of "our Dhamma" and "our Buddha", showing that he misunderstood the very basis of the Master's teaching, which sought not to found any sect, but only to show the way by which discord and suffering might be put away and joy and peace might be found. So grave did the Master regard Khanna's distortion of his teaching that, before he died, he said that the Order should disown Khanna and impose the higher penalty upon him by refusing to hold converse with him. When Ananda told the Order of the Master's wish, Kassapa at once bade Ananda be the one to go to Khanna. Ananda took a boat up the River Ganges to Kosambi, ill-fated Kosambi, once more the scene of discord and wrong doing.

He landed near King Udena's park when the King was enjoying himself there, attended by certain of the ladies of the palace, who at once asked his permission to wait upon their teacher. Afterwards they presented him with many robes. The King, on hearing of their gift, was indignant. He went to Ananda and asked him with sarcasm whether he intended to set up as a hawker. Ananda replied with straightforwardness and courtesy that the robes would be given to those of the Order whose robes were worn out. 'And the worn-out robes, what do you do with them?' asked the King. 'Make them into bedspreads, sire,' said Ananda. 'And the old bedspreads?' asked the King. Then Ananda told him, how old bedspreads were used for bolster-cases, old bolster-cases for carpets, old carpets for towels and dusters, and how the last were finally torn into shreds and beaten up with mud to make flooring clay. The King was so impressed by Ananda that he gave more robes and thereafter held the Order in greater respect.

After talking with the King, Ananda went to Khanna and delivered the Master's verdict, that his offences had been so grave that the higher penalty had been imposed upon him, and that no Brother might now speak to him nor admit him to the assemblies of the Order. So gently and gravely did Ananda speak, that Khanna was smitten with remorse at what he had done, saying that he was like a slain man. He went away alone, and strove for liberation from lust and selfhood, and attained. He then returned to Ananda and asked him to remove the higher penalty. Ananda replied:

'From the moment you realized freedom from lust and selfhood, that penalty was removed from you by yourself.'

If Kassapa's example had caused Fat-Tissa to fall away from the homeless life, many others did the example of Ananda bring back to it. After he left Kosambi that time, we heard no more of discords within it. Wherever he went, men turned from their errors, and gentle speech and kindly acts followed his footsteps, as green things sprout up after the coming of the rains.

Ananda was the greatest of all the lights the Master had lit and who lived on after his death. But as I travelled around the country-side, I met many humble people whose hearts had been touched by the Master and their lives transformed. And they in turn touched others, and awakened the light, one after the other, to the uttermost confines of the earth. He was, as it were, a great lamp shining in the darkness, and from that great lamp little lamps were lit and from them others again.

Chapter XXV—Sources

Digha-Nikaya—S. B. East, vol. XI (after death)

Digha-Nikaya—*Dialogues of the Buddha*, II—S. B. Buddhists, vol. 3, p. 183 (after death)

Vinaya—S. B. East, vol. XX, p. 370 (Council), p. 381 (Khanna)

Vinaya—*Book of Discipline*, V—S. B. Buddhists, vol. 20, p. 393 (Council), pp. 30 and 405 (Khanna)

Theragatha—*Psalms of the Brethren*—Pali Text, vol. 4, p. 70 (Khanna)

Anguttara-Nikaya—*Gradual Sayings*, I—Pali Text, vol. 22, p. 210 (monk not learning rules)

Samyutta-Nikaya—*Kindred Sayings*, II—Pali Text, vol. 10, pp. 145 and 146 (Ananda and Kassapa)

FOUR NOBLE TRUTHS AND THE NOBLE EIGHTFOLD WAY

THE essential teaching of the Buddha is set out systematically in what he called the Four Noble Truths and the Noble Eightfold Way.

The First Truth is the acceptance of the fact that ill, suffering and discord (dukkha) are inherent in the transient life of earth. Why the Universe should have been so constructed, we do not know, and it is as foolish to inquire, as it would be for a man to refuse to let a doctor take a poisoned arrow out of his flesh until he had first inquired the kind of bow which shot the arrow, the type of feather on the arrow, the tribe of the man who shot it, and so on. "Long before that man found out those things," said the Buddha in effect, "that man would have died. But I come to show you how to take the poisoned arrow out." In other words, the Buddha started with the same conclusion that Job reached, that suffering is. We must "take up our cross" and accept it.

The Second Truth is that suffering, ill and discord (dukkha) arise because we desire, crave, want the things of earth which are all transient (anicca). To cling to things that are forever changing is as painful as it would be to cling to an ever-revolving wheel.

The Third Truth is that suffering, ill and discord (dukkha) end when we give up our wants, desires and cravings. Now, our wants, desires and cravings arise from the illusion that we are separate, individual entities or selves. But there is no evidence for this, for everything within us is as ceaselessly changing as are the things without. There is no permanent individual self. It is only our ignorance that prevents us from seeing that we are selfless (anatta). When we practise unselfishness and finally become selfless (when we "deny" ourselves), then suffering, ill and discord are transcended, and we find Nirvana, the Great Peace (the "peace that passeth understanding", "which the world cannot give and cannot take away") and Amata, Deathlessness (the Kingdom of God—as some Christians understand it).

Dukkha (suffering), Anicca (impermanence) and Anatta (self-lessness) sum up the facts of our earthly universe—the Buddha refused to discuss any non-earthly universe—and we have to accept them, however little we may like them.

The Fourth Truth is the Noble Eightfold Way, the practical method, or way to Nirvana.

The Eightfold Way commences with Right Views, the acceptance of the Four Truths, for "all that we are is the result of what we have thought". Hence the things we believe are vital. What is often over-looked is that the same truth can be expressed in many different ways; the Buddhist terminology is one, the Christian and Hindu are others, and should be regarded merely as different languages, each trying to describe an inner experience, which cannot really be expressed in words.

The rest of the Eightfold Way is the practical application, in all aspects of life, of moral and spiritual values—right aspiration or thought, right speech, right action, right livelihood, right effort, right mindfulness, and right meditation or contemplation.

Right aspiration or thought is setting the mind towards self-renunciation (anatta), loving friendship (metta) and truth.

Right speech is kindly, gentle speech, which avoids backbiting, harsh and unkind words, and also avoids idle gossip.

Right action is conduct which does not injure another (ahimsa); it includes non-killing: non-killing not only of human beings, but also of the lower orders; not taking what is not given, and control of the sexual passion. Some destruction of life is necessary if any life is to survive, but if there is reverence for all life, including that of the tiniest insect, and the grass and trees, then the "rape of the earth", which is threatening us with world-wide starvation, could not take place.

Right livelihood is implied in right action, but the Buddha made this explicit. We cannot find the ending of sorrow, if we gain our livelihood in a manner injurious to others. What is injurious, each must decide for himself, but certain professions were definitely prescribed by the Buddha—the soldier's, butcher's, and hunter's, and the trades of manufacturing intoxicants, poisons, and weapons of death.

Right effort means persistent practice, not straining and striving with our own surface will, but ceaselessly continuing with our endeavours despite countless failures.

Right mindfulness, or awareness, including self-knowledge, involves constant watchfulness and truthfulness with ourselves. Modern psychologists have shown the disastrous consequences of lack of self-knowledge, and its necessity in making for integration and inner peace. But right mindfulness means even more than this —a ceaseless awareness of the component parts of our thoughts, minds and bodies, so that we gradually free ourselves from the illusion of being separate self-contained units.

The final section, right meditation or contemplation, or "calming the heart within" was called "mental prayer" by Christian mystics, and in former times was practised in the West, but its practice is almost unknown today. It means learning to prevent diffuseness of thought, by centring on something suited to the individual temperament—anything will serve from a snow-white napkin (which the Buddha gave to a young novice), or the respiration, to the Buddha, or Christ, or Deathlessness. By centring the thoughts, the veil of separateness is pierced and oneness discovered.

The end or object of treading the Eightfold Path is Nirvana, the going-out, cooling, or extinguishing of the asavas, the influxes (five or six) urges, tendencies or biases with which we are born—urge to seek gratification of the five senses, and sixth sense, the intellect or thinking-ability, urge for preservation of the individual life including procreation and individual immortality, urge to regard ourselves as separate entities (source of selfishness), urge to strive for happiness and blind ourselves to the fact of suffering, its arising and its ending. When these are extinguished, we find "Amata" or Deathlessness.

SOURCES

PALI TEXT SOCIETY'S TRANSLATION SERIES (LUZAC)

Vol. 1. *Psalms of the Sisters* (Therigatha), Mrs. Rhys Davids.

4. *Psalms of the Brethren* (Theragatha), Mrs. Rhys Davids.

7. *The Book of Kindred Sayings* (Samyutta-Nikaya), vol. I, Mrs. Rhys Davids.

10. *The Book of Kindred Sayings* (Samyutta-Nikaya), vol. II, Mrs. Rhys Davids.

13. *The Book of Kindred Sayings* (Samyutta-Nikaya), vol. III, F. L. Woodward.

14. *The Book of Kindred Sayings* (Samyutta-Nikaya), vol. IV, F. L. Woodward.

16. *The Book of Kindred Sayings* (Samyutta Nikaya), vol. V, F. L. Woodward.

22. *The Book of the Gradual Sayings* (Anguttara-Nikaya), vol. I, F. L. Woodward.

24. *The Book of the Gradual Sayings* (Anguttara-Nikaya), vol. II, F. L. Woodward.

25. *The Book of the Gradual Sayings* (Anguttara-Nikaya), vol. III, E. M. Hare.

26. *The Book of the Gradual Sayings* (Anguttara-Nikaya), vol. IV, E. M. Hare.

27. *The Book of the Gradual Sayings* (Anguttara-Nikaya), vol. V, F. L. Woodward.

29. *The Middle Length Sayings* (Majjhima-Nikaya), vol. I, I. B. Horner.

30. *The Middle Length Sayings* (Majjhima-Nikaya), vol. II, I. B. Horner.

31. *The Middle Length Sayings* (Majjhima-Nikaya), vol. III, I. B. Horner.

SACRED BOOKS OF THE BUDDHISTS SERIES (LUZAC)

Vol. 1. *Jatakamala* (Garland of Birth Stories), J. S. Speyer.

2. *Dialogues of the Buddha* (Digha-Nikaya), vol. I, T. W. Rhys Davids.

3. *Dialogues of the Buddha* (Digha-Nikaya), vol. II, T. W. and Mrs. Rhys Davids.

Vol. 4.   *Dialogues of the Buddha* (Digha-Nikaya), vol. III, Mrs. Rhys Davids.

5.   *Further Dialogues of the Buddha* (Majjhima-Nikaya), Lord Chalmers.

6.   *Further Dialogues of the Buddha* (Majjhima-Nikaya), Lord Chalmers.

7.   *Minor Anthologies:* vol. I (Dhammapada, Khuddaka-patha), Text and Translation, Mrs. Rhys Davids.

8.   *Minor Anthologies:* vol. II, Udana: Verses of Uplift, and Itivuttaka: As it was said. F. L. Woodward.

10.   *The Book of the Discipline* (Vinaya, Sattavibhanga), vol. I, I. B. Horner.

11.   *The Book of the Discipline* (Vinaya, Suttavibhanga), vol. II, I. B. Horner.

12.   *Minor Anthologies:* vol. IV (Vimanavatthu: Stories of the Mansions, and Petavatthu, Stories of the Departed, Jean Kennedy and H. S. Gehman respectively.

13.   *The Book of the Discipline* (Vinaya, Suttavibhanga), vol. III, I. B. Horner.

14.   *The Book of the Discipline* (Mahavagga), vol. IV, I. B. Horner.

15.   *Woven Cadences* (Suttanipata), E. M. Hare.

16.   *Mahavastu Translation*, vol. I, J. J. Jones.

17.   *Sasanavamsa Translation*, B. C. Law.

18.   *Mahavastu Translation*, vol. II, J. J. Jones.

19.   *Mahavastu Translation*, vol. III, J. J. Jones.

20.   *The Book of the Discipline* (*Cullavagga*), vol. V, I. B. Horner.

For full particulars Pali Text Translation Series (Luzac), refer to Pali Text Society, 30 Dawson Place, London W.2.

SACRED BOOKS OF THE EAST (Ed. Max Muller)

Vol. x.   *Dhammapada.*

XI.   *Maha-Parinibbana*—The Great Decease—also extracts from the Anguttara Nikaya, Digha Nikaya and Majjhima Nikaya.

XIII.   *Selections from the Vinaya.*

XVII.   *Selections from the Vinaya.*

XIX.   *Fo-Sho-Hing-Tsan-King* (Chinese Life of the Buddha).

XX.   *Selections from the Vinaya* (including Devadatta's schism).

XXXVII.   *Sutta Nipata.*

HARVARD ORIENTAL SERIES (Ed. Lanman)

Vol. 3. *Buddhism in Translations*, by H. C. Warren—an anthology.
Vols. 28, 29 and 30. *Buddhists Legends*—The Dhammapada Commentary by E. W. Burlingame.
Vol. 37. *Buddha's Teaching*—The Sutta Nipata by Chalmers.

Bigandet, P. *The Life or Legend of Gautama*—The Burmese Life of the Buddha.
Jataka Stories—Ed. Cowell—Six Volumes (Oxford).
The Sutra of 42 Sections and Two Other Scriptures of the Mahayana School—Tr. by Chu Ch'an (Buddhist Society).
The Jewel of Transendental Wisdom (Chin Kang Ching)—Tr. by A. F. Price (Buddhist Society).
Sutra of the Teachings Left by the Buddha—From Chinese (Koyata Yamamoto).

ANTHOLOGIES

Beal, S.—*A Catena of Buddhist Scriptures from the Chinese.*
Brewster, E. H.—*The Life of Gautama the Buddha* (Kegan Paul) (excerpts arranged in the form of a biography).
Coomaraswamy, A. K. and Horner, I. B.—*Living Thoughts of Gautama the Buddha* (Cassell) (makes the teaching of the Buddha more comprehensible to the Westerner by spelling Self with a capital when appropriate).
Davids, Mrs. Rhys—*Poems of Cloister and Jungle* (Wisdom of East) (from the *Psalms of the Brethren and Sisters*).
Goddard, Dwight—*A Buddhist Bible* (selections, each complete in itself from Pali Sanskrit, Chinese, Tibetan and Modern Sources).
Jennings, J. G.—*Vedantic Buddhism of the Buddha* (a very extensive collection translated with a Vedantic slant—not easy to read but invaluable for reference purposes).
Silicara—*Lotus Blossoms* (Theosophical) (very short extracts with excellent introductory remarks to each section—perhaps the best introduction to the teaching of the Buddha).

Thomas, E. J.—*The Road to Nirvana* (Wisdom of East) (selections from the Pali).

Thomas, E. J.—*The Quest of Enlightenment* (Wisdom of East) (selections from the Sanskrit).

Woodward, F. L.—*Some Sayings of the Buddha* (Oxford) (a handy pocket edition and deservedly the best known of all the anthologies).

Yutang, Lin—*Wisdom of India* (contains Muller's translation of the Dhammapada and some other selections).

GENERAL

Davids, Rhys—*Buddhist India* (Story of the Nations).

Horner, I. B.—*Women Under Primitive Buddhism*.

Nyanatiloka—*Buddhist Dictionary*—(Manual of Buddhist Terms and Doctrine).

Thomas, E. J.—*The Life of the Buddha as Legend and History*.

INDEX

p. 153   Meditation